PRAISE FOR
THE UNDERGROUND GIRLS OF KABUL

"Through extensive interviews with former *bacha posh*, observation of present ones, and conversations with doctors and teachers, Nordberg unearths details of a dynamic that one suspects will be news to the armies of aid workers and gender experts in post-invasion Afghanistan."

—*New York Times Book Review*

"Five years of intensive reporting have yielded this gritty, poignant, and provocative collage of intimate portraits.... Nordberg conveys captivating nuance and complexity; just when you feel some kind of judgment or conclusive opinion is within reach, she deftly turns the tables, leaving us to reexamine our own prejudices and societal norms as we struggle with questions that are perhaps unanswerable."

—*Elle*

"Nordberg's book is riveting, bringing a practice previously unknown to the West to light and continuing to elucidate the plight of Afghan women, whose supposed inferiority is so ingrained in their culture that Western feminism can make few inroads."

—*Minneapolis Star Tribune*

"Nordberg's intimate exploration leaves us rooting for her brave subjects."

—*Mother Jones*

"Nordberg creates a moving intimacy with these stories, weaving them into the bigger picture of contemporary Afghanistan. Diving deep into the lives and hearts of people who are usually ignored, she reveals the enormity of a localized struggle even while grounding it in broader human experience, never allowing the reader to reduce her subjects to curiosities."

—DallasMorningNews.com

"In clear, simple prose, Nordberg describes her encounters with several current or former *bacha posh*. . . . The book raises provocative questions about gender roles in Afghanistan and beyond."

—*Columbus Dispatch*

"Fascinating . . . Nordberg manages to capture the strength of these women, as well as their vulnerabilities, to show the psychological toll *bacha posh* has on those who endure it and the ability of women to adapt to the constricts society places on them."

—ForeignPolicy.com

"In fluid narrative style, Nordberg explores the [*bacha posh*] phenomenon through compelling individual portraits. . . . In addition to presenting a rare glimpse of Afghan life, *The Underground Girls of Kabul* explores the ways that gender identity is shaped and policed. Extending well beyond Afghanistan, this book compels the reader to rethink gender differences."

—Straight.com

"*The Underground Girls of Kabul* is an outstanding work of journalism that uncovers new information about an important subject. It's also an extraordinarily well-written book, full of riveting stories about the real lives of girls and women in Afghanistan today."

—*PopMatters*

"Five years of research, and an almost novelistic approach to her findings, has produced a book full of fresh stories."

—Razia Iqbal, *Independent*

"Nordberg's hopeful yet heartbreaking account offers a dazzling picture of Afghan life. . . . Refreshingly nonjudgmental . . . Thanks to this book, a little more light has been shone on a country and society so often misunderstood."

—*Independent on Sunday*

"Partly a reflection on the politics of sex and gender . . . but it is also a tale of discovery."

—*Sunday Telegraph*

"This powerful account of powerlessness resonates with the most silenced voices in society."

—*Observer*

"[A] searing exposé ... Nordberg's subtle, sympathetic reportage makes this one of the most convincing portraits of Afghan culture in print."

—*Publishers Weekly*, starred review

"A stunning book ... Nordberg has done some staggering work in this unique, important, and compelling chronicle. Book clubs will be riveted, and will talk for hours."

—*Booklist*, starred review

"As affecting as the stories of these women are, Nordberg's conclusion—that women's rights are essential to 'building peaceful civilizations'—is the most powerful message of this compelling book. Intelligent and timely."

—*Kirkus Reviews*

"*The Underground Girls of Kabul* is a groundbreaking feat of reportage, a kaleidoscopic investigation into gender, resistance, and the limits of cross-cultural understanding. Jenny Nordberg is a riveting storyteller and she has an astonishing tale to tell."

—Michelle Goldberg, author of *The Means of Reproduction: Sex, Power, and the Future of the World*

"Jenny Nordberg has given us a fascinating look into a hidden phenomenon of extreme patriarchal societies: a form of gender-bending far riskier and more rewarding than Western academia's trendy, abstract gender categories. Nordberg's reporting is thorough and sensitive, her writing vivid and insightful. You will not forget this book; it will haunt you."

—Robin Morgan

"Brilliant, urgent, groundbreaking ... It is a call to action, and a reminder that even under the greatest abuses of power women have found ways to fight and flourish. The inspiring story of the *bacha posh* is not just a tale of ingenuity and survival in Afghanistan. It is an excavation of the deep and insidious roots of global misogyny, and an offering of hope."

—Cara Hoffman, author of *Be Safe I Love You*

"A tremendous feat of reporting and storytelling: Until [Nordberg's] work on the custom of *bacha posh* was published in the *New York Times*, the practice had never been systematically documented, and her narrative is so finely observed that it often reads like fiction. Nordberg's curiosity, her humor, and her genuine warmth for her subjects come through on every page."

—Katherine Zoepf, fellow, New America Foundation

"A riveting firsthand account of what life as a girl is like in Afghanistan and how it often means becoming a boy. Jenny Nordberg has written a compelling and important work that exposes the profound gender prejudice that exists, in different forms, all over the world."

—Jennifer Clement, author of *Prayers for the Stolen*

"Forget everything you thought you knew about gender and what it means to be a woman or man. Jenny Nordberg's exquisitely reported look at why Afghans choose to raise their girls as boys is nothing less than heartbreaking, mind-bending, and mesmerizing—not to mention timely."

—Lauren Wolfe, director, Women's Media Center's Women Under Siege

"Nordberg brings to light a world that no Afghan speaks of, but everyone knows: the world of girls raised as boys, usually until puberty. In a society where being a girl means living as chattel, and where families without boys are shamed, the *bacha posh* tradition arose, as it has in other highly patriarchal societies. Going deeper, Nordberg discovers that the *bacha posh*, once adults, become a subversive force: Having tasted freedom and opportunity, these women can never go back. They stand up—for themselves, their daughters, and their country. The former *bacha posh* may yet change Afghanistan for the better.... Nordberg's book is a pioneering effort to understand this hidden world."

—Valerie M. Hudson, professor and George H. W. Bush Chair, Bush School of Government and Public Service, Texas A&M University

"The investigation into *bacha posh* gives a new and unique perspective on the women's situation, gender, and resistance in Afghanistan. [Nordberg] tells the story with empathy and respect for the women who have let her into their lives. This book will interest both those who want to learn about Afghanistan and those wanting to understand how gender works.... A must-read for both Afghanistan and gender specialists."

—Sari Kouvo, codirector, Afghanistan Analysts Network

"*The Underground Girls of Kabul* is an amazing book. The fact that Nordberg brings this to light is eye-opening to everyone—even to Afghans.... Many Afghans live with it as part of their life."

—Naheed Bahram, program director, Women for Afghan Women

THE UNDERGROUND
GIRLS OF KABUL

IN SEARCH OF A HIDDEN RESISTANCE
IN AFGHANISTAN

JENNY NORDBERG

B\D\W\Y
BROADWAY BOOKS
NEW YORK

Library of Congress Cataloging-in-Publication Data
Nordberg, Jenny.
The underground girls of Kabul: in search of a hidden resistance in
Afghanistan / Jenny Nordberg.—First edition.
pages cm
1. Gender Identity—Afghanistan. 2. Sex role—Afghanistan. 3. Male
impersonators—Afghanistan. 4. Women—Afghanistan—Social conditions.
5. Girls—Afghanistan—Social conditions. I. Title.
HQ1075.5.A3N67 2014
305.309581—dc23   2014000295

ISBN 978-0-307-95250-9
eBook ISBN 978-0-307-95251-6

Printed in the United States of America

Book design by Lauren Dong
Cover design by Elena Giavaldi
Cover photography by Adam Ferguson

10 9 8 7

First Paperback Edition

To every girl

who figured out that she could run faster,

and climb higher, in pants

This story was reported from Afghanistan, Sweden, and the United States between 2009 and 2014. Most of the book's events take place in 2010 and 2011. I have told the stories of the characters as they have been told to me, attempting to corroborate any details I have not observed in person. Each person has consented to being interviewed for the purposes of the book, and has exercised a choice over whether or not to remain anonymous. In some cases, names or identifying details have been changed or left out to protect the identity of a subject. None of the characters were offered or have received money for their participation. Translators have been paid for their work. Any errors due to translation or my own limitations are my responsibility.

This is a subjective account.

CONTENTS

BUT NOT AN AFGHAN WOMAN

I would love to be anything in this world
But not a woman

I could be a parrot
I could be a female sheep
I could be a deer or
A sparrow living in a tree

But not an Afghan woman.

I could be a Turkish lady
With a kind brother to take my hand
I could be Tajik
or I could be Iranian
or I could be an Arab
With a husband to tell me
I am beautiful

But I am an Afghan woman.

When there is need
I stand beside it
When there is risk
I stand in front
When there is sorrow
I grab it
When there are rights
I stand behind them

Might is right and
I am a woman
Always alone
Always an example of weakness
My shoulders are heavy
with the weight of pains.

When I want to talk
My tongue is blamed
My voice causes pain
Crazy ears can't tolerate me
My hands are useless
I can't do anything with
My foolish legs
I walk with
No destination.

Until what time must I accept to suffer?
When will nature announce my release?
Where is Justice's house?
Who wrote my destiny?
Tell him
Tell him
Tell him

I would love to be anything in nature
But not a woman
Not an Afghan woman.

ROYA
Kabul, 2009

THE UNDERGROUND
GIRLS OF KABUL

PROLOGUE

THE TRANSITION BEGINS here.

I remove the black head scarf and tuck it into my backpack. My hair stays in a knotted bun on the back of my head. We will be in the air soon enough. I straighten my back and sit up a little taller, allowing my body to fill a larger space. I do not think of war. I think of ice cream in Dubai.

We crowd the small vinyl-clad chairs in the departure hall of Kabul International Airport. My visa expires in a few hours. A particularly festive group of British expatriates celebrate, for the first time in months, a break from life behind barbed wire and armed guards. Three female aid workers in jeans and slinky tops speak excitedly of a beach resort. A piece of black jersey has fallen off a shoulder, exposing a patch of already tanned skin.

I stare at the unfamiliar display of flesh. For the past few months, I have hardly seen my own body.

It is the summer of 2011, and the exodus of foreigners from Kabul has been under way for more than a year. Despite a final push, Afghanistan feels lost to many in both the military and in the foreign aid community. Since President Obama announced that U.S. troops would begin to withdraw from Afghanistan by 2014, the international caravan has been in a rush to move on. Kabul airport is the first stop on the way to freedom for those confined, bored, almost-gone-mad consultants, contractors, and diplomats. The tradespeople of peace and international development look forward to new postings, where any experimentation with "nation building" or "poverty reduction" has not yet gone awry. Already, they reminisce over the early, hopeful days almost a decade ago, when the Taliban had just been defeated and everything seemed possible. When Afghanistan was going to be renovated into a secular, Western-style democracy.

THE AIRPORT RUNWAY is flooded with afternoon light. My cell phone catches a pocket of reception by one of the windows, and I dial Azita's number again. With a small click, we connect.

She is giddy after a meeting with the attorney general and some other public officials. The press attended, too. As a politician, that is when Azita is in her element. I hear her smiling when she describes her outfit: "I made myself fashionable. And diplomatic. They all took my picture. The BBC, Voice of America, and Tolo TV. I had the turquoise scarf—the one you saw the other day. You know it. And the black jacket."

She pauses. "And a lot of makeup. Big makeup."

I breathe in deeply. I am the journalist. She is the subject. The rule is to show no emotion.

Azita hears my silence and immediately begins to reassure me. Things will get better soon. She is sure of it. No need to worry.

My flight is called. I have to go. We say the usual things: "Only for now. Not good-bye. Yes. See you soon."

As I rise up from the floor, where I have pressed myself to the window so as not to lose the connection, I fantasize about turning back. It could be the last scene of a film. That moment when an epiphany makes for a desperate sprint through the airport to set everything right. To get the good ending. So what if I spend another afternoon in Colonel Hotak's office, being lectured about my expired visa? Some tea, a stamp in my passport, and he will let me go.

As I go through each step in my head, I know I will never do it. And how would this—my last act—play out? Would I storm into Azita's house flanked by American troops? Afghanistan's Human Rights Commission? Or just by myself, with my pocketknife and my negotiation skills, fueled by rage and a conviction that anything can be fixed with just a little more effort?

As I walk through the gate, the scenarios fade away. They always do. I follow the others and once more, I do what we all do.

I get on the plane and just leave.

PART ONE
BOYS

Adam Ferguson

AZITA AND MEHRAN

CHAPTER ONE

THE REBEL MOTHER

Azita, a few years earlier

O UR BROTHER IS really a girl."

One of the eager-looking twins nods to reaffirm her words. Then she turns to her sister. She agrees. Yes, it is true. She can confirm it.

They are two ten-year-old identical girls, each with black hair, squirrel eyes, and a few small freckles. Moments ago, we danced to my iPod set to shuffle as we waited for their mother to finish a phone conversation in the other room. We passed the headphones between us, showing off our best moves. Though I failed to match their elaborate hip rolls, some of my most inspired sing-along was met with approval. It actually sounded pretty good bouncing off the ice-cold cement walls of the apartment in the Soviet-built maze that is home to a chunk of Kabul's small middle class.

Now we sit on the gold-embroidered sofa, where the twins have set up a tea service consisting of glass mugs and a pump thermos on a silver-plated tray. The *mehman khana* is the most opulent room in an Afghan home, meant to show off the wealth and good moral character of its owners. Cassette tapes with Koran verses and peach-colored fabric flowers sit on a corner table where a crack has been soldered with Scotch tape. The twin sisters, their legs neatly folded underneath them on the sofa, are a little offended by my lack of reaction to their big reveal. Twin number two leans forward: "It's *true*. He is our little sister."

I smile at them, and nod again. "Yes." Sure.

A framed picture on a side table shows their brother posing in a V-neck sweater and tie, with his grinning, mustached father. It is the only photo on display in the living room. His oldest daughters speak a shaky but enthusiastic English, picked up from textbooks and satellite television from a dish on the balcony. We just have a language barrier here, perhaps.

"Okay," I say, wanting to be friendly. "I understand. Your *sister*. Now, what is your favorite color, Benafsha?"

She goes back and forth between red and purple before passing the question to her sister, where it gets equally serious consideration. The twins, both dressed in orange cardigans and green pants, seem to do most things in perfect girly synchronicity. Their bobbing heads are topped with glittery hair scrunchies, and only when one speaks will the other's scrunchie be still for a few seconds. Those moments are a beginner's chance to tell them apart: A small birthmark on Beheshta's cheek is the key. Benafsha means "flower"; Beheshta, "paradise."

"I want to be a teacher when I grow up," Beheshta volunteers for our next topic.

When it becomes each of the twins' turns to ask a question, they both want to know the same thing: Am I married?

My response mystifies them, since—as they point out—I am very old. I am even a few years *older* than their mother, who at thirty-three is a married mother of four. The twins have another sister, too, in addition to their little brother. Their mother is also in the national parliament, I say to the twins. So there are many things I am not, compared to her. They seem to appreciate that framing.

Their brother suddenly appears in the doorway.

Mehran, age six, has a tanned, round face, deep dimples, eyebrows that go up and down as he grimaces, and a wide gap between his front teeth. His hair is as black as that of his sisters, but short and spiky. In a tight red denim shirt and blue pants, chin forward, hands on hips, he swaggers confidently into the room, looking directly at me and pointing a toy gun in my face. Then he pulls the trigger and exclaims his greeting: *phow*. When I fail to die or shoot back, he takes out a plastic superhero from his back pocket. The wingman has blond hair, shiny white teeth, two gun belts slung across his bulging chest, and is armed with a machine gun. Mehran says something in Dari to the figurine and then listens intently to him. They seem to agree: The assault has been a success.

Benafsha comes alive at my side, seeing the chance to finally prove her point. She waves her arms to call her brother's attention: "Tell her, Mehran. Tell her *you are our sister.*"

The corners of Mehran's mouth turn downward. He sticks his tongue out in a grimace before bolting, almost crashing into his mother as she walks into the room.

Azita's eyes are lined with black kohl, and she wears a little bit of blush. Or perhaps it is the effect of having had a cell phone pressed to her ear. She is ready now, she exclaims in my direction. To tell me what I came to ask about—what it is like, almost a decade into America's longest war and one of the largest foreign aid efforts of a generation, to be an Afghan woman here.

WHEN WE FIRST meet, on this day, I am researching a television piece on Afghan women and Azita has been a member of the country's fairly new parliament for four years. Elected to the Wolesi Jirga, one of the legislative branches installed a few years after the 2001 defeat of the Taliban, she had promised her rural voters in Badghis province that she would direct more of the foreign aid influx to their poor, far-flung corner of Afghanistan.

The parliament she entered was heavily populated with drug kingpins and warlords and seemed to be in a state of paralysis due to deeply entrenched corruption, but it was at least an attempt at democracy that many Afghans expressed hope for. It followed many forms of failed governance during the last century: absolute monarchy, communism, and an Islamic emirate under the Taliban. Or no government at all in times of civil war.

As some foreign diplomats and aid workers around Kabul came to know Azita as an educated female parliamentarian who not only spoke Dari, Pashto, Urdu, and Russian, but also English, and who seemed relatively liberal, invitations to events poured in from the outside world. She was flown to several European countries and to Yale University in the United States, where she spoke of life under the Taliban.

It was not unusual for Azita to invite foreigners to her rented home in Macroyan, either, to show her version of normal life in a Kabul neighborhood. Here, laundry flutters on the balconies of dirt-gray four-story buildings, interrupted by the occasional patch of greenery, and in the early mornings, women gather at the hole-in-the-wall bakeries while men perform stiff gymnastic exercises on the football field. Azita takes pride in being a host and showing herself off as an exception to the way Afghan women are portrayed in the outside world—as secluded inside their homes, with little connection to society, often illiterate and under the spell of demonizing husbands who do not allow them any daylight. And definitely not receiving visits from *farangee,* or foreigners, as the historical invaders were once dubbed by Afghans. These days, foreigners usually go under *amrican,* regardless of their passport.

Azita enjoys demonstrating her running water, the electricity, the television set in her bedroom; all paid for with money she has made as the breadwinner of the house. She knows that impresses foreigners. Especially female foreigners. With her glowing cheeks, sharp features, and military-grade posture, elegantly draped in black fabric from head to toe, and exuding a warm scent of musk mixed with something sweet, Azita does look different from Afghanistan's majority of women. At five feet six—perhaps a little taller in her pointy size-eleven sling-back heels—she even towers over some visitors.

Those usually arrive in more practical shoes, as if on a trek some-where.

ON THE TOPIC of progress for women since 2001, Azita expresses little satisfaction to visiting foreigners, of which I am just the lat-est: Yes, more women are seen on the streets of Kabul and a few other larger cities than when the Taliban was in power, and more girls are enrolled in school, but just as in earlier eras when reforms were attempted, most progress for women is limited to the capital and a handful of other urban areas. Much of what the Taliban had banned and decreed regarding women is still effectively law in large parts of this mostly illiterate country, enforced by conservative tradi-tion. In many provinces, burkas are still commonplace, and women rarely work or leave the house without their husbands. The major-ity of marriages are still forced, honor killings are not unusual, and any involvement of the justice system in a rape case usually means that only the victim goes to jail, charged with adultery or with having had premarital sex—unless she, as a commonly imposed solution, is forced to marry her rapist. Women burn themselves to death using cooking fuel to escape domestic abuse here, and daughters are still a viable, informal currency used by fathers to pay off debts and settle disputes.

Azita is one of few women with a voice, but to many, she remains a provocation, since her life is different from that of most women in Afghanistan and a threat to those who subjugate them. In her words: "If you go to the remote areas of Afghanistan, you will see *nothing* has changed in women's lives. They are still like servants. Like animals. We have a long time before the woman is considered a human in this society."

Azita pushes her emerald green head scarf back to reveal a short black ponytail, and rubs her hair. I shake off my scarf, too, and let it fall down on my neck. She looks at me for a moment, where we sit in her bedroom. "I never want my daughters to suffer in the ways I have suffered. I had to kill many of my dreams. I have four daughters. I am very happy for that."

Four daughters. Only four daughters? What is going on in this family? I hold my breath for a moment, hoping Azita will take the lead and help me understand.

And she does.

"Would you like to see our family album?"

WE MOVE BACK into the living room, where she pulls out two albums from under a rickety little desk. The children look at these photos often. They tell the story of how Azita's family came to be.

First: a series of shots from Azita's engagement party in the summer of 1997. Azita's first cousin, whom she is to marry, is young and lanky. On his face, small patches of hair are still struggling to meet in the middle as a full beard; a requirement under Taliban rule at that time. The fiancé wears a turban and a brown wool vest over a traditional white *peran tonban*—a long shirt and loose pants. None of the one hundred or so guests are smiling. By Afghan standards, where a party can number more than a thousand, it was a small and unimpressive gathering. It is a snapshot of the city meeting the village. Azita is the elite-educated daughter of a Kabul University professor. Her husband-to-be: the illiterate son of a farmer.

A few staged moments are captured. The fiancé attempts to feed his future wife some of the pink and yellow cake. She turns her head away. At nineteen, Azita is a thinner and more serious version of her later self, in a cobalt blue silk caftan with rounded shoulder pads. Her fingernails have been painted a bright red to match crimson lips, set off by a white-powdered face that reads as a mask. Her hair is a hard, sprayed bird's nest. In another shot, her future husband offers her a celebratory goblet from which she is expected to drink. She stares into the camera. Her matte, powdery face is streaked with vertical lines running from dark brown eyes.

A few album pages later, the twins pose with Azita's mother, a woman with high cheekbones and a strong nose in a deeply lined face. Both Benafsha and Beheshta blow kisses onto their *bibi-jan,* who still lives with their grandfather in the northwest of Afghanistan. Soon, a third little girl makes her appearance in the photos. Middle sister Mehrangis has pigtails and a slightly rounder face. She poses next to the twin mini-Azitas, who suddenly look very grown up in their white ruffle dresses.

Azita flips the page: *Nowruz,* the Persian New Year, in 2005. Four little girls in cream-colored dresses. All ordered by size. The shortest has a bow in her hair. It is Mehran. Azita puts her finger on the picture. Without looking up, she says: "You know my youngest is also a girl, yes? We dress her like a boy."

I glance in the direction of Mehran, who has been skidding around the periphery as we have talked. She has hopped into another chair and is talking to the plastic figurine again.

"They gossip about my family. When you have no sons, it is a big missing, and everyone feels sad for you."

Azita says this as if it is a simple explanation.

Having at least one son is mandatory for good standing and reputation here. A family is not only incomplete without one; in a country lacking rule of law, it is also seen as weak and vulnerable. So it is incumbent upon every married woman to quickly bear a son—it is her absolute purpose in life, and if she does not fulfill it, there is clearly something wrong with her in the eyes of others. She could be dismissed as a *dokhtar zai,* or "she who only brings daughters." Still, this is not as grave an insult as what an entirely childless woman could be called—a *sanda* or *khoshk,* meaning "dry" in Dari. But a woman who cannot birth a son in a patrilineal culture is—in the eyes of society and often herself—fundamentally flawed.

The literacy rate is no more than 10 percent in most areas, and many unfounded truths swirl around without being challenged. Among them is the commonly held belief that a woman can *choose* the sex of her unborn baby simply by making up her mind about it. As a consequence, a woman's inability to bear sons does not elicit much sympathy. Instead, she is condemned both by society and her own husband as someone who has just not desired a son strongly enough. Women, too, often resort to blaming their own bodies and weak minds for failing to deliver sons.

The character flaws often add up about such a woman in the eyes of others: She is surely difficult and obnoxious. Perhaps even evil. The fact that the *father* actually determines the sex of a child, as the male sperm carries the chromosome makeup for each child and determines whether a boy or a girl will be born, is unknown to most.

For Azita, the lack of a son stood to impede all she was trying to accomplish as a politician. When she arrived with her family in Kabul in 2005, sneers and suspicion about her lack of a son soon inevitably extended to her abilities as a lawmaker and a public figure. Her visitors would offer their condolences when they learned about her four daughters. She found herself being cast as an incomplete woman. Fellow parliamentarians, constituents, and her own extended family were unsympathetic: How could she be trusted to accomplish anything at all in politics when she could not even give her husband a son? Without a boy to show off to the constant stream of visiting political power brokers, her husband also grew increasingly embarrassed.

Azita and her husband approached their youngest daughter with a proposition: "Do you want to look like a boy and dress like a boy, and do more fun things like boys do, like bicycling, soccer, and cricket? And would you like to be like your father?"

She absolutely did. It was a splendid offer.

All it took was a haircut, a pair of pants from the bazaar, and a denim shirt with "superstar" printed on the back. In a single afternoon, the family went from having four daughters to being blessed with three little girls and a spiky-haired boy. Their youngest would no longer answer to *Mahnoush,* meaning "moonlight," but to the boy's name *Mehran.* To the outside world—and especially to Azita's constituents back in Badghis—the family was finally complete.

Some, of course, knew the truth. But they, too, congratulated

Azita. Having a made-up son was better than none, and people com-
plimented her on her ingenuity. When Azita traveled back to her
province—a more conservative place than Kabul—she took Mehran
with her. In the company of her six-year-old son, she found she was
met with more approval.

The switch also satisfied Azita's husband. Tongues would now
cease to wag about this unlucky man burdened with four daughters,
who would need to find husbands for all of them, and have his line
end with him. In Pashto, Afghanistan's second official language,
there is even a deprecating name for a man who has no sons: He is a
meraat, referring to the system where an inheritance, such as land assets, is almost exclusively passed on through a male lineage. But since
the family's youngest took on the role of a son the child has become
a source of pride to her father. Mehran's revised status has also afforded her siblings considerably more freedom, as they can leave the
house, go to the playground, and even wander to the next block, if
Mehran is along as an escort.

There was one additional reason for the transition. Azita says it
with a burst of low laughter, leaning in a little closer to disclose her
small act of rebellion: "I wanted to show my youngest what life is like
on the other side."

That life can include flying a kite, running as fast as you can,
laughing hysterically, jumping up and down because it feels good,
climbing trees to feel the thrill of hanging on. It is to speak to another boy, to sit with your father and his friends, to ride in the front
seat of a car and watch people out on the street. To look them in the
eye. To speak up without fear and to be listened to, and rarely have
anyone question why you are out on your own in comfortable clothes
that allow for any kind of movement. All unthinkable for an Afghan
girl.

But what will happen when puberty hits?

"You mean when he grows up?" Azita says, her hands tracing the
shape of a woman in the air. "It's not a problem. We change her into
a girl again."

CHAPTER TWO
THE FOREIGNER

Carol

T HERE IS A small restaurant favored by Kabul's unlikely ladies
who lunch, where local riffs on quiche lorraine and delicate little
sandwiches are served as a war rages on unseen in the provinces.
The yellow house with a small garden is tucked into a small alleyway
behind a government ministry and flanked by enough roadblocks to
make it an acceptable outing for foreign diplomats and aid professionals. As in many other places, the electricity goes out every half
hour or so, but guests quickly pick up the habit of carrying on their
conversations in absolute darkness until the switch between generators brings the small lamps up again—all while keeping calm when
small creatures occasionally skitter past their feet under the table. I
had come here to meet the grande dame of Kabul expatriates in the
hope that she could shed some light on what seemed to be yet another
of Afghanistan's many secrets.

Thus far, I had mostly met resistance.

After my first visit to Azita's family, I scoured the Internet and
newspaper archives, thinking that I had missed something fundamental in my homework on the country. But my searches turned up
nothing on any other girls who dressed as boys in Afghanistan. Was
Azita just an unusually creative woman? Or could it be, as I still sus-

pected, that more Afghan families turned their daughters into sons, as a way of both conceding to and defying an impossibly rigid society?

I had also consulted the experts. There were many to choose from.

Girls and women had become one of several urgent causes to the international aid community after the fall of the Taliban, with numerous specialists on the topic of Afghan women shuttling in and out of the country on short-term rotations from Washington, D.C., and various European capitals. Since many donor countries required development projects—from agriculture to politics—to consider specifically how the lives of Afghan women were to be improved, Kabul had turned into a place brimming with "gender experts"—a term encompassing many of the foreign-born aid workers, sociologists, consultants, and researchers with degrees in everything from conflict resolution to feminist theory.

After observing, but largely ignoring, the Taliban's vicious treatment of women for years, consensus among foreigners now converged on the need to quickly usher Afghan women closer to a Western version of equality. A "gender workshop" seemed to be taking place at every upscale hotel in Kabul, where European and American women in ethnic jewelry and embroidered tunics held seminars and drew circles on whiteboards around words like "empowerment" and "awareness." Throughout Afghanistan, hundreds of disparate aid projects were under way, whose euphemistically stated goals were to enlighten Afghans on topics such as "gender mainstreaming" and "gender dialogue."

But senior officials at the United Nations and experts from both government and independent aid organizations delivered a unanimous dismissal when I approached them: Afghans did not dress daughters as sons to counter their segregated society. Why would they ever do that? Had more girls like Mehran existed, these experts, heavily invested in the plight of Afghan women, would certainly know about it, I was told. Anthropologists, psychologists, and historians would surely also have taken note, as such a thing would seem to go against the common understanding of Afghanistan's culture, where one dresses strictly according to gender. Books would have been written and academic studies would have been made. Ergo, such a practice—if it was really a practice and not just an oddity—*must* not exist. Gender segregation in Afghanistan is among the strictest in the world, I was repeatedly told, making such an act unthinkable. Dangerous, even.

But persistent inquiries among Afghans offered a different, if muddled, view. My male translator casually remarked that he had heard of a distant girl cousin who dressed as a boy, but had never understood or thought much of it. Other Afghans echoed occasional rumors of such girls but uniformly advised that I better leave it alone; poking into the private affairs and traditions of families was never a good idea for a foreigner.

An Afghan diplomat eventually offered a firsthand sighting, remembering a friend on his neighborhood football team during the Taliban era in the 1990s. One day the friend just disappeared and a number of his teammates went to his house in search of the boy. His father stepped out of the doorway and said that unfortunately their friend would not be returning. She had changed back to being a girl. The team's twelve-year-olds on the street outside were stunned.

This, however, was an *anomaly,* the diplomat assured me. Any such desperate and uncivilized measures could be blamed solely on the horrors of the Taliban era. A 2003 Afghan feature film, *Osama,* had actually told a story of a young girl who disguised herself as a boy under Taliban rule. But that was fiction, of course. And besides, these were new, enlightened times in Afghanistan, the diplomat said.

But were they really?

To a reporter, the aggressive pushback by expert foreigners and Afghans alike was intriguing. What if this pointed to something bigger than just Azita's family—something that might raise questions about what else we were missing in our decade-long quest to understand Afghanistan and its culture?

I was hoping Carol le Duc might have some input on the topic. With her red hair and jewel-toned silk *shalwars,* Carol never seemed to offer the same confident and often-repeated theses about Afghans or what their country needed in terms of basic understanding of Western values. "I would never call myself a feminist," she had said, for instance, when I first met her. "No, no, I leave that to the others."

Instead, Carol is of a kind that eschews the expat crowd, preferring to socialize with the Afghan families she befriended many years ago, when fewer foreigners were allowed into the country under Taliban rule. She is believed by many to have the sharpest institutional memory in Kabul and is famous for having been one of few women to have negotiated with the Taliban when they were in power.

Carol arrived in this part of the world in 1989 after a divorce. She could have been perfectly comfortable back in England for the rest of her life. But she chose not to. "I hate traveling and passing through places. I like to get to know people. To go deeper," she had told me. "And I realized I was a completely free woman at forty-nine." In her almost two decades in Afghanistan and Pakistan since, she has worked for nongovernmental organizations and as a consultant to government ministries. With a degree in anthropology from Oxford, she has been involved in many studies involving Afghan women, children, and politics.

Holding a firm belief that tea scented with crushed cardamom served in fine bone china cups makes any disaster—and Kabul has seen its share—a little more bearable, she lives in modest grandeur in a peach-colored stone house surrounded by a well-tended garden with two peacocks "because they are beautiful to look at." In winter, her fireplace is a rare find in Kabul; it actually works. And in summer, her large rattan chairs under a slow-moving ceiling fan render August slightly more livable. Every Afghan working for the taxi services that cater to foreigners in residence knows her walled home on a muddy Kabul street simply as "the Carol House," and locals speak of her with a fondness and respect reserved for those who have come to be part of their own history, reaching further back than the most recent war.

At times, though, Kabul becomes a bit much even for Carol, and she hops on a flight to her "country cottage" in Peshawar, a violent Pakistani city formerly under British control, where the Afghan king used to summer. Today Peshawar is considered one of the most dangerous places in the world. It is so infested by Islamic extremists that few Westerners visit voluntarily, and when they do, it is usually with military-grade protection. But to Carol, accustomed to walking Kabul by foot with absolute disregard for what foreigners call "security," and refusing to contain her firecracker hair under a head scarf, Peshawar offers only a marginally more complicated existence. The airport, of course, is a "huge kerfuffle," in her words, where, in place of a hospitality desk, a "Mr. Intelligence" will always approach, presuming she is American. And each time, Carol takes great pleasure in stating she is *British*. And nothing else.

"Now, would you like the special white tea, or should we try the special red?" she asks me at the restaurant, after listening to my quandary. After a nod from Carol, the server pours the illegal red wine from a chubby blue teapot.

That an Afghan girl is being brought up as a boy makes complete sense to Carol: "As a woman, why *wouldn't* you want to cross over to the other side, in a country like Afghanistan?" she exclaims. In fact, she is entertained by the idea; it appeals to her contrarian side.

While she has never observed the practice among children, she does recall a field trip several years prior with a small team of aid workers to Ghazni province, a Taliban stronghold. The men and women of one tribal village lived strictly separated, and when Carol was invited for tea in the women's quarters, she was surprised to find a man living among them. The women called him "Uncle," and he appeared to enjoy a special status in the village. The women served his tea and treated him with great respect. Uncle's appearance was rugged, but he had a slightly softer face than the other men. It took a while, as well as a few helpful whispers, for Carol to understand that Uncle was actually an adult woman in a turban and men's clothing.

In the small village, Uncle functioned as an intermediary between men and women, and served as an honorary male who could convey messages and escort other women when they needed to travel, posing no threat because she herself was a woman.

Like Azita's daughter Mehran, Uncle had been raised as a boy, Carol was told. It was the local mullah's doing, apparently: Uncle had been born as the seventh daughter in a family of no sons. As the spiritual leader of the village, the mullah had taken pity on the parents. So he simply designated the infant girl to be her parents' son only hours after she was born. He gave the child a boy's name, and then promptly dispatched her parents to present what was now their son. The mullah's official proclamation that a son had been born was gratefully accepted by the parents—it both heightened their status and released them from the inevitable scorn of their village.

But why hadn't Uncle ultimately reverted to her birth sex with the onset of puberty? How did she escape being married off? And did she appear pleased with this arrangement? Carol shrugs at my questions; she really doesn't know. Uncle did not have a husband or children of her own, but she certainly enjoyed a higher status than the women. She was "an in-between figure."

That no one seems to have documented any historical or contemporary appearances of other "Uncles" or little girls dressing as boys is entirely understandable, in Carol's view. Even if they should exist, little documentation has survived Kabul's various wars and revolving-door regimes. Afghans are not particularly fond of being queried about their families either: Government officials and their institutions are at best regarded with suspicion.

The closest thing to an Afghan national archive is, in fact, overseen by a longtime American resident in Kabul whom I had also consulted: expatriate Nancy Duprée, the quick-witted American historian in her eighties, affectionately known to many as the "grandmother of Afghanistan." Celebrated for publishing several travel guides to the most remote parts of Afghanistan in the 1970s, she documented Afghanistan's culture and history together with her late husband, archaeologist Louis Duprée. That said, Nancy had neither seen nor heard of girls who dressed as boys and could think of no documentation on the topic through all her time in Afghanistan, dating back to the country's last king, who was ousted in 1973. But she was "not the least bit surprised" by my story of one little girl being brought up as a boy. Similar to Carol's take on the subject, it made a certain sense to Nancy: "Segregation calls for creativity," she had told me.

Nancy also offered up an old photograph left in her care by the former Afghan royal court. In the yellowed black-and-white shot taken in the early years of the twentieth century, women dressed in men's clothing stand guard in Ḥabībullāh Khan's harem. The harem could not be supervised by men because they posed a potential threat to the women's chastity and the king's bloodline. These women dressed as men solved the dilemma, indicating that such solutions may have been used historically in the highest echelons of Afghan society as well.

But what goes on in the secluded lives of Afghan families may never have been open to much investigation by foreigners, Carol suggests. Especially not during this latest deluge of outsiders who want to change Afghanistan. Just like a longtime local who mourns the loss of a neighborhood's soul, Carol describes what Kabul has become in recent years: a cement-gray fortress, where regular Afghans have been driven out of their own city due to an inflated war economy and skyrocketing rents that few but foreigners paid by international organizations can afford. They have created a place where the fear and rumors that drive expatriate communication circulate in a closed loop.

"Most foreigners in Kabul live much like the most shielded Afghan women they are trying to liberate," Carol sarcastically remarks.

AFGHANISTAN HAS A culture of thousand-year-old customs and codes passed down through generations. The history of its women has been sparsely recorded. The history of many countries is often a history of their wars, only occasionally spearheaded by the rare queen. Most sociological research in Afghanistan has been done by foreigners—almost exclusively men—who rarely had access to women, and learned only what Afghan husbands, brothers, and fathers told them.

In Afghanistan, there is no child protection agency to call, no reliable office that retains statistics, no established research university. No one can even say with much certainty how many people *live* in Afghanistan—figures ranging from twenty-three to twenty-nine million are thrown around by the large aid agencies.

The first and only census in Afghanistan was conducted in 1979, and later attempts to actually count Afghans have been both controversial and riddled with difficulty. Three decades of constant war and the movement of large refugee populations make accuracy impossible. The task is further complicated by the complex ethnic makeup of Afghans and the ongoing debate over the exact location of the border with Pakistan.

Those who try to be diplomatic often say that Afghanistan is made up of a collection of minorities, a visible legacy from the many conquerors who came in from different directions throughout history. The largest minority, roughly estimated to make up 40 percent of the population, is the mostly Sunni Islam Pashtun group, many of whom consider themselves to be ethnic Afghans. They dominate the south and the east. The second largest minority is the Tajiks, who are strongest in northern and central Afghanistan. The Hazara people are believed by many to be ancestors of Mongols and were ruthlessly persecuted during the Taliban era as followers of the Shia strain of Islam. Mostly up north, there are also Afghans of Uzbek, Turkoman, and Kyrgyz ethnicity. The country also has Kuchi nomads. While alliances have been formed and broken between groups of ethnicities, those within each group are often suspicious about other ethnicities. This is another reason that little voluntary information, for instance, about how many children are born in a certain area, or within one group, is offered, not least what sex they are.

In Carol's view, the West may also be more obsessed with

children's gender roles than what Afghans are. Although Afghan society is strictly built on the separation of sexes, gender in childhood in a way matters *less* here than in the West. "Here," Carol says, "people are driven by something much more basic—sexuality. Everything before puberty is just preparation for *procreation*. That is the main purpose of life here."

And perhaps we need to set aside what we in the West think of as the order of things to even begin to understand Afghanistan. Where a long lineage of tribal organization is far more powerful than any form of government, where language is poetry and few can read or write but it is common for an illiterate person to have memorized the work of Pashto and Persian poets and to speak more than one language, parameters for established truths and knowledge are manifested in other ways than those outsiders easily recognize. In Carol's words, in a nation of poets and storytellers, "what matters here are the shared fantasies."

For that reason, to find anything out in Afghanistan, one must instead look to the informal structures. For example, those who know Afghan women most intimately are not foreigners, nor Afghan men, but other Afghan women—and the doctors, teachers, and midwives who witness firsthand the desperation for sons and what women will do in order to have them. And no secrets will be offered up immediately, Carol cautions. "You must listen to what they never say."

For effect, the restaurant generator gives up for the third time and we are in the dark again. I inhale deeply. In the darkness, Carol's powerful scent of mandarin and black currant becomes more pronounced and I finally ask about the cloud of cologne that we are both ensconced in. My question delights her.

"Ah, yes. There is this man in Peshawar . . . he deals in essences and oils. He told me they deliver to a French perfumer who makes something rather famous out of this one. That's just talk, of course, but it is pleasant, no?"

I nod, and cannot bring myself to tell Carol that her purveyor is telling the truth. It's a scent I know quite well. As the lights come on

I smile. I, too, am a completely free woman, and just as Carol once decided to do, I have time to go deeper.

BUT COULD I even write about Azita's family, to start? Over the course of a few months, she and I have several takes of the same conversation.

"You told me that you have four daughters," I began my first such call to her. "You also told me about the family's son . . ."

It was a chance just to take it all back and tell me never to return. I almost hoped she would take it. It was only later that I understood she had already made up her mind.

"I think we should tell the reality."

"But this is your secret. Are you sure?"

"I think so. It could be interesting for people. This is the reality of Afghanistan."

With that, I was invited back to her house. And into her family.

CHAPTER THREE

THE CHOSEN ONE

Azita

A T FIVE A.M., she forces herself to rise from the pallet of long, bulky pillows on the floor of the dining room, which also serves as a bedroom.

Before she makes the push to rally her children for the day, she flips through a carousel of images in her mind, aiming to remember five good minutes from the day before, to wake up her spirits with good thoughts. Perhaps she spoke without being interrupted by one of her fellow parliamentarians. Or maybe one of the girls showed her a new painting, and it was really quite accomplished.

Only then does she walk across the hallway to wake her four daughters sleeping in their bunk beds under blue Winnie-the-Pooh covers. A small war over the bathroom usually ensues between Mehrangis and Mehran. The twins will eat some yogurt and naan bread left over from the day before. Mehran will likely refuse breakfast but agree to a roll or sugary cookies or an orange.

The three eldest girls will dress in below-the-knee black dresses and white head scarves over shiny black ponytails. The youngest will don pants, a white shirt, and a red necktie. All four will grab one of the identical large nylon backpacks. Mehran's is far too big for her, but she carries it with pride, just like her older siblings do. Their father will walk his children to the school bus, holding only Mehran's hand.

Azita has fifteen minutes left to get ready. But she is fast. In that time, she transforms herself. As soon as she steps out of the house, she will be upholding the honor of not only her husband and her family, but also her province and her country. Her appearance is a big part of that. She must dress carefully: to divert rather than to attract attention.

Reputation is more than symbolic in Afghanistan; it is a commodity that is hard to restore once it has been damaged. Much like a credit score, it should constantly be preserved and ideally also improved upon, forcing both males and females to adhere to a web of strict social rules. In choosing each detail of her outfit, Azita considers the fundamentals of Afghanistan's honor culture, where a woman's purity is linked to the reputation of her family at all times. The Taliban no longer rules in Kabul, but the dress code for women is still very conservative. Carol le Duc clarified for me the informal but very real penalty system: "A woman who attracts improper attention to herself is inevitably a *whore*."

For a woman, being likened to a whore for dressing the wrong way or being seen speaking to a man who is not her husband can be of great consequence: Her neighbors will talk, her parents may be devastated, and shame will fall over her relatives and potentially tarnish their reputation and standing in society. For a female politician, this game is even more complicated, because politics by its nature requires some degree of visibility.

In the eyes of conservatives, if an Afghan woman must work, she should, at most, be a teacher in an all-female class. Any profession in which a woman interacts with or can be observed by other men is more problematic, as it risks tarnishing her family's reputation. Women who work with foreigners, with their different customs, are even more suspect. Sitting on the national assembly, in the burning glare of the public eye, Azita provokes reactions on many levels.

Her work uniform consists of an Iranian-style full-length black *abaya* with a thin black head scarf, meant to exude authority and dignity. She hopes to display a sense of refinement as well as deep conservatism; no contour of her body must be evident as she moves. The black garment features a small gold trim; any further display of color would be out of the question. In another universe, in another life, Azita's color of choice would be bright red—but that is an impossible color in Afghanistan. The color of fire is considered to be overtly sexual, meant to arrest the eyes of men. It is for someone who means to be flamboyant. Admired. Brightly colored dress was outright banned by the Taliban, but it still would be unthinkable, potentially even dangerous, in Afghanistan's conservative culture. No respectable Kabul woman wears red outside the house, and Azita owns no red clothing.

It takes her seconds to draw thick lines with black kohl around her eyes and dust herself with a beige powder. There are usually cameras in parliament, and she knows by now that matte skin photographs better. As she leaves the house, she puts on a pair of gold-ornamented dark sunglasses. A friend bought them for her in Dubai. She allows herself a few more special effects: two Arabic rose-gold rings and a knockoff designer handbag. Gold is not so much decoration as a display of portable cash, signifying a woman's status as a good wife and mother. He who has a good, respectable, and fertile wife will honor her with gold for all to see. Azita has paid for her own rings, but this no one needs to know.

AFTER SHE IS settled in the backseat, her car is soon absorbed into Kabul's dense morning mash of wheels and dented bumpers. The usual fifteen-minute drive to the national assembly in Karte Seh takes at least one hour in the mornings. White Toyota Corollas patiently pop in and out of large potholes, navigating labyrinths of roadblocks and stretches of no road at all. Spring, or the beginning of *fighting season,* as it's called here—when Taliban and "insurgents" will spring into more aggressive battle—is still a few months away. The hard, icy ground is not yet covered with dust, and red pomegranates from Kandahar are still being cracked open in stalls by the roadside.

Azita's driver avoids getting too close to Afghan police transports, the green Ford Ranger pickup trucks crammed with blue-clad police officers, their assault rifles poking out in every direction. Afghan police are among the most popular targets for suicide bombers and improvised explosive devices known as IEDs. Officers patrolling Kabul are killed at twice the rate of military men, who are harder to get close to. In the eyes of insurgents, both are considered traitors working for the foreign-backed government. Early mornings—when the conviction of martyrdom and the prospect of virgins waiting in paradise is still fresh—are a favorite time for suicide bombers to attack, since dense traffic promises the reward of a high death count.

Azita subscribes to the regular Afghan argument: When your time is up, it's up. God decides when that may be. She cannot spend every morning ride to work thinking of whether the moment has arrived. Azita and her driver have missed explosions by seconds before. Each day, she takes a risk just by stepping out of her house. She logs about two anonymous death threats a week at her office or at home, when she is warned to quit parliament. Or else. To avoid the threats and the inconvenience, she regularly buys new SIM cards for her mobile phone to get a new number, but they keep calling. Her transgressions are clear: She is a woman who dares to serve in parliament and she is a prominent symbol of a controversial, Western-supported government. The threats have become routine. Sometimes she argues with the caller, lecturing him on how the Koran does not condone murder. And it is always a he. "We know you don't care about your own life, but think of your children," they once said. That time, the threat was accompanied by the sound of gunfire. The one time Azita attempted to report threats to the police, they advised her "not to worry." After all, they added, there is little they can do.

There have been direct attempts on her life: A year earlier, two men on a motorbike attempted to throw a hand grenade into the yard of her Badghis house. It exploded against the outside stone wall. When Azita ran out from the kitchen, she found her daughters hiding in a corner of the small garden.

Wealthier politicians travel by armored car, surrounded by

gunmen with shortwave radios. Those with investments in the illegal yet flourishing poppy trade—Afghanistan is the world's largest producer of opium—usually have a follow car as well, to better the odds in case of a kidnap attempt. Azita cannot afford much more than her Toyota Corolla with a driver, who has taped a small glass bottle onto the dashboard—holy water from Mecca. It helps him focus; not even those who make sudden U-turns or drive toward him in the wrong direction merit a honk of his horn.

Azita did employ a bodyguard when she first started, as several colleagues told her it would look unseemly to always arrive without a male escort. But the bodyguard had a tendency to fall asleep as soon as he sat down, so she fired him. Along with all the other members of parliament, Azita has been issued a handgun for her own protection. With no intention of ever using it, she hid it somewhere in her apartment. She often reminds herself that she must find it before the children do.

In the car, she takes out her phone and attempts to bring up CNN's website on the small display, but she does not get far on the spotty Afghan networks.

She looks out the window instead, on the merchants who slowly push their carts toward the marketplace and the motorbikes with at least two and often three or four people clinging on, their faces protected against Kabul's beige-colored air with wraparound scarves. Pairs of Afghan ladies, wearing sandals with socks, hold hands and jump over open sewers. Not much is really white here, and few things are crisp, except for brand-new Land Rovers shipped in for foreigners and rich Afghans. Sooner rather than later, most things turn a shade of mud or khaki. Khaki and cement are the primary colors of Kabul, the monotony broken only by the poppy-funded houses that are painted a cream-infused red, a warm pink, or even green, with glimpses of tasseled pastel curtains—the deceptively cheery narcotecture of Kabul.

Chlorophyll is in short supply here; most trees have either died from pollution or have been burned for fuel by the indigent. A splash of matte red sometimes also filters through the Kabul gray, in an old mural or another Cold War—reminder of those who tried to control the capital before both the Taliban and the Americans.

To AZITA, "THE Russian time," as she refers to it, was not the protracted and brutal struggle painted by English-language memoirs of what Afghans call "the Soviet war" of the 1980s. To her, it was the backdrop of a reasonably charmed childhood.

Her father had been a member of a large but not wealthy clan, and was the first man from Badghis said to have pursued a master's degree in Kabul. He carried that distinction when he returned to his province to marry. He had first met Azita's mother, Siddiqua, when she was only twelve, and according to family legend, had fallen in love with her at first sight. They waited seven years to marry, and in 1977, their first child arrived, a much-loved and longed-for daughter. They named her after the Persian word derived from fire, or *azar*. Soon after celebrating Azita's first birthday the family returned to build a life in Kabul, arriving just in time for the Saur Revolution, when the Communist People's Democratic Party took over the Afghan government.

With ideological and financial backing from Moscow, the new leadership proclaimed aggressive reforms, setting out to replace religious law with a more secular system, promoting state atheism, and forcefully trying to establish a more modern society. Each business sector and each official institution was to be overhauled, from agriculture and the legal system to health care and—most controversially— family law.

The Russians were not the first to try to effect gender parity in Afghanistan, nor would they be the last.

Amanollah Khan had tried to assert rights for women in the 1920s, together with his queen Soraya, who famously cast off her veil in public. The royal couple also began promoting the education of girls, banned the selling of them for marriage, and put restrictions on polygyny. The backlash was severe. To many Afghans, and particularly to the majority who did not live in Kabul, the reforms seemed outrageous: Tribal men would lose future income if daughters could no longer be sold or traded as wives. In 1929, under threat of a coup, the king was forced to abdicate.

Three decades later, King Mohammad Zahir Shah made another, more cautious push for educating and emancipating women, proposing to grant them equal rights in the Constitution of 1964, and the right to vote. Privileged Afghan women were sent abroad for university studies, returning to become professionals and academics.

Arline Lederman, an American development professional who taught at Kabul University in the early 1970s, remembers "a thrilling time" when elite Afghan women were more sophisticated than most of their liberal American counterparts. Women of Kabul's royal family who wore raincoats, sunglasses, and Hermès head scarves and gloves "could have passed for Jackie Kennedy's friends on an autumn day in Boston," she observed.

Those advances of a small group of elite women were significant, but they were exclusive to Kabul and a handful of other urban areas. In the rest of the country, women's roles were largely stagnant.

When Communist-era reforms rolled out on a large scale in the 1980s, however, they did not settle for the small elite in Kabul. In this new era, women and girls would no longer live in seclusion—they would receive mandatory educations, freely choose whom to marry, and be active participants in a new society. After the massive Soviet military force arrived to prop up the fragile Kabul Communist government, thousands of government-employed Russians also landed in Kabul to help execute Moscow's idealized plan for a new Afghanistan.

Agrarians, engineers, aid workers, teachers, and architects began to set up large-scale foreign aid projects with Soviet expertise. The programs were targeted toward turning around the whole country, and quickly. The Soviet leadership, which prided itself on having built an ideal, superior society at home, initially did not place much weight on historical references or failures by others who had come before them.

One clearly stated goal was to educate and introduce more women in the workforce. The idea was sound: Only by gaining real economic power would women have the chance to gain real rights and redress imbalances. The execution would eventually prove to be as misguided as in previous attempts, with only a gradual and late understanding of the deep-rooted economics of patriarchy in the countryside.

But in Kabul, a few female Afghan ministers and parliamentarians were appointed. Others took up work as doctors and journalists, police and army officers, and lawyers. Unions and associations were formed, and, occasionally, women led them. In the capital, segregation at restaurants and on public transportation was banned.

In that progressive environment, Azita's family settled into an upper-middle-class existence, where her father taught geography and history at the university and eventually invested in a small neighborhood store, selling paper goods, dried fruit, nuts, and other household staples. When he realized his daughter had a knack for languages, he bought her a small television set, so she could watch state newscasts broadcast in Russian and eventually translate parts of them for her parents. When Azita's skill became known to teachers, she was singled out as a particularly talented child.

With that, she had been chosen for a special purpose.

As in any long game of invasion and nation building, the Soviets wanted to train the next generation of Afghan leaders and secure their loyalty to Moscow. Little Azita, who possessed a quick mind and a willingness to study, was moved to a more demanding school, with foreign teachers and Russian as the official language. She and other handpicked students would ascend through the new system's most elite institutions—the breeding facilities for Afghanistan's future power cluster. Their education would be crowned by a year or two of higher studies at the best universities of Moscow or Leningrad.

Azita remembers this time being "like Europe," in Kabul, where she would take an electric tram car to school, operated by a female driver. The female school uniform was a brown dress, a white apron, and brown shoes with white kneesocks. On their heads, the girl students wore only brown velvet bows.

To the delight of her Russian teachers, teenage Azita was athletic, too, and she was made captain of the girls' volleyball team. She planned to take her father's academic legacy a step further, and make him even more proud of his firstborn. It did not matter that she had not been born a boy—this newly reformed country that promoted women was on her side. She would become a doctor. Failing that—which did not seem likely—she saw herself as a news anchor, inspired by the unveiled, modern women she saw on her television set. Azita was the Soviet plan for a new Afghanistan incarnate.

But tradition still ruled in the provinces, where the political manifesto mandating equality between the sexes directly contradicted much of Pashtun tradition around inheritance and ownership. Rapid attempts at reforming society and culture were met with great resistance and fury aimed at the government for again issuing decrees to ban child marriage and the lucrative trading of women and girls, and for stating that no women should be sold for marriage, or married against her will. Once more tribal men saw the risk of losing both cash and influence. If women were to be educated and work outside the home, they would "dishonor" their families by being seen in public and potentially develop other, even more subversive ideas. And who would care for the children if women took over the tasks of men? Society would undoubtedly fall apart. Worst of all, another proposed decree would allow women to initiate divorce more easily. Clearly, foreign influence brought decadence and subverted Afghan traditions. The reforms were declared un-Islamic by many religious mullahs.

Meanwhile, armed resistance to the Soviet occupation built around the country. Parts of the mujahideen opposition to the Soviet occupation had found a sympathetic ally in the Pashtuns next door in Pakistan, who were eager to exert influence in Afghanistan. The Soviet-instituted reforms proved to be an efficient pretext for recruiting followers: Women's education as well as all women's rights were despicable, pernicious poison-pill notions that stood to destroy the very fundament of Afghanistan's culture and way of life.

Power has always been held by those who manage to control the origins of life by controlling women's bodies. The old Afghan expression *zan, zar waa, zamin* summarizes the ever-present threat against men's personal property, which was always the main reason for taking up arms: Women. Gold. And land. In that order.

Resistance against the Soviets was boosted by generous financing and logistical help from abroad: U.S. president Jimmy Carter had declared that the Soviet invasion of Afghanistan constituted "the greatest threat to peace since the Second World War." As the fight against Communism was a battle between good and evil, Islamic fundamentalists made excellent partners in this mission as they, too, had clear views of good and evil, albeit from a slightly different perspective.

And so the gains of women in Afghanistan once again directly contributed to war, as their fate was mixed into the powder keg of tension between reformers and hardliners, between foreigners and Afghans, and between the urban centers and the countryside.

Yet, the outside world did not seem to notice the central controversy of Afghan women. The foreign powers instead seemed to agree that there were much bigger problems with Afghanistan than such a peripheral issue, which would have to be revisited at some other time, when the men had stopped fighting. The threat of Communism—and the need to contain it—ensured American dollars and arms kept flowing to the Soviet opposition, moderates and extremists alike.

AZITA'S FAMILY HELD out in Kabul for a while, through violence and power struggles following the eventual Soviet troop withdrawal, when mujahideen groups fought for control of the capital. When the violence shut down schools and many areas of the city, a routine was established for the now seventeen-year-old's rare outings with her father. Azita always carried a note with the phone numbers for relatives in her pocket and a few bills in one of her shoes, in case an attack should separate them.

In the spring of 1992, Kabul erupted into full-blown civil war. Azita gradually trained herself not to panic when a first blast set off a series of explosions, or when she, like most other children in Kabul at the time, saw body parts and corpses on the streets. Her memories from that time largely revolve around shock waves, vibrating buildings, and the fires that ensued: "It started from everywhere. Shooting, bombarding, blasting, killing. Everywhere, there was something. One day we had fifteen or sixteen rocket blasts in our neighborhood. The house was shaking all the time."

Her father, Mourtaza, decided the family had to leave. His family had grown, with three more daughters and one son arriving after Azita, and he could not find a way to take them to Pakistan. Instead, they made a difficult journey back to their remote home province of Badghis. The apartment in Kabul was boarded up, the store left behind. It would be ransacked, but there was nothing they could do to stop it—everyone they knew was fleeing, too. After packing all they could in a small car, the family drove off as refugees in their own country. As their car became a target for snipers the family abandoned it by the road, continuing for eighteen days by bus and by foot, sleeping in mosques and trying to avoid rebels and looters along the way. Those are days Azita cannot recall anymore; her brain has buried them somewhere.

When they reached what they saw as a semblance of civilization again—the city of Herat in western Afghanistan—they were certain of survival, as war had not yet reached nearby Badghis. Her youth would end there, and she would not return to Kabul for many years.

She remembers being angry about the war, and that she had not been able to take any of her books with her, from the small library her father kept in the house.

"Did you have a favorite book?" I ask her in the car, as she describes her last days in Kabul.

"Of course. *Love Story*."

"Oh. I read that, too." I had found it at my grandmother's house once, in my mother's collection of books. "Do you remember the quote at the end? 'Love means never having to say you're sorry'?"

"Yes, yes." Azita smiles and her eyes drift off a little. "It was difficult for me to understand, but I cried a lot in the end when she died. I cried a lot. When I grew up I understood the exact meaning. I watched the movie, too, several times."

"Have you ever been in love?"

She looks at me, silent for a moment before she speaks.

"I love my husband, Jenny."

CHAPTER FOUR
THE SON MAKER

Dr. Fareiba

THOSE WHO MAKE it here are the lucky ones.

Most often, the promise of new life arrives by car. Poor hydraulics and patchy road make the heavily pregnant patients under powder-blue burkas sway in the backseat of the battered Toyota Corollas. The sign on the gate shows a crossed-out machine gun: No weapons allowed. That rule will be disregarded, as most everywhere else in Afghanistan. The guards, who have watched each car barrel down the hillside, give a nod to swing open the steel doors. Inside is a two-story hospital, where a handful of doctors work in shifts at this sole medical clinic in a largely Taliban-controlled area of thirty-two thousand people. Some patients are nomads; most are from poor, rural families.

On average, one hundred and sixty-six new Afghans are born in the maternity ward here each month, according to the hospital's records. It rests in the middle of a quiet flat plateau in the Wardak province, about an hour's drive from Kabul. Quiet, that is, on a good day: A few miles north of the hospital is an American military base—the primary target for rocket attacks by insurgents, as all resistance to foreign troops is dubbed. Those insurgent fighters take aim at the foreign enemy from several angles, the hospital squatting between themselves and the target. When fired, the rockets arc through the sky above the little hospital and often hit just outside the grounds. At times, they fall a bit short and hit the hospital.

Thermal cameras on unmanned drones hum in the air above, trying to discover the rockets while they are still on the ground, often mounted on makeshift piles of stones and sticks, connected to batteries and timers. If the drone operator spots something of interest, an attack helicopter armed with machine guns, rockets, and missiles can be dispatched in a preemptive attack.

Regardless of who aims to kill whom out there, most efforts inside the clinic frantically revolve around life. Nobody will ask patients what family or clan they belong to, or who they may have been fighting outside the gate. Every ragged, hollow-eyed child is cared for, every pregnant woman is ushered inside. The men will wait outside, leaning back in rows on benches along a yellow stone wall with a backdrop of snowy mountains, while the fate of their families plays out in the hospital. Most are in the typical villager dress of white cotton pants, vests, and plaid turbans, with open sandals or plastic shower shoes also in the iciest of winter.

Inside, layers of burkas, hijabs, and shawls are pulled back by sun-burned henna-painted hands. The hands often look older than the faces underneath, with their soft cheeks and unwrinkled eyes. A few mothers-to-be have only recently become teenagers. Every few hours, a woman's struggle to have a son ends here, inside a white-tiled room, where three gynecological chairs have been covered with black plastic bags. A baby boy is triumph, success. A baby girl is humiliation, failure. He is a *bacha,* the word for child. A boy. She is the "other": a *dokhtar.* A daughter.

The woman who returns home with a son can be celebrated with a *nashrah* ceremony, where music is played and prayers are said. Food and drink will be brought out in abundance. The new mother will be presented with gifts: a dozen chickens or a goat to celebrate her achievement. She may even be offered a few pounds of butter to help her breast-feed her baby boy to become healthy and strong. She is elevated to a higher status among women. She who can deliver sons is a successful, enviable woman; she represents both good luck and a good wife.

If a daughter is born, it is not uncommon for a new mother to leave this delivery room in tears. She will return to the village, her head bowed in shame, where she may be derided by relatives and neighbors. She could be denied food for several days. She could be beaten and relegated to the outhouse to sleep with the animals as punishment for bringing the family another burden. And if the mother of a newborn has several daughters already, her husband may be ridiculed as a weakling with whom nature refuses to cooperate, a *mada posht*. Translation: "He whose woman will only deliver girls."

One kind of child arrives with the promise of ownership and a world waiting outside. The other is born with a single asset, which must be strictly curtailed and controlled: the ability to one day give birth to sons of her own. She, like her mother before her, has arrived in what the United Nations calls the worst place in the world to be born. And the most dangerous place in which to be a woman.

"WE ARE THE Pashtun people. *We need the son.*"

Dr. Fareiba emphasizes each word in hoarse, broken English. It should not be too hard, even for a foreigner, to understand this fundamental fact of her country. As with many women here, her weathered face betrays no precise age, nor will she offer a number. But she will gladly speak of everything else in short, assertive bursts with one corner of her mouth perpetually turned into an upward smirk. She has brought me through a back door into the disinfectant-smelling, bare-bones hospital for an education on the need for sons after extracting a promise that I will not attempt to speak to any of the husbands outside, which could alert them to the presence of a foreigner and endanger the hospital.

Dr. Fareiba's patients share many circumstances with the majority of Afghanistan's women, whose lives are far removed from that of Azita and others in Kabul. These are the invisible women, now only temporarily out of the view of their husbands. For some, it is the only time they are allowed to have contact with people outside their own family. Most are illiterate and very shy, even in front of other women. Some hold hands and hesitate to step up to the examination table for the first time, where bulging bellies are carefully touched by doctor's hands.

Dr. Fareiba is known by reputation. She is greeted with respect as she sweeps around the corridors in her work uniform: a burgundy leather coat and a floor-length velvet skirt. She peeks into every room, where women nurse their newborns under thick polyester fleece blankets, or line up along the walls to see the gynecologist. Some smile; others hide their faces. The children, who have come with their mothers, do not smile. Much of the donated brightly colored clothing they wear is either too large or too small. None of them have anything resembling overcoats, and they, too, wear open sandals on soil- and dust-blackened feet. Only one little girl has a pair of red rubber boots. She looks to be around six years of age, with a matted mop of brown hair. Her pale gray eyes quietly follow the movements of the younger siblings left in her charge while their mother is seen by one of the doctors.

Dr. Fareiba asks a few questions of each patient, smiles, and then turns around to give me a matter-of-fact summary. Each contains a life story:

"The husband left her after three of her babies died. Now remarried as a second wife. She is twenty-five, and pregnant again."

"Seventeen. First child. Married to her older uncle."

"Twenty-one. Three children. Her husband is a powerful man, with many wives."

Birth control is available for free at the hospital. The doctors urge patients to wait at least three months between pregnancies for a better chance of carrying a child to term. Whether patients actually use any form of contraception has less to do with ideology or a conservative husband and more with the practical circumstances of life here. Too much snow, heavy rain, or a mudslide in the spring may block the roads from a small village when time comes to refill a prescription or submit to another injection. Or there simply may be no car, or no gas for the car, or no one to drive it. That also contributes to eighteen thousand Afghan women dying each year of complications from childbirth; about fifty women per day, or one every half hour.

In another room, three women from the same village are in various stages of pregnancy with complications, but the cost of a car ride could not be justified for just one, or even two of them. So the first two had to wait for the third to go into labor. Only then were they all three driven together, as fast as the car would go. Despite efforts to stem maternal mortality, Afghanistan still ranks among the world's worst countries to give birth in, on par with the poorest and most war-torn nations in Africa. But the odds for survival at this clinic, in the middle of a battlefield, are better than at a home birth.

"She is forty," Dr. Fareiba says of a patient in a postdelivery room. The woman is lacking several front teeth, and has bracelets stacked up on each arm. "A miscarriage. But she has ten live children. Only girls. So she tries for a son, again and again."

When a new wife is blessed with two or three sons as her first children, she will not be pressured to have many more after that. If a few girls follow, that is fine, too. But at a streak of only "girl, girl, girl," in the doctor's words, most women will keep trying for a son. It's a one-sentence explanation to the population question: A total of four or five children is perfectly acceptable to most parents in Afghanistan—but only if that number includes mostly boys. The life expectancy of a woman here is forty-four years, and she spends much of it being pregnant. Most couples know how to limit pregnancies if they want to, but the pressure to have another son often overrides any concern for a woman's survival.

Dr. Fareiba pokes into the blanket of a new mother, who lies on a bed facing the wall. She has been silent since her delivery. The doctor sweeps up the small bundle from her side and turns to the nurse trailing her every step. They nod at each other: Yes, it's a girl.

She is only a few hours old, and she does not have a name yet. Her eyes have been lined with kohl, "for magical luck," and to protect her from the evil eye. The baby blinks a little, and her tiny mouth gasps a few times. She is perfect, down to her tiny, grasping fingers. Yet to many in Afghanistan, she is *naqis-ul-aql,* or "stupid by birth," as a woman equals a creature lacking wisdom due to her weak brain. If she survives, she may often go hungry, because feeding a girl is secondary to feeding a son in the family, who will be given the best and most plentiful food. If, in her family, there is a chance of the children going to school, her brothers will have priority. Her husband will be chosen for her, often before she reaches puberty. As an adult, very few of life's decisions will be her own.

LOOKING AT THE revered Dr. Fareiba, though, it is hard to imagine that she would allow a man to rule any aspect of her existence. She herself has defied tradition by working under almost every form of government in the past twenty years, as well as no government at all, since there was always a need for female doctors. Dr. Fareiba has delivered "maybe one thousand babies," by her own estimate.

"But why do only sons count here? What is it that women cannot do?" I ask.

Dr. Fareiba raises her hands in the air to express frustration. She already explained this: It is not about capability. Men and women just have different roles and different tasks. It is about how society is arranged and what works. It is about how it's always been.

The pressure for sons is not just perpetuated by men, either. Women need sons just as much, Dr. Fareiba says, using herself as the example. Her three sons are not only her proudest achievement; they are essential to the survival of her family. Who other than a son protects and cares for his parents, should they survive to old age? If the family needs to flee from yet another war? In case of a dispute, or a violent conflict, with another family? There is no social security, little health care, and virtually no rule of law in Afghanistan. There is just unemployment, poverty, and constant war. In this environment, the number of sons equals a family's strength, both financially and socially. They are insurance. A 401(k). A bank. Dr. Fareiba's sons will support and ensure not only her life but her family's longevity and legacy.

Dr. Fareiba has a daughter, too. But she will be married off to a man of her parents' choice, and move away to live with her husband's family. The ownership of an Afghan girl is literally passed on from one male—her father—to the one who becomes her husband. He will take over the ruling of her life, down to the smallest details if he is so inclined. Dr. Fareiba may not even see her daughter again, if her future son-in-law and his family decide to move far away. On the other hand, when her own sons marry, they will take their new brides back to Dr. Fareiba's house to start new families there. More sons will hopefully be born, and her family will grow larger and stronger.

"The daughter is never ours. But the son," says Dr. Fareiba in a matter-of-fact tone, "will stay with us forever."

It is how things always worked in this country, where tribal law and strict patrilineal tradition have historically offered a higher degree of stability than most governments. In Afghanistan, not much is for certain other than an open sky and eventual death. In between the two is family.

Dr. Fareiba leaves it at that.

But the patriarchal system, with the idea that women should be subordinate to men, and that sons are more valuable than daughters, was in fact never a "natural" nor a God-given order that always existed. It can be traced back to entirely human-created historical events.

When American scholar Gerda Lerner pioneered the study of women's history in the 1980s, her research provided both evidence and an explanation for how patriarchy originally began to form. It was not until around the dawn of agriculture, when humans transitioned from being hunters and gatherers to becoming herders and farmers, in the fourth to second millennium BC, that notions of personal property and ownership also created the need to control reproduction. Specifically that meant the wombs of women, since those with the most children gained an advantage. Both children, who could be used for labor, and women, who could produce the children, became resources that could be bought and sold to create alliances and thereby expand upon personal ownership. Land as well as capital was passed down solely through male heirs, creating an absolute need for sons to preserve wealth and build legacies. Many societies grew out of this raw version of the patriarchal system, which is still very much in place in the world's most conservative countries, and has visible remnants in most other societies.

In addition to Gerda Lerner's historical explanations of the origins of patriarchy, one may inch closer to an understanding of Afghanistan's honor culture and the standing of women by considering the struggles of women in Western societies only a few generations ago. A tried-and-true reporter's strategy is also useful: to follow the money, and observe how those who control it will use every worldly and otherworldly argument for not sharing it.

BUT HOW DOES someone like Dr. Fareiba come to exist in this environment, where most Afghan women—and men, for that matter—have seen little diversion from the original version of patriarchy?

In reality, almost every truth about Afghanistan can be easily contradicted, and almost every rule can be bent—when it is practical. There have always been fathers with more liberal minds who had daughters and urged them to take on the world outside. Dr. Fareiba is one of those daughters, having been born into a well-off Pashtun family, which allowed her to complete most of her education during the Communist period. Her father, also a doctor, her four brothers, and her seven sisters all graduated from university. Their family could afford it and saw no reason to differentiate between the education of sons and daughters. Dr. Fareiba's husband is also a physician, carefully chosen by her parents because he would allow their daughter to work.

Still, she must respect the rules of life here, even those she finds frustrating, and she cuts me off when I question the system of male inheritance and forced marriages. "This is our society. Our culture."

It's typical. Even though an Afghan may privately declare that something is illogical, illegal, silly, or just plain wrong, he or she can at the same time make an argument for why it must be adhered to: Society demands it; society is not ready to accept any diversion. This is the meaning of the frustrated shrug, the "I wish it would be different, but . . ." explanation.

The punishment for going "against society" is "gossip" and with it the threat of losing one's good reputation and family honor. Too much gossip makes life complicated and dangerous. The disapproval of neighbors, friends, and even one's own family can make accomplishing basic things for a man—getting a job, marrying a daughter into a good family, or borrowing money to build a bigger house— almost impossible. In a place where the state hardly exists and few institutions function, reputation is one of few valid currencies, and preserving it must always take priority. With the consequence that sons must be had at all costs.

"THEY CALL ME the maker of sons," says Dr. Fareiba as we sit down for tea at a later time, unwrapping dusty caramels from a glass tray. She will put one behind her front teeth and suck her tea through it to make it sweet, the way many Afghans do.

Making sons is a specialty, and one she says she shares with some other Afghan doctors, who are known to offer it as a service on the side. It costs a little extra. Dr. Fareiba is well aware that the male sperm decides the sex of the fetus, but she still believes that "changing conditions" inside a woman's body can make the environment more or less favorable for the "right" sperm—those carrying the male chromosome combination. The man needs no special treatment, however. His body is already complete and ready to produce sons.

Dr. Fareiba makes a reference to her own sister, who has a university degree and a husband who is an engineer. But they were pitied as they didn't have a son, only four daughters. So she came to Dr. Fareiba.

"She asked me: 'Why don't you get any girls—you get boys? What is the problem with me?' And I treated them one year ago, and now thanks God she has a son."

Dr. Fareiba beams. Her nephew, now seven months old, was conceived after his mother was put on Dr. Fareiba's special regimen of certain foods, homemade potions, and sexual positions. "I made him for you," she is fond of telling her sister.

Those tried-and-tested methods for creating sons have been passed down to her from female relatives through generations and finessed through experimentation and by trading tips with fellow Afghan doctors.

"Hot foods make boys," Dr. Fareiba explains, citing the various dishes, black tea, and dried fruits she prescribes for the woman who needs a son. Eating yogurt, melon, and green tea, on the other hand, count as "cold" foods, and are more likely to result in girls. Creams and powders can also help. Dr. Fareiba makes most of them at home and trades them with other doctors. Her female patients are instructed to insert the potions into their vaginas, meant to help along those sperms carrying the male-determining Y chromosome.

Conventional medicine does acknowledge that male sperm swim faster and tire sooner, while the female-chromosome-carrying sperm are slower but have more stamina and stay alive longer in the uterus.

Dr. Fareiba also advises her female patients to lie flat after intercourse, to allow the precious male sperm every advantage without gravity derailing things. According to conventional medicine, however, there is only one way to ensure conception of a specific sex: to remove the egg and vet the sperm in advance before implanting a fertilized embryo back into a woman's womb. When I tell Dr. Fareiba this, she just smiles. She has too successful a track record, and her science is ancient: "Tell me," she says. "What do *you* believe?"

I will remember her question. In Afghanistan, as Carol first suggested, believing can be more important than anything else, and mythos counts as much as logos.

But even Dr. Fareiba concedes that failure must sometimes be declared. After she and other experts have done all they can, parents do resort to other solutions.

Yes, she says, there may be other girls like Mehran, who masquerade as boys. Simply because everybody knows that a made-up son is better than none at all. Dr. Fareiba lowers her voice when she speaks of a certain type of family. As a physician, she has attended several births where an infant girl is announced as a son. The child is then presumably brought back to the village and reared as a boy for as long as the lie will hold, or as long as the community goes along with it, knowing that it is merely an honorary boy. Dr. Fareiba and her colleagues have also learned not to ask too many questions when young boys have been brought to the hospital's emergency room, only for the doctor on call to make a startling discovery when examining the child. They all keep face, in a silent agreement with the parents.

Children's rights are a concept unacknowledged in Afghanistan. If parents want a girl to look like a boy, then it is within the right of the parents to make that happen, Dr. Fareiba believes. This temporarily experimental condition will right itself later on. Children, just as Carol le Duc mentioned, take a predetermined path in life. For girls, that means marrying and having children of their own. For boys, it means supporting a family.

Dr. Fareiba does not imagine there is any documentation about what she refers to as the private circumstances of each family. Nor is she keen on offering referrals to anyone who might know more about it. The creation of such a son would be the parents' decision, and their choice should be respected. And what does it matter, anyway? These girls are hidden, and that is exactly the point. To everyone on the outside, they are just *bachas*.

CHAPTER FIVE
THE POLITICIAN

Azita

I T WAS TEMPORARY, she was told.

As the oldest sister, Azita was immediately put to work when she arrived at her grandparents' house in Badghis in 1995. For laundry to be done, a wood fire first had to be kindled and tended to. Fresh water then had to be hauled from a long walk away with two heavy buckets. Homemade lye was extracted by pouring ashes in salt water. The lye took the dirt out of fabric—and the skin from hands. The student from an elite school in Kabul found herself in what is still today one of the country's most rural and undeveloped provinces. Close to Iran and bordering on Turkmenistan, Badghis is named after the strong winds that come across the mountains and blow across its deserts and scattered pistachio forests. Most residents are farmers. Few can read or write.

Without functioning schools to go to, there was not much to do, and Azita's parents insisted that when the war was over, they would return to the capital and resume a normal life. Azita would become a doctor and she would travel abroad. All according to plan.

But the eighteen-year-old's prospects gradually turned darker. Badghis is dominated by Tajik tribes and has a Pashtun minority, and the Taliban was closing in, ferociously fighting to take full control of the province. At the house, where Azita spent most of her time, the windows had to be covered, so no passersby could see her shadow. When she left the house, always with a male escort, she viewed the outside world through the thick grid of a burka that made quick turns of the head disorienting and breathing more difficult. It had taken a week of burka training at the house before she mastered pulling the fabric tight over her face so that she could navigate past what little she saw while walking. She learned to move more slowly, making sure she did not flash her ankles.

While local rulers in Badghis in peacetime had not taken a very liberal view of women, nor did the warlords who followed, the Taliban who eventually came to control most of Afghanistan had a particular hatred for half the population.

In his book *Taliban*, Pakistani author Ahmed Rashid describes those who fought for the Taliban: Many were orphaned young men, mostly between fourteen and twenty-four, educated in an extremist version of Islam by illiterate mullahs in Pakistan, and having no sense of their own history. They were Afghan refugees who had grown up in camps and knew very little about a regular society and how to run it, having been taught that women were an unnecessary and, at most, tempting distraction. For that reason, there was no need to include them in decision making and other important matters. The Taliban leadership also argued for sexual abstinence and maintained that contact between men and women in society should be avoided, as it would only serve to weaken warriors.

Controlling and diminishing women became a twisted symbol of manhood in the Taliban's culture of war, where men were increasingly segregated from women and had no families of their own. Taliban policies toward women were so harsh that even an Iranian ayatollah protested and said they were defaming Islam. And once again, the role and treatment of women became a critical conflict, both in a monetary sense and in an ideological one, as Afghanistan's leadership became increasingly isolated from the rest of the world. To them, when Western powers criticized the Taliban view of women, it confirmed that it was correct to segregate the sexes, since any Western idea, invention, or opinion was decidedly un-Islamic. That designation, of course, excluded advanced weaponry and other modern perks exclusive to the male leadership.

To quell the boredom in what was virtually a form of house arrest in Badghis, Azita took it upon herself to carry on the education of her younger sisters. With time, other girls from the neighborhood discreetly joined them. Officially, they were just gathering to read and reread the Koran many times over, but Azita offered lessons in math, geography, and language. Books posed a risk—both to carry around and to keep at the house—so teachings mostly consisted of Azita's own recollections from her Kabul school.

Around the same time, Azita began to quiet herself in the presence of her father, Mourtaza. She had always been his confidant and vice versa. They would sit together and talk about politics, history, and literature. But as the war raged on and the Taliban gradually began to dominate Badghis, Mourtaza changed. He became irritable. At night, he was restless and did not sleep much. The children tried to steer clear of him during the day, but it was difficult in the small house when the girls could not venture outside. It confused Azita that her father seemed to have lost interest in their conversations, and she was sad that he did not give her the attention he used to.

Two years into the family's stay in Badghis, Mourtaza received an offer of marriage for his eldest daughter. It came from one of his nephews and was delivered by his widowed sister-in-law. Marriage between first cousins is both favored and common in Afghanistan, as a way to keep property and other assets within the extended family. Most important, such marriages are thought to strengthen family bonds by avoiding dilution by outside blood.

Azita had been regularly targeted for marriage by both relatives and sons of entirely unknown families since the family had settled in Badghis. She did not give it much thought; in her mind, people had no way of knowing she just wasn't available on the Badghis bride market. At least not yet. She was on a different track—in Badghis, she considered herself merely on hiatus from the rest of her life. Several of her classmates in Kabul had nurtured forbidden fantasies about marrying for love and having fairy-tale wedding parties. But Azita had remained fairly oblivious of the idea throughout her teenage years. If anything, she had been guilty of pride and raw ambition. In her staked-out immediate future, there was no time for boys. She had never even met those who proposed marriage in Badghis—they were received by her parents, who had a stock answer for anyone who came asking for their daughter: "She is going to be educated, and we don't want to waste her talent." And certainly not on an illiterate farmer like her cousin—to Azita, that was almost too obvious.

SHE WAS UNPREPARED for the conversation she overheard one evening. Mourtaza was angry again. He had been fooling himself that Kabul would return to normal any time soon, he told his wife. It put him in an impossible situation. He could not maintain the family with just their ten-year-old son. If Azita had been a boy, she heard him say, it would have been different. The family would have been stronger and more respected. Azita's younger sisters only added to the difficulty, and made Mourtaza weak, with a weak family, exposing him to threats from outsiders and with few prospects for future income.

For nineteen years, Azita had hoped her father was not angry she had been born a girl. But it was what he said next that took her breath away. He had changed his mind about the initial proposal from Azita's cousin. Mourtaza would accept it. Azita was to be married.

Her knees buckled, and she sank to the floor.

It would solve their problems, Mourtaza continued. Marrying his daughter to a relative would tie another adult male to his family and carry them all through these hard times. It would ensure the safety of both Azita and her younger sisters: If the eldest was married, at least, it showed his resolve to others; that he had a plan for his daughters. She must agree, he said to his wife, that it was better to have Azita safely married to a man they knew than to risk the family's future.

But Azita's mother, Siddiqua, did not remotely agree. She begged her husband to change his mind. She even raised her voice to him. It would not be a good marriage, she said. What would become of their daughter if she married into an illiterate family from the village? The argument escalated into a fight, and Mourtaza threatened to leave Siddiqua if she did not support him. His decision stood firm, and he demanded that she bring Azita the news. It is how it should be done, he told her: It is a mother's task to tell a daughter she is to marry and who her parents have chosen for her.

When Siddiqua came to her daughter the next day, she began by asking her forgiveness. She had lost the battle, she said. She cried as she told Azita that she would soon be a wife. After more than two decades with Mourtaza, she could not go against him but had to keep the family together. Siddiqua bowed her head in sorrow before her daughter, pleading that she would honor her parents' decision.

"This is your destiny," she told her daughter. "You must accept it."

Azita rebelled as best she could. She screamed. She cried. She was silent and refused to eat for days. She existed in a delirium between sleep and the barest consciousness from lack of food and complete exhaustion. Some things she dreamed and some were real; she could not tell it apart. There was little she could do—if she had run away, she would most likely have been arrested, beaten, and imprisoned as soon as she left the house. She knew escape was not an option. To refuse her parents would draw shame over the entire family, and her father would be disgraced.

She needed at least ten more years, she told her mother as she tried to negotiate. The situation in Afghanistan would change. She could go on to university, just as they had planned. Make them proud, and become extraordinarily successful.

"I will do whatever you want. Just give me more time," she implored her mother.

"I am sorry, my child," Siddiqua responded. "I cannot do anything more. It is over."

Later, Azita thought she had perhaps been naive. She had only vaguely imagined getting married someday, to a man who would share

her goals in agreement with her parents. It would be someone educated, like herself, and they would both work. Perhaps an academic,
like her father. Someone to look up to, who in turn supported her
own ambition. But her illiterate cousin, whom she had not seen since
they were toddlers?

A few months later, Azita left her parents' home with her new
husband. She was carried away on a donkey, headed for her mother-
in-law's house in a remote village. As a bride price, Azita's father received a small piece of land and one thousand American dollars.

TODAY, AS SHE steps out of her morning ride in dark sunglasses and
nods at the security guards, Azita represents the law in the Islamic
Republic of Afghanistan. Today, like any other day, tribal elders from
her province will come and ask for her favors. Leaders of political fac-
tions will try to court her vote. Businessmen will attempt to negotiate
her support.

She receives them all in a parliament annex, presiding over meetings at the head of a long mahogany conference table. Meetings are
rarely timed or scheduled and have no set agenda, but just keep rolling throughout her day; there is always another group of men waiting
outside. She is paid two thousand dollars a month to sit in the national assembly's lower house, tasked with creating and ratifying laws
and approving members of government.

A visitor can reach the steps of the yellow building only after
being approved for passage through four sandbagged roadblocks; the
final checkpoint is flanked by two American Humvees, with machine
gunners sticking their heads out on top. The guards may be local, but
this government, as well as the very state itself, is upheld by 130,000
troops from forty-eight countries, though most are American. They
are positioned just beyond the mountains in the distance, above the
thick walls that surround the compound, with a single Afghan flag
on a pole fluttering high in the air.

The government was created using the standard playbook of

"state building" by Western countries after a regime is removed. At a conference near the former West German capital of Bonn in November 2001, a few dozen Afghans selected from those who had aligned themselves with Americans were brought in to design the first national government since the Soviet invasion of 1979, and to draft a new constitution. It was largely a gathering of winners, most notably of those Afghans representing the armed Northern Alliance, which had helped U.S. Special Forces to topple the Taliban. Leaders of several major Pashtun tribes deemed by foreigners to be close to the Taliban were not invited. Back then, no compromises were to be made in the planning and execution of a brand-new country.

Around the same time, the liberation of women began to be described by politicians in the United States and Europe as one more rationale for the war in Afghanistan, almost equal to that of fighting terrorism. In the new country that was to be created, half of the population would be granted heretofore unthinkable concessions: After years of being unable to peer out of any window, Afghan women would be allowed to leave their homes without a blood relative escort. They should also be represented in government by the mandated 25-percent-minimum female share of seats; surpassing at the time both the United Kingdom, with 22 percent, and the United States, with 17 percent.

A ministry for women's affairs was created, and the new constitution stated, just as the Koran does, that men and women are equal. Western countries also soon set out to propel one of the world's poorest countries into a shiny new state with the help of a massive infusion of foreign aid money and expertise. At the time of Azita's entry into Kabul's 249-member lower house in 2005, she personified the new American plan for Afghanistan.

ON THIS DAY, she opens her first meeting by inviting three men visiting from Badghis to speak. They have come to argue on behalf of a brother, who has been sentenced to sixteen years in prison for drug smuggling. He is innocent, they tell Azita.

She nods. Can she see the court documents? The men produce them. They also hand her another document, which they have written in advance, stating that a member of parliament knows their brother is innocent and that he should be released immediately. Could she please sign it, so they can take it to the provincial governor and just have him back?

It doesn't work like that, Azita explains. What the court has decided, she cannot change. She is a member of parliament, not a judge. The men are bewildered: "But you are our representative. You have this power. You should do this for us!"

Azita suggests a compromise—she will help them appeal the brother's case in the supreme court in Kabul. "That's all I can do. I will ask them to investigate the case again. I will ask this of them and also tell them that you are my villagers."

There is no other way, she assures them while gently laying out the basic structure of the justice system, switching between Pashto and Dari so that all those present will understand. Another man from Badghis speaks up, offering a new detail about the situation: The jailed man has not only been found guilty of drug smuggling, he has also been sentenced for assisting the Taliban in the production of a roadside bomb.

With that, Azita becomes impatient. "Is lunch ready?" she asks of a worker who has wandered in to wipe the table, midmeeting. She reassures her visitors that she will inquire with a lawyer whether the case can be appealed. Then she invites them to stay and eat with her.

In the afternoon, she attends one of the daily drawn-out, sometimes chaotic assembly sessions inside the main building that still smells of paint and new carpentry. Inside the dimly lit theater, where participation is overwhelmingly male, sessions are frequently interrupted by procedural details, such as translations between the two official languages, and the fact that many of the representatives cannot read and need to have documents read aloud to them. And then there are the frequent power outages, where everything will go dark before spare generators rumble alive again.

The chairman will not often grant Azita permission to speak, and when he does, others will protest or just interrupt her. When she proposes something, she is often ignored, only to later hear a similar plan discussed by others.

Her sixty-two female peers, scattered in small groups throughout the assembly, can hardly be described as a sisterhood. They share no common cause vis-à-vis women's rights. Some openly serve as placeholders recruited by wealthy and powerful warlords looking to strengthen their own influence. With some notable exceptions, the women in parliament generally remain silent. In their almost five years in office so far, they have seen laws ratified that actually discriminate against women, and like the male members, they have not objected when amnesty has been handed out for war crimes.

Azita thinks of herself as a political pragmatist, trying to wisely use what little capital and room to maneuver she has, as she represents a remote province and lacks a personal fortune. For the campaign that brought her here, a supporter lent her two hundred dollars to register as a candidate. The fear of not being able to repay the money stayed with her throughout her campaign. With little experience campaigning, she did what she could to get her name out to the parts of her province where it was too dangerous to travel—where the Taliban or local warlords were in control. Azita believes her command of Pashto helped her win the seat in parliament, since some of the elder tribesmen cast their vote for her. She hopes at least a small share of the women in her province voted for her as well, with the permission of their husbands or fathers.

Now, after being cut off and even ridiculed for daring to speak at the Ministry of Education on another day I was in the audience, she sits stoically on her assigned chair and just looks out into the air. In Azita's reasoning, it is better to exist on the inside, where she at least has a vote, than to only shout about women's rights from outside the barricades, where few but the foreign press might listen.

Like Carol le Duc, Azita would never call herself a feminist. It's a far too inflammatory word, and one associated with foreigners. Her own brand of resistance is slightly different. For instance, she never misses an opportunity to be on camera. The young and spirited Afghan press corps, much of which operates with foreign aid money, often ask Azita to comment on parliamentary negotiations, and she always accepts. She prefers to be interviewed on the lawn outside, as the plenum usually disrupts in angry murmurs and complaints at the sight of a video camera, although photography is indeed allowed. Azita never confronts colleagues who argue women should not appear on television, but to her, that is exactly the point. If a young boy or girl somewhere in Afghanistan catches a glimpse of a woman on television, and an elected politician at that, it has some small value. To show them that at least she exists. That she is a possibility.

Azita guards her mannerisms carefully, on-screen and off, well aware that her appearance and personal life are thoroughly scrutinized. What she actually says, or how she negotiates, matters less. A slip of the scarf, an offhand remark, laughing out loud—it would all be inappropriate for a serious politician. The personal is always political here. She monitors and studies her female colleagues, constantly adjusting her own behavior to the unspoken demands and questions: *What is she wearing? Is she too loud? Does she move her hands too much when she speaks? Does she walk too confidently? Is she a good wife and mother? How many sons does she have? Does she look like a devout, modest Muslim woman? Does she pray? How many times a day?*

The Islamic Republic of Afghanistan is most often described as a strict Muslim society. Regardless of personal beliefs, the *appearance* of being anything other than very pious here can harm one's reputation and present dangers. To complicate things further in a largely illiterate society, Afghans often differ on what exactly constitutes "a good Muslim." The largest religious authority in the country, the National Council of Religious Scholars, or the Ulama Council, consists of three thousand members from around the country—most of whom have a mujahideen background from the 1980s. The council has been known to preach whatever suits its members' shifting alliances and political purposes, frequently denouncing the presence of foreigners and issuing harsh decrees to limit the role of women in society.

Louis Duprée described this contradiction in his work on Afghanistan: "Islam, in essence, is not a backward, anti-progressive, anti-modern religion, although many of its interpreters, the human, action component, may be backward and anti-progressive." It is the classic curse of organized religion—when its *interpretation* is hijacked by mortals as a means to control others.

To Azita faith is, and should be, personal: "I go to mosque. I go to the general prayer on Fridays. I believe when I pray that God listens, and that if you help others, God will love you more. Sometimes for my work, I go to the embassies, where people smoke and drink. I don't do that. But I would not say anything bad about those people who do. I believe everyone can have their own idea, their own belief. So that is my version."

WHEN SHE RETURNS home at the end of the day, various suppliants have already lined up outside her apartment complex, where there are no guards or any other security provisions. One needs a job. Another asks her to broker a family conflict. They will all expect a meal and a place to sleep for the night, in her two-bedroom apartment. In Azita's words: "As an MP, you are a guesthouse, a restaurant, a hospital, and a bank."

Constituents regularly ask to borrow money. Azita has no savings, but to decline without at least trying to offer a small travel contribution, for instance, could be seen as hostile. But it would not be as bad as turning someone away who needed a place to sleep. That is simply not done. It would risk having someone go back to Badghis saying Azita is a lazy and haughty representative who does not care about her people.

She learned this quickly on the job: "A woman politician's work is very different from a man's. You are a politician during the day, and then when you reach the door of your house, you have to be a good mother and a housewife as well. I have to take care of my children: Do homework, cook for them, make dinner, and clean. Then I have to receive my guests and be a good host for them."

She cheers herself up as she cooks dinner for ten most nights of the week. "I compare myself to other political ladies in the world. We all have to work very hard and ignore those people who say we should not be here."

BY MIDNIGHT, SHE is finally alone again, in the same corner of the bedroom where she began her day. Only now she is in jeans, a short ponytail, and a loose tunic. She rubs Pond's cold cream onto her face to remove the powder now alloyed with dust and oil from the gas burner on the kitchen floor. Without makeup, her face is softer, younger.

Her dinner guests included eight men from Pakistan and their children, some of whom are now asleep on the floor in the other room. The guests were appropriately honored, both by the generous portions of meat served and by the hospitality extended to them by the men of the house: Mehran, barefoot in a crisp white *peran tonban,* seated next to her father, who wore an identical outfit. Glowing from the attention and excitedly chatting with the men gathered, Mehran also managed to follow a wrestling match on the corner television. They laughed together while Azita kept the serving plates heaped with rice and stew coming from the kitchen.

"After five or ten minutes, they used to ask about my son, and the entire discussion was about why I don't have a son. 'We are sorry for you. Why you don't try next time to have a son,' they would say. And I want to stop this talking inside my home. They think you are weaker without a son. So now I give them this image."

"So they are all fooled by this? And nobody else knows?"

Her family and relatives know. Some neighbors may have a clue, too. But no one has commented on it.

"What if someone asks you outright whether Mehran is a boy or a girl?" I ask.

"Then I don't lie. But it almost never happens."

But if it became known to a wider circle? Would it shame her? And what of any danger to Mehran from religious extremists? Or just from some of the many who comment on how people should live their lives in accordance with Islam?

None of that applies, according to Azita. Perhaps because the absolute need for a son trumps everything else, a disguised girl in Afghanistan, or any other collective secret, exists under the same policy as gays in the United States military used to do: "Don't ask, don't tell."

Afghanistan has many other worries on its mind. A girl who grows up in boys' clothing is not an affront—in fact, it only confirms the established order, in which men have all the privileges. And as Carol le Duc said: "Shared deceit at some point no longer constitutes deceit."

Like Carol le Duc and Dr. Fareiba have done, Azita gently hints at the possibility that I may be more caught up in questions of gender than she, or any Afghan, is. After all, she points out, we are just talking about a child. Why is it important to manifest her female gender, especially when it marks the little girl as a weaker, more constrained, child, of lesser value? Instead, just like Harry Potter when he dons his invisibility cloak, Mehran can move about freely in pants with a cropped haircut. A girl always stands out—she is a target, for which special rules and regulations apply.

That Western idea of "being yourself" does not apply for adults here, either. In her eighteen-hour workdays, Azita too plays a role, keeping what she thinks of as her own persona under wraps:

"Most of the time now, I am a politician. Not Azita."

"What is the other one like?"

She rolls her eyes. "The other one is more fun. She is happy and she has more time to live in her own way. Not in the way other people want. People don't look at her all the time. She is a better mother. In

Afghanistan, you have to kill everything inside you and adapt yourself to society. It is the only way to survive."

"Do you think Mehran would have been turned into a boy if you had not been a politician?"

"Honestly? No."

"But don't you worry about Mehran? Don't you think of what it's like for her, and what will happen to her?"

"I think of that every day. Every day I wonder if this is right."

CHAPTER SIX
THE UNDERGROUND GIRLS

I T IS SIMPLE MATH—if she is caught, no one eats. And every day she fears discovery.

All that Niima is ordered to do, she does very quickly. She climbs to fetch store offerings from the top shelf. She dives under stacked crates of imported Pakistani oranges to pull out boxes of tea. She squeezes her small, flexible body between tightly packed bags of flour behind the counter. She tries never to look directly at customers. If they looked into her eyes, she imagines, they would see she is not a real boy.

With her short hair and gray tunic, ten-year-old Niima plays her part perfectly. But her soft voice gives her away. That's why she rarely speaks when she is Abdul Mateen, as she is mostly known outside the mud wall of her home in one of Kabul's poorest neighborhoods, where an open sewer runs alongside cinder block houses. Niima attends school for two hours each morning in a dress and a head scarf. Then she returns to the house, changes into work clothes, and goes to work as a shop assistant in a small grocery store near the family's house. On an average day, she brings home the equivalent of $1.30. It supports her Pashtun family of eight sisters and their mother.

Niima poses as a boy purely for the survival of her family. There is nothing voluntary about it and her act hardly contains an element of freedom.

At Niima's house, shoes and sandals lying outside are separated from the inside by only a thin, frayed curtain. Niima's father is an unemployed mason who is often away and spends most money he manages to get hold of on drugs, says Niima's mother.

It was the shopkeeper's idea to turn Niima into a boy—the shopkeeper is a friend of the family—and she is a few years into her part-time boyhood now.

"He advised us to do it. And he said she can bring bread for our home," her mother explains.

Niima could never work in the store as a girl, nor could her mother, even if she wanted to. It would be impossible for a Pashtun woman, according to the family's rules. "It's our tradition that women don't work like this."

The relatives would be embarrassed. And her husband would never condone it.

Niima displays no enthusiasm for being a boy. To her, it is hard work, with little upside. She would rather look like a girl. At home, she likes to borrow her sisters' clothing. Every day she complains to her mother: "I'm not comfortable around the boys in the store."

Her mother consoles her, saying it will only be a few more years before she can change back into being a girl again. The family's future survival is already mapped out: When Niima gets too old for working in the shop, her younger sister will take her place. And after that, the next sister.

SHUBNUM'S TOO-EARLY transition to become a girl has already begun. The eight-year-old is still in a *peran tonban,* but her hair is being allowed to grow out. It was not supposed to happen until she turned thirteen, but her manner, her fits of giggles, and her long fluttery lashes made it impossible for her to pass any longer. When she was found out in the boys' school she attended together with her older brother, the teachers did not object. But Shubnum had to endure plenty of teasing in class after the others guessed she was a girl.

When I visit her mother, Nahid, in her two-room apartment

close to Kabul University, Jack Bauer of *24* is torturing a suspected Muslim terrorist with the electrical current from a broken lamp on the grainy television. Shubnum and her brother watch intently. Their older sister, in a head scarf with a shy smile, stays in a corner, mostly looking down at her hands.

Although Nahid has one son, circumstances dictated she needed another one. When her abusive husband of seventeen years asked her to cover herself completely and stay at home, Nahid chose to walk away with nothing. Her father struck a very unusual and costly deal with her husband at the time of the separation: Their family money would go to him in exchange for the children. Husbands otherwise have an absolute right to the children, which is why the divorce rate is close to zero in Afghanistan. With support from her family, Nahid moved to another part of the city and began her life anew. She found a job and an apartment. But as a single mother of three—which is almost unheard of in Kabul—she had to balance her family with an extra son, in order for them all to feel safer.

As a divorcée, she was seen as a loose, available woman, risking threats and violent approaches by men, as well as plenty of direct and indirect condemnation by other women. As a woman with two sons, however, she is considered a slightly more respectable creature.

It would have worked out well had Shubnum not been so reluctant and not so terminally girly. Each time she was taken to the barber for a haircut, she cried. Afterward, she would tug at her short hair to make it grow out faster, and at home, she would obsessively try on her older sister's dresses.

Eventually, Nahid gave up. She blames herself—perhaps she did not make being a boy alluring enough for Shubnum.

When asked which gender she prefers, Shubnum is unhesitant. "A girl," she responds, with a big smile and cocked head. She glances over at the television, now showing an intense performance of Indian bhangra dance. "So I can wear jewelry and dance."

Her wish will be granted. At her future wedding, if not before.

SLOWLY, I HAVE BEGUN to drill through the layered secrets of Kabul in search of more girls of Mehran's kind. Shubnum and Niima are two of the first I find. I locate them through Kabul's plentiful maze of gossip, where firsthand information is rarely offered up at once, and only in face-to-face meetings.

Officially, they do not exist, but one degree beyond the foreign-educated Kabul elite, many Afghans can indeed recall a former neighbor, a relative, a colleague, or someone in their extended family with a daughter growing up as a boy. At first, there are rarely names, and never much by way of an address. But the wealth of human knowledge embedded in a system of tight social control stands in place of a phone book, a database, and a map.

With the help of Omar and Setareh, two young Afghan translators with few fears but an abundance of street smarts between them, I slowly craft chains of referrals, confidences, and introductions that over time begin to prove that more girls actually live as boys in and around Kabul. Many more.

One lives "next to the third house where the tree was cut down." Another is thought to be "on the first floor in the house without windows next to the bazaar." Or "on the other side of the refugee camp, just up the road, inside the blue gate with barbed wire." There is one in a certain middle school; another is thought to be in a particular neighborhood. Someone's daughter has been known to play football on a field, and to help out in her father's tailoring shop.

In our search, we are often confused and at times completely lost, circling alleys and neighborhoods that always lack street signs for hours. But once we finally come upon the right family and discreetly inquire whether their son may possibly be *a girl,* an invitation for tea is usually extended by the ever-polite and hospitable Afghans, regardless of whether they live in elegant villas or in houses made from tarps and mud. After lengthy introductions, always with some fine diplomacy by Omar or Setareh, often with questions about Sweden and my own family—particularly about my father—and many refills of tea, we are permitted to meet and speak to the family's made-up son.

Setareh and I soon begin to challenge each other on spotting the common traits of the girls in disguise. Some are given away by softer features. Or the occasional giggle. Others are show-offs, trying a little too hard with the boyish attitude and displays of aggression. But most often, we recognize the steady, challenging gaze, as though we had a secret in common. It happens that a little boy will give either of us a sly smile, out on the street or in school, only to later, in private or with her parents, confirm that she is indeed a little different from the crowd she moves with.

Although none of the girls chose their boyhood voluntarily, most say they enjoy their borrowed status. It all depends on what they get to *do* with it. For each child, it boils down to perks versus burdens. Those who, like Mehran, are part of upper- or middle-class families, are often their families' token of prestige and honor, thriving on speaking up at school and playing violent outdoor games in the neighborhood.

Others, in poor families, are broken down by forced child labor, just as the actual boys in the same position often are. "This can be an awful place to be a woman. But it's not particularly good for a man, either," Carol le Duc is fond of observing. Among street children in the merchant business, selling chewing gum, polishing shoes, or offering to wash car windows on the streets, some are actual boys, and others are girls in disguise. They are all part of Kabul's underbelly and, to those who pass them by, mostly just invisible.

I even find that there is a name for those children who are not actually here. The colloquialism for the child who is not a son or a daughter is *bacha posh*. Together with a translator, I settle on that spelling in the Roman alphabet, as there are no existing written references. It literally translates as "dressed like a boy" in Dari. In Pashto, this third kind of child can also be referred to as *alakaana*. That the term exists and is well-known indicates that these children are not unusual. Nor is it a new phenomenon.

At times in our search for the *bacha posh* we get it entirely wrong, approaching the wrong family or arriving at the wrong house in the wrong neighborhood. And at times, we find something quite different from what we were looking for.

THERE IS NO electricity in the house at the compound built for handicapped war veterans near Kabul airport. The sun set several hours ago, and in one of the family's small, dark rooms, twelve-year-old Esmaeel has been introduced as "the only son" among ten siblings. Esmaeel has dark hair, bushy eyebrows, and even a hint of black hair on his upper lip. There is nothing feminine about him, and I feel both impatient and confused. We may simply have been misinformed about this family.

But it would be rude to leave now that we have been invited in, so we sit for tea while Esmaeel's mother tells her story. She moves slowly, supporting herself on a homemade crutch wrapped in pieces of cloth. She has only one leg. The other was lost in a bomb explosion in 1985. Her ten children, ranging in age from one to twenty, gather around her on the thin carpet covering the cement floor. The eldest grew up under the Taliban, and like many girls that age she is illiterate. She is far less confident than her younger sisters, who have attended school since 2002 and excitedly speak of becoming doctors or lawyers when they grow up.

But their mother hushes them. All she wants to talk about is Esmaeel. He is the most intelligent of them all, and whatever money the family can spare will go toward his higher education. The girls will have to wait their turn, if there's anything left. Esmaeel is her "light," his mother says. "I don't want to make any difference between my children, but I know that Esmaeel will reach a high position in society."

Esmaeel came to the family through divine intervention, she explains. When her sixth daughter was born, this desperate mother decided that the child should be presented to the world as a son. She told everyone her new little girl was, in fact, her firstborn son. The made-up baby boy held no practical purpose for the family as an infant. But she held a *magical* one. Her mother had been told by friends and neighbors that if she were to turn her girl into a boy, it would bring her good luck. Good luck, in this case, was a *real* son. The maneuver had helped many families before her: Through visual manifestation, when a woman looks at the image of a male child every day, her body will eventually conceive a son.

With that, the coin finally drops: Esmaeel is not a girl disguised as a boy—he *is* the family's only son. Telling her story of giving birth to a son after dressing a daughter as a boy for two years, the mother looks immensely pleased. Her sixth daughter, who had been a *bacha posh,* died shortly after her third birthday, but she had fulfilled a greater purpose.

Trying to grasp this new and additional motif for turning a girl into a boy, I shift my position on the floor. The room goes silent, indicating that we have once again entered the realm where my kind of logic or science is no longer valid.

"Okay. But how can you know this works—"

Esmaeel's mother cuts me off with a quick gesture toward her son.

"Look at him. You can see it for yourself."

"OF COURSE." IT is one of the most common ways to produce a son, Dr. Fareiba confirms when when I locate her in Kabul later that week. Certainly not as foolproof as her tips and tricks, but an oft-employed method in the villages throughout Afghanistan, where there is no access to Dr. Fareiba's level of expertise.

She is in fine form on this day, leading a workshop at a run-down guesthouse in the Shar-e-Naw neighborhood for dozens of Afghan medical workers from the country's far-flung provinces.

High on the agenda is the issue of breast-feeding: A problem has arisen in the provinces where aid organizations have been distributing milk powder. The original recipients of the milk powder, the poorest women, resell it at markets, enabling those of slightly better means to buy it, considering it a sign of wealth not to breast-feed. In an attempt to fix an aid initiative gone wrong, Dr. Fareiba and her colleagues are trying to reverse the trend and talk women into at least trying to breast-feed their newborns for a few months.

Kabul is having an early spring, and the female participants have retired to a room at the back with two chubby sofas and a plastic fan on the floor pushing the air around. The male health workers eat elsewhere. Dr. Fareiba invites us to join the lunch, where eight female Afghan doctors and midwives from eight different provinces are passing around watermelon slices on glass plates. As I sit down with Setareh, they all want to offer us the best bites. Predictably, the oldest woman gets to serve us, and offers an entire pile. But there is something I want more than watermelon: I wonder if the *bacha posh* are all around Afghanistan, in their provinces too?

After a careful introduction to the topic by Setareh, and some nudging by Dr. Fareiba, the women tell one story after another of newborn girls announced as boys at birth in their villages.

Families can be rich, poor, educated, uneducated, Pashtuns, Tajiks, Hazara, or Turkoman—it doesn't matter, they tell me. The only thing that binds the girls together is their family's *need* for a son. These women have met girls who live as boys because the family needed another income through a child who worked, because the road to school was dangerous and a boy's disguise provided some safety, or because the family lacked sons and needed to present as a complete family to the village. Often, as we have seen in Kabul, it is a combination of factors. A poor family may need a son for different reasons than a rich family, but no ethnic or geographical reasons set them apart. They are all Afghans, living in a society that demands sons at almost any cost.

And to most of them, the health workers say, having a *bacha posh* in the family is an accepted and uncontroversial practice, provided the girl is turned back to a woman before she enters puberty, when she must marry and have children of her own. Waiting too long to turn someone back could have consequences for a girl's reputation. A teenage girl should not be anywhere near teenage boys, even in disguise. She could mistakenly touch them or rather be touched by them, and be seen as a loose and impure girl by those who know her secret. It could ruin her chances of getting married, and she would be seen as a tarnished offering. The entire family's reputation could be sullied.

So how many *bacha posh* children are there in Afghanistan?

No one knows. They are a minority, but it is "not uncommon" to see them in the villages throughout the country. There are usually one or two in a school. Often one as a helper in a small store. And the health workers have all known them to appear at clinics, escorting a mother or a sister, or as a patient who has proven to be of another birth sex than first presumed. The health workers have all witnessed it and agree that every family with only daughters will consider switching one to a boy. In their view, it is mostly to the girl's advantage to live a few years as a boy, before the other, hardship life of childrearing of her own begins.

One of the doctors, this one from Helmand, is four months pregnant. She has four sons already. The others joke she is in the clear. She would like a girl this time. Her husband supports her wish. It is the first time I've heard someone say they actually want a daughter. The other women congratulate the doctor. They love girls, they say. But they are also women and realists. There is a deep and personal knowledge of the difficulty of bringing another girl into a country such as their own. The future of a daughter here depends on her father. A Wardak midwife lays it out clearly: "It's only good to have a girl with a good man. With a bad man, you don't want to have any girls, because they will suffer, like their mother."

For instance, she says, if a husband abuses his wife, he will most likely abuse the daughters, too. That's when you, as a woman, pray intensely for all your children to be sons. In her line of work, one of the hardest things to watch is when an abused woman gives birth to another girl. They know the girl will be brought into an abusive home. Nine out of ten Afghan women will experience domestic abuse in some form, according to surveys from the United Nations and several human rights organizations.

In neighboring countries such as India, where sons are similarly much preferred over daughters, ultrasound machines are among the most sought-after equipment by doctors and patients. According to Mara Hvistendahl in *Unnatural Selection: Choosing Boys over Girls, and the Consequences of a World Full of Men,* 160 million female fetuses have already been aborted throughout Asia, skewing the demographic for generations to come and creating acute problems for societies lacking women. Although both ultrasound screenings and secret late-term abortions are available in Kabul for those who can pay, most rural parts of Afghanistan are not there yet. Women in these areas just have Dr. Fareiba's low-tech, ancient recipes to depend on, for now, as they hope to avoid bringing too many daughters into this world.

To FURTHER THAT mission, the health workers also each have at least one example of *magical* son making from their home provinces. They confirm that the prevailing reason to create a *bacha posh* might very well be to beget a real son. The young midwife from Wardak in a bright orange scarf says her cousin was dressed as a boy for nine years, until her mother finally gave birth to a son. It often happens that a daughter will remain a boy only until a real son is born; he will then replace the *bacha posh* as their parents' pride.

This mystical way of ensuring sons has parallels with the new-age concept "power of positive thinking," used to such great effect by athletes and salesmen. *See it, believe it, and it will happen.* The Afghan version is a form of prayer that doesn't quite fit into any of the religious practices I am aware of in Afghanistan. It's just magic, the women explain. But is God still involved, somehow? I inquire, as they refer to a divine intervention.

They look at each other. Magic is *magic*. And there is no God except Allah.

An uncomfortable silence follows. Demonstrations have been held in the previous few weeks based on the persistent rumor that foreign aid workers had tried to convert Muslims to Christianity.

Dr. Fareiba gives me the "move on" nod. She may have agreed to reveal some of her secrets thus far, but religion is a topic best not discussed with a foreigner.

CHAPTER SEVEN
THE NAUGHTY ONE

Mehran and Azita

*A*rms up! Arms out! Touch your toes! Make a wave! Swim into the air! Big circles! Again! Now the salute! Salute and honor your country!"

Morning gymnastics have a touch of both Montessori and military discipline. About one hundred small children make a very serious attempt at synchronicity on a recently defrosted lawn, where patches of grass have sprung up in the dry mud.

It has taken the headmaster about twenty minutes to form her troops and move through the attendance call. When she calls a name, an arm shoots up with a loud *"bale"* from boys, and a softer version from the girls inside the densely packed crowd of six- to ten-year-olds.

The head boy at the top of each S-shaped line is keeping order, and Mehran stands next to one such fellow second-grader in shirt and tie. After the wobbly gymnastics is done the two friends adopt identical poses—hands in pockets, hips forward, resting broad-legged and bored looking. Behind them, boys in pants and girls in shift dresses—but no head scarves—line up. The required school uniform color is green, and it comes in as many nuances as the school has students, since every mother outfits her own child from whatever green fabric is available at the bazaar. Mehran's belly exceeds her pants; the front button above the zipper has been replaced by an uncomfortable safety pin. Her toes are bare in her sandals, and in one pocket is a leftover cookie from breakfast.

The students are mostly children of Kabul's recent-vintage professional class. Many of their parents are educated, and drop their children off here before going to work in government or for international organizations. The private institution offers English instruction and teachers who have graduated from high school. A few even hold degrees from a teaching academy.

When the headmaster calls out for a volunteer student to perform a solo song before the students, Mehran stares blankly. A girl humbly walks up to face the crowd of students, her head bowed and her hands clasped together in front of her. Mehran, still with hands in pockets, leans over to her friend and whispers something, with a nod at the girl in front of them. The friend grins widely in agreement and they giggle, before being urged to join in singing the national anthem. A few Koran verses follow, and the headmaster offers her daily nugget of life advice for the children: "Brush your teeth, cut your nails, and never lie."

Older students are dismissed first, and they slowly pour into the two-story stone building and up the stairs, where an elderly helper has placed a red bucket of water and brown pressed soap under posters of Russian fighter jets and an Iranian passenger airline. The old woman rinses each child's hands with a splash from a red plastic pitcher and sends them off to their classrooms. Mehran's teacher declares that in honor of the foreign visitors on this day, she will begin with the English lesson—a class, it turns out, that will be conducted without books, and entirely in Dari.

MEHRAN FIRST ARRIVED here, to the school's kindergarten, as Mahnoush, in pigtails and a pistachio dress. When school shut down for a break she left and never returned. Instead short-haired, tie-wearing Mehran began first grade with the other children. Nothing else changed much. Some teachers were surprised but did not comment except to one another. When the male Koran teacher demanded Mehran cover her head in his class, a baseball cap solved the problem. The other children did not seem to pay much attention. The school's high turnover of students helped, as did the school's coed policy of not separating boys and girls for lessons or play.

Miss Momand, who started her job as a teacher after Mehran's change, remembers being startled when a boy was brought into the girls' room for afternoon nap time. As she helped Mehran undress it was clear she was a girl. Miss Momand was so confused she called Azita to ask why she had sent her child to school looking as she did. Azita simply explained that she had only daughters, and that Mehran went as the family's son. It was all Miss Momand needed to hear— she understood perfectly. She herself used to have a friend at school who was a family's only child and had assumed the role of a son.

Mehran seems to have adapted well to her new role, in the eyes of her teacher. A little too well, perhaps. She takes every opportunity to tell those around her that she is a boy. She will refuse such activities as sewing and doll play in favor of cycling, football, and running. According to Miss Momand, Mehran has fully become a boy, and neither her exterior nor her behavior is distinguishable from another boy's. All the teachers play along and help protect her secret by letting her change clothes in a separate room when necessary.

"So is this all normal to you? Common, even?" I ask Miss Momand.

"Not exactly. But it is not a problem."

The rules are clear: dresses for girls, pants for boys. There are no other cross-dressers attending school. But it is not for the school to get involved in a family matter, she explains. Whatever gender the parents decide upon, the school should help perpetuate. Even when it is a lie. The school has other things to worry about, such as how many armed guards are needed by the front gate. The teacher expresses some solidarity with Azita: "Mehran's mother is in parliament. She is a good woman. We do what we must."

"We women, or we Afghans?"

"Both."

As for academic skills, Mehran is "intelligent, but a little lazy," according to her teacher. She is quick to smile, and equally quick to put on an angry-looking, annoyed face when she is not immediately understood or agreed with. A few years after leaving Mahnoush behind, Mehran's personality has grown louder. She spends breaks floating in and out of the boys' football games and other outdoor activities, depending on where the action seems to be at the moment. And whereas most other students want to stick to friends their own age, Mehran appears eager to catch the attention of older boys, often trying to impress them and seek some attention by being obnoxious. She will yell, touch, and push those around her. Most of the time she is ignored, but at times she needs to be pulled away from a clash with an older boy. Mehran is well aware she is a girl, according to the teachers. But she always introduces herself as a boy to newcomers. Since Mehran was a girl for several years before she was remade into a boy, there should be little confusion to her in that regard.

Sigmund Freud claimed that children are not even aware of genital differences until around the age of four or five, but in the 1980s, Dr. Eleanor Galenson and Dr. Herman Roiphe proved that children's understanding of a sexual identity begins much earlier. According to their findings, a child can be aware of his or her birth sex as early as fifteen months.

Yet in Afghanistan, there is a certain interest in keeping children in the dark or at least blurring the lines about boys and girls. Specifics about anatomical differences are purposely not explained by many parents, in order to keep the minds of children—and especially those of little girls—"pure" for as long as possible before they marry.

It goes along with how my mother once told me the story of how she, as a ten-year-old in a more conservative version of Sweden of the 1950s, proclaimed to her mother that she intended to become a boy when she grew up. My mother had only one sister and a dim view of differences between men and women, never having seen her father or any other men without clothes. My grandmother scoffed at her daughter and called her stupid but did not offer any explanation for why the plan wasn't feasible.

At Mehran's school, children are never supposed to see the opposite sex naked, either; that is absolutely forbidden. The headmaster tells me that at this stage, she is certain that to most students, what sets little boys and girls apart is all exterior: pants versus skirts.

That, and the knowledge that those with pants always come first.

ON FEBRUARY 7, 1999, Azita knew she had failed, but she was too exhausted to speak or to show any reaction at all. She had just given birth—twice. She was in her mother-in-law's small freezing house, insulated only with dried grass baked into the mud walls. The first twin had been born after almost three days and three nights of labor, one month prematurely. She weighed a mere 2.6 pounds and her breathing was shallow. Ten minutes later, her face had turned blue and she showed few signs of life as her sister arrived. She, too, was unconscious. The women who had helped Azita deliver her children did not wash the babies. Instead, they just handed them to her wrapped in cloth—it was too obvious to all those present that the children would not make it.

When her mother-in-law began to cry, Azita knew it was not from fear that her granddaughters might not survive. The old woman was disappointed. "Why," she cried, according to Azita, "are we getting more girls in the family? What will I tell the neighbors? And the villagers?"

Azita felt nothing. The year before, she had crossed the doorstep of her primitive new home as the property of a poor farming family, carrying only one thing of value—a womb. Her husband already had a wife whose womb was the very reason Azita had been drafted as wife number two. The first wife had given birth to a daughter, but her second child—a son—had died. After that, she had only miscarried. It was what had prompted the mother-in-law to seek out a second young and healthy wife for her son. With Azita came the promise of a better future for the family in a small farming village perched on a hillside and even more isolated from the outside world than Badghis's provincial capital of Qala-e-Naw. At the time it was reachable only by horse or donkey, or by foot.

The ten-person household, with two husbands who were brothers, their three wives, and all the children, was run by Azita's mother-in-law. She wielded her power down to the smallest details of the lives of her sons' wives. She decided how chores were distributed among them; when they ate and what; who spoke and what the conversation should be about. She also held the keys to the food pantry. Following her rules meant the difference between eating and going hungry.

When Azita first arrived, she was tasked with several jobs. She soon learned how to handle the cows—one for milking and three for fieldwork—the ten sheep, and the flock of chickens. In the spirit of an older sister and as someone who had grown up very differently, she soon began offering opinions and ideas on how the family did things. Azita suggested they wash their hands before eating, that they cut their nails, and that they help one another with the children. She advocated for them all to join forces and bring much more water into the house, to combat poor hygiene and disease. She suggested that the men and women of the family share meals—a radical idea in a household that strictly separated men and women except at night, when a husband was expected to sleep together with one of his wives. Having more contact within the family made sense, Azita argued, and it was how she had been brought up.

None of her ideas were well received.

A particular provocation was the many dresses Azita had brought with her from her family home. Each woman in the village household owned only two dresses—one that was for special occasions such as weddings and should not be worn otherwise, and the other a regular dress that was to be worn for ten days before it would be washed, since water was so scarce. Azita was told that if she wanted to wear fresh clothes more often, she could fetch her own water from the far-away well.

Next, Azita protested her mother-in-law's system for keeping the wives in check, when any sign of insubordination rendered a response by her walking stick. The first wife was beaten most often, as she made the most mistakes. It upset Azita, and she argued against it. That escalated to yelling and finally, one day, Azita stepped in to shield her husband's first wife, jerking the stick away and breaking it in two. Infuriated, she threatened her mother-in-law: "I will beat you back. I am not afraid of the Taliban, and I am absolutely not afraid of you."

Islam does not condone the beating of wives, she added. Women should not beat other women, either. The old woman stared at her daughters-in-law, silently fuming before turning around and leaving them both. The family's longtime ruler of its women had no plans to abdicate. Mute obedience was not only expected of the family's wives—it was the norm and a prerequisite for their lives to work. As Azita had taken it upon herself to shelter her husband's illiterate and shy first wife, things threatened to spiral out of control. So the mother-in-law took the issue to her sons, who agreed something needed to be done. Since Azita was from the city, they concluded, whatever evil she had picked up there needed to be stemmed. There was still time for the newcomer to be recalibrated into a normal wife, and to remove whatever ideas a decadent Kabul upbringing had instilled in her.

They were to be beaten out of her.

THE FIRST BLOW came as a surprise to Azita. She had never seen her father beat her mother, and she had rarely been slapped as a child. Now, her husband would use a wooden stick or a metal wire, when one was available, for regular preemptive beatings without a specific cause, just to make sure there would be no arguing with his mother. Sometimes, he just used his fists.

"On the body. On the face. I tried to stop him. I asked him to stop. Sometimes I didn't."

"And sexually?"

Azita goes silent.

"It is not called rape in Afghanistan if your husband forces himself on you," she says. "People would think you are a stupid woman if you call it that."

A woman's body is always available to her husband, not only for procreation, but for recreation as well, since male sexuality is seen as a good and necessary thing. If a wife does not submit, the husband could feel frustrated and look elsewhere, the thinking goes, which would then endanger the fundament of a family and with that society as a whole. Predominantly Christian countries did not recognize marital rape as illegal, either, until fairly recently, as one of the original purposes of marriage itself was to legalize sex. In the United States, marital rape was not criminalized in all states until 1993; in the United Kingdom, 1991.

Early on in her marriage, after the physical beating had begun, to everyone's relief, Azita became pregnant. With that, she had taken the first step toward fulfilling her purpose. Expecting a son, the family left her alone as she grew bigger. "Look at her—she is so fat and healthy. Surely, she will have a son," they said.

Azita was grateful for the semblance of peace. She, too, prayed for a son.

Delivering the twin girls was not only a disappointment; Azita had almost made a mockery of the family. Azita's brother-in-law had also only fathered girls; it was as if the family was cursed. The one consolation was that the premature twins might not live long.

Not even Azita felt any love for her daughters at first. It was a different emotion that made her fight for her tiny newborns: pity. The doctor who had come from town offered no congratulations when she examined the twins after a few days. They still had little chance of making it, she decided. She turned to Azita and said, simply, "I am sorry."

Azita accepted the doctor's prognosis, but being unable to breastfeed, she still begged her mother-in-law for some milk from one of the cows. After Azita offered to pay for the milk, which her mother-in-law argued could have been sold for a profit, she was able to spoon-feed her two daughters. Slowly, their condition improved. After two months, they smiled a little, and that's when Azita began to love them. They became her reason for living in those first years of marriage.

When Azita's younger brother came to check on her on behalf of their parents, she tried to be upbeat and assure him it was not so bad. She hoped he would bring their parents good news, not making them think of her as a quitter. It was only when her father, Mourtaza, came to visit that the veneer cracked. She told him she hated her life. When he showed no reaction, her fury grew in a way that she had never dared to show her father before. As he walked out the door to leave, she followed and screamed at him from the doorstep: "*Thank you very much!* Because of you, I am suffering every day. You told me to educate myself. I did, and now I am treated worse than a donkey, or a cow. You did this."

Mourtaza looked at her in silence. Then he spoke. "Yes. I did this to you. I am so sorry."

It was the only time she had seen her father cry.

IN CURRENT-DAY KABUL, when Mehran returns home from school in the late afternoon, her special snack is already set out on the kitchen counter: two oranges on a plate, with a little knife to peel them. She attacks the oranges in a frenzy, and then, her hands still sticky, she crawls up onto her mother's lap. The goal is to convince Azita to release her laptop so the sisters can watch a film. While her sisters smile as they gently make a request, Mehran is loud and insistent. Her right ear sports a large Band-Aid, after a failed attempt to pierce herself with a needle inspired by the male Bollywood action hero Salman Khan, who wears just one earring.

"He is very much a boy right now," Azita mutters, trying to hush Mehran while she is on the phone. "The other day I came home, and he was trying to take apart my computer, saying he was looking for the games inside." She laughs. "Mehran is not like the girls. He is my naughty one."

Azita caresses her daughter's arm while switching between two cell phones and three languages. "I will try," she tells one caller. "I will call the principal and discuss it with him." A colleague has had a child expelled from school and asks that Azita pull some strings. There are some things she won't do: suggest young unmarried girls as wives for constituents or their children, for example. She never says "no" outright but will always take time to explain that she may not be entirely suited to help with some tasks.

Azita's daughters spend this afternoon like most others—in frustrated boredom between the apartment's yellow walls, watching Indian television or favorites Hannah Montana and Harry Potter on DVD. They will raise the volume, as well as the level of bickering, as each hour slowly passes. Mehran needs to do her homework, and until it is done, the girls have been told no one goes outside. When the twins find a pirated Tajik CD with pop music under Azita's desk and begin to dance, Azita becomes worried. The neighbors might hear, and a parliamentarian's family can't be suspected of listening to something like that.

Azita loves to dance, but she does not do it often. Dancing falls into the same category as poetry for a woman—it equals dreaming, which may inspire thoughts about such banned topics as love and desire. Any woman reading, writing, or citing poetry is a woman who may harbor strange ideas about love and romance in her head, and thus is a potential whore. When Azita once posted a poem on her Facebook page, she immediately received comments suggesting she was inappropriate.

Though the sun has already begun to set, Azita decides to allow the girls an hour of outside play, on the condition that they stay within her range of vision from the window. The four girls almost fall over one another as they slip on their sandals and tumble down the stairs and into the small yard. The neighborhood crew of two older boys and a cadre of smaller children are already there, all in bright-colored clothing emblazoned with cartoon characters. No other girls of Benafsha and Beheshta's age are present. Allowing young girls outside is uncommon, even in less conservative neighborhoods, and Azita's ten-year-old twins may be able to go, at most, three more years without head scarves. Their father has let it be known that he would prefer they cover themselves already now.

On the grass, a few boys toss a weathered football between them, and when the ice cream man comes cycling by with his cart, its one speaker playing a monotonous little melody, the scene is momentarily peaceful.

Benafsha and Beheshta do not envy Mehran, they assure me. Why would they want to play football and get dirty like Mehran? Scream and yell and fight with the boys? Mehran may be their much-cuddled younger sister who rules the family with her temper, but they would not want to trade places with her. With Mehran's boyhood, she has become the most spoiled child of the family. Or perhaps, as the baby of the family, she always was. The twins only know they have a much harder time extracting money from their father, who seems to give Mehran anything she asks for. To the twins, he appears to listen more attentively when Mehran speaks and to laugh a little louder at her jokes.

In eight-year-old middle child Mehrangis's view, on the other hand, Mehran absolutely has the better deal. Mehrangis is not included in the twins' giggly camaraderie, where they always have each other's backs, and she receives less attention for her appearance. She reveals a proposal she recently made to her parents: "They say I am a little bit fat, so I told my mother that maybe it was best they make me a boy, too, since I am not pretty."

But her parents denied her wish to cross over to boyhood. Mehrangis had actually been her father's first choice for *bacha posh,* but since she is older and would have had to become a woman sooner, they decided against it. Mehran would last them longer as a son. Mehrangis shrugs her shoulders when she tells the story; it didn't happen for her, and that's just the way it is. She knows she is not considered as charming or as cute as her older sisters. But because Mehran goes as a boy, at least no one talks about her being fat or not pretty enough.

For Mehran, there is no need to play well behaved, adorable, or pleasing. There is no expectation of grace or adoring smiles. When I take pictures of the girls, or when they take pictures of one another with my camera, Benafsha and Beheshta strike well-rehearsed poses, pouting their lips and batting big flirty eyelashes, sometimes pointing fingers at each other and swirling their arms as they perform a little Bollywood-style dance routine. At times Mehrangis attempts to emulate them, but it mostly earns her mockery. Mehran goes in the exact opposite direction—looking angry, staring into the camera, hands on her hips. When she does smile, it is a big grin, showing off the large gap between her two front teeth. Her clothes barely hold together at times, especially after she has been rolling around outside for a few hours. And she is the biggest eater in the family, after her father.

Benafsha pulls my sleeve. She wants to say something, but we must move away from the others. We move closer to the wire fence toward the road, and she says it quickly, her voice low and her face down.

"Two of my friends call her a girl. They know I have a sister and not a brother." Not only that: "She fights a lot. The boys, the older neighbors' boys, they say 'You are a girl.' She tells them 'No, I am a boy.' But they know."

The twins try their best to comfort Mehran when it happens, Benafsha says. But sometimes she becomes too upset, and they do not know what to do. Certainly, Mehran annoys the twins at times, but what upsets them more is when other children gossip about her.

"She was quiet before," Benafsha says. "Now she's naughty, and she fights. Now, she cries a lot. When we go to sleep I ask her 'Why do you cry?' She says, 'Because they say I am a girl.'"

Luckily, Benafsha feels, it will all be over soon. In a few years, Mehran will have to change back into being a girl. They all know it—their mother has told them several times. At some point soon, whatever privileges Mehran now enjoys will end.

Not sure what to say, I look up at the building. Three windows are full of faces wrapped in head scarves, smiling and waving down at us. The girls are too old—too close to puberty—to be allowed outside.

WHEN A STORM arrived from over the mountains to her small village in Badghis, Azita used to imagine the clouds came from Kabul. As a child, she had been scolded by her mother for running around in rainstorms and getting sick. In those early years as a married woman, she would stand on the doorstep of the village house, her eyes closed, and let the rain pour over her face. In her mind, she would go up to the locked gates at the end of the yard. She would open them, and just keep walking.

It would be years before she began to dream of a big future again, but with time, she extracted permission to do more things beyond caring for her children. By teaching neighboring women to cook the exotic dishes she had learned to make in Kabul, she gained a reputation as the mashed-potato lady. Based on her preparatory studies for medical school back in Kabul, in Badghis, she also began receiving villagers for small health care needs. Volunteering for the Red Crescent, she administered shots to children and diagnosed the most common illnesses. Villagers paid what they could—often nothing, but sometimes a few onions or tomatoes, even a chicken. Most of the time, Azita used them as trade with her mother-in-law, in return for fresh milk from the family's cow for her daughters. She also taught basic writing and reading in Dari to any girl in the neighborhood who would come over, under the guise of reading the Koran.

WHEN THE UNITED States, the United Kingdom, France, and Australia launched the attack in Afghanistan on October 7, 2001, it was a direct message to Azita that her world might open up again. As the Taliban leadership crumbled, she began an attack of her own, to convince her husband that the family should leave the village and move to the provincial capital of Badghis. In Qala-e-Naw, she would be able to work now that the Taliban was no longer in power, and the family could make a better life from that income. Her husband had already invested in a small street stall that sold chewing gum and phone cards, but profits were not enough to sustain them. If Azita were allowed to work, he would no longer need to labor in the family's small plot of land, she argued. She knew there would be ways to make money now that she could go outside.

Eventually he agreed to leave his mother's house behind, on the condition that Azita would support the family. They moved into a borrowed house, sharing it with another family. In the beginning, food was scarce. Benafsha and Beheshta still remember the luxury of tasting biscuits from a bakery for the very first time when their grandfather brought them as a gift.

Azita quickly lined up two jobs: During the day, she would teach in a middle school, and in the evenings, she offered even more classes for those girls who had been left illiterate during the years of war and Taliban rule. By now, Azita had three children of her own who came with her or stayed with neighbors when she worked.

But the real opportunities, she realized, lay with the foreigners.

She took it upon herself to learn some English—memorizing twenty words a day—and within a few months, she landed a third job as a translator for a German aid organization. They offered her the most she had ever made—$180 per month. It was enough to turn the family's life around completely, and almost overnight, they moved several steps up society's ladder. As one of the few women with an education in her province, Azita was well served by the influx of foreigners and cash that came with a wartime economy. She soon could even dangle the prospect of a house of their own before her husband. She was determined to make their marriage work, too, and once out from under her mother-in-law, they did get along better.

As a fourth enterprise, Azita expanded her health services in the evenings.

There was still very little health care available, and even though

Azita was rarely able to charge her patients, her reputation slowly built in the province, where people would travel from afar to see her for a shot, or to have their children seen by her. She also held preventive health seminars, where she taught simple things, such as the benefits of washing hands, and washing vegetables before eating them. Slowly, she built on her standing in the community, and for the UN-mandated 2002 emergency *loya jirga* meeting, where a transitional government after the Taliban would be agreed upon, Azita was elected as one of the representatives from Badghis province.

The Kabul meeting, where Azita carried her seven-month-old daughter Mehrangis on her hip to negotiations, offered a taste of what she had once imagined her life should have been. More than two thousand delegates from all around Afghanistan gathered for several weeks and Azita was surrounded by those with ambitions similar to hers. The idea of helping to build a new society—one where her daughters would not have their dreams crushed by authoritarian regimes and war—seemed perhaps less of a calling and more of a responsibility she should take on. The childhood dream of becoming a doctor would mean going back to school, and as she now had a family to support, she needed full-time work. As women were to be allowed into Afghan politics, it held the promise of an area where she could revive that old dream of making an impact, of becoming a leader.

Three years later, after getting her degree from a teaching academy in Badghis while working for a United Nations office as a translator, a friend offered to lend her the two hundred dollars needed to register to run for parliament in the first national elections. At twenty-eight, and now a mother of four, Azita decided it was more money than she could afford to repay if she lost. She simply had to win.

AMID THE ENDLESS cement, blast-protecting sandbags, and dust of Kabul, the desire for beauty can become overwhelming. To those who make the five-hour journey past the infamous Bagram air base, where Afghans have been tortured to death by U.S. forces, through several Taliban-controlled areas, and down a dirt road where small homemade bombs frequently disrupt traffic, an untouched fairy-tale world is said to open up.

On this Friday, Azita has sent her husband and the girls off to that place for a picnic outing. While they are gone, she will rest. As she waves good-bye to her family from the third-floor window, she sees that Mehran has taken the front seat next to her father. The older girls, bubbly with excitement, share the backseat as long lines of cars head out of town early in the morning. Friday is the day for prayer, but it is also a day off that families can spend together. Going on a "picnic" is a much appreciated way for less conservative Afghans to meet, and for some to clandestinely drink, away from neighbors and other gossips in Kabul. Alcohol is banned, but that rule is freely bent, just as many other cultural and religious decrees in Afghanistan often are.

Our Friday morning convoy also includes a local fire chief, who is an old friend of Azita's husband. His car is followed by two trucks with young Kalashnikov-carrying firefighter escorts.

The destination we arrive at is Kapisa province, an old mujahideen stronghold, where large stone formations and hills break up a dwindling green landscape just on the verge of bursting into full summer. Harsh winters have made knotty branches on century-old trees more resistant, and they reign over almost invisible paths through high grass and into fields where children herd sheep. On the other side of a hill are fields of shell peas and cucumbers, where a river feeds the thick, dark soil. Next to it, spread out on the grass, picnicgoers from Kabul sit together in groups. Some women have removed their head scarves and laugh loudly.

The young chain-smoking firefighters unload a large plastic sheet, two heavy Oriental rugs, and several large baskets and buckets from their trucks. They carry it all, plus guns and ammunition belts, across the pretty streams by jumping from stone to stone. When Mehran, dressed in white just like her father, falls and plunges knees-first into the water, she is swung back up and carried on his shoulders. She rides triumphantly, overlooking the procession at the tail end of which her sisters slip in their flat sandals, struggling to pick up the pace.

The firefighters act as pathfinders, who after a half-hour trek settle on the perfect tree, unfurling large plastic sheets underneath it. In this traditional rite of spring, the tree soon begins to vibrate, and clusters of little white and red berries patter down on the plastic sheet, held by two of them. A third firefighter, who has climbed up to the top of the tree, and wrapped his legs around a thick branch, lets out a loud, satisfied laugh when he is asked to give the branch another shake. And the mulberries rain down again, making their way from the plastic sheet into baskets. Our caravan sets off again, and the loot is carried to the side of a river stream that holds another little secret. A hole has been carved into the ground and lined with stones, allowing water from the stream to flow in. Baskets are emptied into the bathtub-like reservoir filled with ice-cold, clear water, and everyone squats around the tub to greedily scoop up the dark purple berries, scarfing them down by the handful. When all have eaten more than they can really stomach, hand-knotted rugs are spread out on the grass. For the prescribed digestive routine, several of the berry eaters go from cross-legged to fully lying down while large containers of runny yogurt are passed around.

AZITA'S HUSBAND OF thirteen years smiles broadly and turns his face toward the sun. In search of attention, Mehran crawls up onto him, only to be carefully pushed off his very full belly. It is rare for him to get out of Kabul, and to show his children much other than the apartment where they all spend most of their time.

He tells me he married Azita because she was his cousin, but also because he loved her. But mostly, he explains, he did his uncle and his family a favor. Otherwise Azita could have been forced to marry a stranger in wartime.

"That is why I stepped in. The whole family agreed it was the best thing."

"But you already had a wife?"

"Yes. But Azita is the daughter of my uncle. Since I lost my father, he became like a father to me. When he said he did not want to lose her to another family, I wanted to help."

He looks at Mehran. "He is completely like a boy, don't you think? He looks like a boy, and he behaves like a boy. He is a good son for us."

I look at Mehran, whose facial features resemble her father's, especially when she wrinkles her forehead or frowns. Grinning, he agrees that Mehran is more pampered than his other children. But she is the youngest, so she just needs a little bit more love—one must remember that, too. It's the same in every family. And Mehran will go back to being a girl; there is certainly no confusion about that. Ten or twelve may be a good age. Or a few years later, depending on how she looks. Her father is not entirely sure: "It is the first time we have done this. Let's see what will happen."

He does not foresee any trouble for Mehran, or believe that her time as a boy will be confusing later on. Planning for or even thinking much about the future is best avoided. Through a turbulent history and several wars he has learned that trying to foresee the future is often just cause for disappointment. "This is the need for today, and I don't know about tomorrow. She knows she is a girl, and when she grows up she will understand the difference better, too."

The deceit has worked so well he has almost fooled himself. "To be honest, I think of him as a boy. When I see him, I see my only son."

He fully expects Mehran to grow up to be a young woman, to marry and have children of her own. Anything else would be strange. "This is life in Afghanistan. Hopefully he will be lucky. Maybe it will be even easier for him since he is a boy now."

At the kebab lunch, Mehran is given the honorable placement between her father and the fire chief. She has become friendly with several of the firefighters, who allow her to hold each of their Kalashnikovs in a wobbly grip. If the firefighters have any clue of her real gender, they are too polite to say. Very politely, they also avert their eyes when the three other girls come their way, and they all make an effort to keep a distance, to avoid any physical collision. None of

the other girls are offered a chance to hold the guns. After ingest-
ing a large amount of food, the fire chief takes out a sweet-smelling
hand-rolled cigarette and lights up. He offers it around to his circle
of escorts, who happily put their guns on their laps and accept. It will
make the drive back to Kabul a little less dull.

On the way home, Mehran falls asleep on her father's shoulder, as
the task of driving is turned over to a firefighter with droopy eyelids.
Mehran has a few more years before the life of an Afghan woman
begins. For now, she is on the side of privilege.

PART TWO
YOUTH

Know then that the body is merely a garment.
Go seek the wearer, not the cloak.

—RUMI,

THIRTEENTH-CENTURY PERSIAN POET

Courtesy of the author

ZAHRA

CHAPTER EIGHT
THE TOMBOY

Zahra

STANDING ON TOP of a table, she was an animal on display. There was cheering and loud laughter. Her body was frozen, and she could not move. When tears rolled down her cheeks she did not lift her hands to wipe them off. That she cried engaged them even more. *"Look, look."* And she was looked at some more. Some clapped their hands with excitement. Finally, she buried her face in her hands, screaming, to block out the sound.

It would become one of her first very illuminated memories, and she would later describe it: "I made the world dark. I thought that when I could not see the world, the world could not see me."

Arriving at kindergarten in Peshawar in the standard uniform for boys had been a mistake. Her mother had brought it to her, and Zahra had managed for a few days before the other children figured her out. The older ones began to taunt her: She was not a real boy, so why would she want to look like one? One of them ran for the teacher, who was not pleased to hear about the charade. Zahra's parents were called over and quietly sat through a lecture about the importance of discipline and obedience in children from a young age. That was both the kindergarten's and the school's mission, and it was not to be made fun of. The parents would need to get a proper girl's uniform for their daughter before she would be allowed to return.

At home, Zahra cried and tried to wriggle out of the blue skirt and white blouse. It was when she returned to school that she was put on a table, to serve as an example before the others.

"This is a girl," the teacher announced. "Look at her. This is what a girl looks like. Do you see? She was never a boy. You will *all* remember this now."

ALMOST TEN YEARS later, standing in the doorway of her family's apartment in Kabul, Zahra has chosen her own outfit: a boxy black jacket, a buttoned-up shirt, and dark pants. She has the look of an elegant young man, walking a fine line on gender, with her round face, full lips, long eyelashes, and a shiny black Tom Cruise hairstyle with a neat side parting. She does not greet us with a smile. Nor does she lower her gaze, an impulse ingrained in most Afghan girls. She is unafraid, looking me straight in the eyes, resting one hand on her hip. And why would she not? Her exterior is of the ruling gender; mine is not.

Through another chain of rumors and introductions, I have found fifteen-year-old Zahra and her family. They are from Andkhoy in the northern Faryab province. There, according to several carpet dealers in Kabul, girls are commonly dressed like boys in order to help out as weavers in carpet production. But Zahra was never a *bacha posh* who did hard labor. Instead, her parents say their daughter just always *wanted* to be a boy. They had nothing to do with it. And just as with many stories of *bacha posh* I have encountered by now, that will turn out to be not entirely true.

Zahra is coming of a dangerous age.

An Afghan girl who is no longer a child but on her way to becoming a woman should immediately be shielded and protected to ensure her virginity and reputation for a future marriage. No matter how athletic, boyish, and buoyant the spirit of a *bacha posh* may have been, puberty—or, according to Dr. Fareiba, ideally sometime before—is the time when the curtain necessarily comes down for most girls. It is when they must be undone, otherwise a *bacha posh* can become "a little strange in the head," in Dr. Fareiba's words, if she presents as something else going into puberty, when gender segregation goes into full effect. For this reason, by remaining in male disguise at fifteen, Zahra is slowly treading into far more complicated territory than a younger *bacha posh*. By her age, girls are commonly taught to focus on becoming proper, shy, and very quiet young women.

But Zahra lacks most traditional feminine traits and speaks for herself right away. She has lived as a boy for as long as she can remember and has no intention of changing. She does not ever want to become an Afghan woman. They are second-class citizens, she explains to me, always beholden to and ruled by men. So why would she want to join them?

"People use bad words for girls; they scream at them on the streets," she says. "When I see that, I don't want to be a girl. When I am a boy, they don't speak to me like that."

Zahra would rather work, support herself, and make her own decisions, without being under the guardianship of a husband, following that of her father, as Afghan culture dictates for women. Other teenage Kabul girls will say similar things as a joking fantasy, as defying one's parents is rarely an option in Afghan culture. But Zahra is serious, and she speaks of the usual path for Afghan women as unthinkable to her. She does not want a family, nor does she desire children of her own. "For always, I want to be a boy and a boy and a boy," she says.

There are no other *bacha posh* in her school, but she has come to this conclusion on her own, through observations of her neighborhood, and her own family. There, eleven people share three rooms, and Zahra sleeps with her sisters. As in many other Afghan households, moments of privacy extend, at most, to the bathroom. One of her eight siblings is always banging on the door to get in, or just banging on the door as they run by.

‒‒◄━►‒‒

WITH THE PERMISSION of Zahra's parents, my female translator Setareh and I begin to stroll around Zahra's Kabul neighborhood with her on some afternoons after she has finished school. She has an exaggerated and clunky way of walking, as if there were something between her legs. With high, tense shoulders, and hands hanging by the thumbs in her pockets, she strides forward in broad, duck-footed steps, in her preferred outfit of an oversize hooded plaid shirt, jeans, and flip-flops. She keeps her head low, face close to her chest, and looks up only if someone directly calls her name. She knows her power is in the exterior, and her walk successfully signals that she is a typical teenage boy with some attitude.

Through this small masquerade, Zahra constitutes a provocation and a challenge to the order of her entire society.

Fashion has always been a way to communicate class, gender, and power. In Afghanistan, gender and power are one and the same. A pair of pants, a haircut, the right walk, and a teenage girl can reach for all kinds of things she is not supposed to have. Just as the Taliban strictly controlled how both men and women looked during their reign—when women could appear in public only when covered from head to toe—specific rules on clothing have been used throughout history by those who want to make sure the patriarchal order stays in place.

King James I of England denounced women dressing like men during his reign in the 1600s to ensure women did not see any undue advantages. France implemented a law in 1800 that said women could not wear pants; it was not formally removed until 2013. The Taliban explicitly forbade women wearing men's clothing, and also for girls to dress as boys, which may indicate that there were enough transgressions of Zahra's kind, and enough *bacha posh,* for them to see a need to ban the practice. Today, there is no official decree that makes any mention of dressing girls as boys.

The Taliban's dress police is also gone, but dress codes for women from puberty onward are still subjected to a strict social control, with many freelance enforcers. A woman must clearly signal her gender through her dress, but there are fluid limits to *how much* of a woman she is allowed to be.

One day just outside Zahra's house, a teenager rides by us on his bike, smacking his lips, uttering something in Dari. Setareh's face twitches in an impulse to yell back, but instead she pulls back, lowering her gaze like a good girl. But Zahra's reaction is swift: First, she hurls some profanities after the biker. Then she turns to Setareh and apologizes profusely on the cyclist's behalf. Both of them refuse to translate the original insult, but soon it creeps out that the offensive line was "I can see the shape of your body," followed by speculation about what kind of woman Setareh might be. No feminine shape should be noticeable when she moves, and her dark green, loose Punjabi-style pants, tunic, and scarf cover everything but her face and her hands. But her tunic is cut with the slightest hint of a waist in the middle, and the ensemble, which is not unusual for a current-day Kabul woman in her twenties, is less conservative than an all-black cloak. Adding to that, in the eyes of the cyclist, she is a lone woman in the company of a foreigner and a young boy—in other words, both suspect and possibly inappropriate company.

I look down at my wide black pants and knee-length black trench coat. "So what am I? Not another woman?"

Zahra and Setareh both look at me. "You," they agree, "are just a foreigner. Nobody cares about you. It is Afghan women they harass. Even the small boys are like the religious police, trained in telling women what they should wear."

As A FOREIGN, non-Muslim female, I am by definition a different species. Therefore, I am in some ways a neuter, which may be just as well under these circumstances. But what I wear still matters, and I am expertly styled to draw a minimum of attention to myself. A few days before the street incident, Setareh had given me a loving makeover. After observing me on our various excursions throughout Kabul, she finally decided to offer some commentary. My clothes were simply not loose *enough*, or wide *enough*, or dark *enough*. The sleeves were a little too short, showing a hint of wrist, and the delicate fabric of my tunic tended to cling to my thighs when I walked. Plus, bare feet in sandals? Everybody was looking at my white feet.

Ten minutes later, after we had dived into my sparse closet, all that was deemed sexual had been removed, and I had been fully turned into a black blob. I had to look almost Afghan? I wondered. Not exactly, Setareh scoffed: "You will never look Afghan."

Even though the new look is much better, it is still decidedly foreign, she explained. The fabrics I wear look too expensive: Afghans wear shiny polyester, imported from Pakistan. My black coat is okay, but the cut is too modern, and not boxy enough. The pants are the worst—made from a high-tech breathable fabric, they look *sporty*. Since when does a proper Afghan woman practice sports? That is a men's thing.

Even if I hid under a burka, my body language would give me away as all but an Afghan woman, Setareh warned. "You wave your hands around when you speak. You sound aggressive. Like you demand something. You put your hands on your hips, like you want to challenge people. It looks very rude for a woman to do that. You walk fast, and you don't look down. You look into people's faces as it pleases you."

She smiled again—as what came next was almost too obvious— the black backpack I sometimes carry my camera in is just as bad as my khaki shoulder bag. They are both such Western giveaways—like I am about to go mountain climbing. No, Setareh explained: A modern Kabul woman strives to look cosmopolitan, like those in advertisements from Dubai, Pakistan, or Iran. She puts on makeup and carries a decent, feminine handbag, and wears heels—not so high that she could get stuck on rainy days when Kabul's dust instantly turns to mud or be unable to jump over sewers, but still delicate enough to be feminine. Practicality in dress is for uncivilized people. And for men.

But the point is not to look good, or for me to resemble an Afghan. In order to work efficiently, we need to blend in and just be as close to nothings—but still women—as possible. Show respect. Afghans make a sport of spotting foreign men in trimmed beards and traditional village garb who ride around together in groups of two or three in regular taxis as they give the native look their best shot. Their expensive sunglasses and hiking boots always give them away. Trying too hard is the ultimate embarrassment, in Setareh's view.

Her friends all spend much time tweaking and trying to expand upon the female dress code, in which they must look like women, but at the same time, not to the point that they seem to be inviting any attention from men.

The hidden body is all about sex—which does not officially exist, other than in marriage for the purpose of procreation. It is why the smallest slip of a fabric can send a provocative signal. When most of the body is hidden, what follows is also that much more becomes sexualized. In an environment where sex is never discussed, where men and women are strictly separated, sex is, ironically and perhaps unfortunately, on everybody's mind all the time. Body parts, fabric, gestures that elsewhere would never seem sexual become loaded. This frustrating contradiction means everyone must be hyperaware.

As a woman, you must shrink both your physical body and any energy that surrounds it, in speech, movement, and gaze. Touching someone of the opposite sex in public, by mistake or as a friendly gesture, must always be avoided. A Swedish diplomat had thoroughly rejected my attempt to grab his arm the week before: Such frivolous affection between foreigners of the opposite sex would be misinterpreted, and send the wrong signals. Afghan male friends, however, are frequently spotted holding hands in Kabul, often while holding the strap to a gun in the other hand.

The responsibility for men's behavior, indeed for civilization itself, rests entirely with *women* here, and in how they dress and behave. Men's animalistic impulses are presumed to be overwhelming and uncontrollable. And as men are brutal, brainless savages, women must hide their bodies to avoid being assaulted. In most societies, a respectable woman, to varying degrees, is expected to cover up. If she doesn't, she is inviting assault. Any woman who gets into "trouble" by drawing too much attention from men will have only herself to blame.

In essence, it is the tired old attempt to dismiss a rape victim—did she wear something provocative? If so, she is responsible, at least in part, for being attacked. The idea that men are savages who can never control themselves was always a great insult to men, as it implies that men have no functioning minds that at any time could overrule very aggressive impulses.

The Koran, just as the Bible, has passages where modesty in clothing is advised for both men and women. But what exactly constitutes a modest, pious, and pure woman is nowhere explicitly prescribed in the Koran, and varies with its many interpreters. Veiling predates Islam and was originally a privilege for noble women only, to symbolize their sexual exclusivity to one man. Setareh, like most women here, covers her head, but when she crosses the border to visit relatives in Pakistan, it is more important that the scarf also obscures her chest. Up north, women sweep big sheets of fabric, the *chadori,* around themselves, sometimes even as an additional layer under a burka. Around Kabul, young women let the scarf slip, and each time we are alone, Setareh shakes out her long, shiny hair and runs her fingers through it to make it come alive, in a gesture of relief and pleasure. Zahra, on the other hand, would have shaved her head, had her mother not forbidden her from doing it.

AS WE PASS a small vegetable stall on our walk around Zahra's neighborhood, where dusty oranges, carrots, and apples are for sale, she proudly mentions that it was the scene of a fight last year, in which she took center stage. She had been walking with one of her younger sisters when they heard a hissing sound behind them; somebody was trying to snare the attention of the younger sister. *"Shht-shht-shht. . . . Shht-shht-shht. . . ."* The sister bowed her head and tried to walk faster, but Zahra would not let the insult pass quietly. She flipped around and yelled at the young man.

"Shame on you—*shame, I say*—you almost have a beard, and you are flirting with a child."

At first, the teenager seemed surprised and took a few steps back. But then he picked up a stone and threw it at Zahra. She ducked, and the stone hit a car behind her. Infuriated, Zahra went on the attack. She kicked him in the stomach and tried to punch his face. The boy fell to the ground but managed to throw another stone. That one hit the side mirror of the parked car. When two policemen from the park came running, Zahra explained the situation. Her eyes were angry and her heart was on fire when she spoke: The older boy had been inappropriate with her sister, who was only twelve.

The police agreed and shared Zahra's indignation after taking a quick look at Zahra's younger sister—she was properly dressed in black, with a head scarf tightly pinned over her hair. She could not be suspected of having provoked the young man's behavior. Concluding that, they began to beat the young boy. A local shopkeeper also joined in. After a few kicks and punches, they dragged the boy away, in the direction of the police station. He would spend the night in jail.

I look to Setareh for guidance, who fills in the blanks as Zahra finishes the story: "It's the role of the bigger brother to protect the honor of younger sisters. A brother should challenge those who are rude to them."

The older brother would be Zahra, in this case. Young girls, in Zahra's opinion, should have no contact with boys before they get engaged or married. A brother's greatest fear can be that his sister will fall in love with some boy of her own choosing. Such a crush would be disastrous for the family. The sister could be tainted and unmarriageable later on.

Young men are not to be trusted, Zahra says. They can make promises to young girls, only to later withdraw them when the girl is already shamed and tarnished from speaking to a boy and thus suspected of no longer having a pure mind.

I ask Zahra, to make sure I understand: "So girls should not be friends with boys before they get married?"

She shakes her head no. Absolutely not.

"But you hang out with boys?"

"Only my neighbors."

Even though Zahra plays the overprotective male with her sisters, she shares no loyalty with other boys. She is not one of them; she despises the way they treat girls.

There is an apparent duality in how she sees herself, and in how she sorts her different personas by tasks and traits: "When I am lifting a heavy carpet, my neighbors say I am strong. Then I feel like a boy. When I clean the house, I feel like a girl. Because I know that's what girls do."

Zahra is the one who moves around the most in her family. She runs all the errands, to the tailor and to the bazaar. She fills the heavy gas canisters and carries them home. Her male side is physical: "Boys are stronger than girls. They can do anything and they are free. When I was a child, everyone was beating me and I cried. But now, if anyone tries to beat me, I hit back. And when I am playing football, and do something wrong, they yell at me. Then, I yell back."

"Why do you think you feel like both?"

"My mother always tells me that I am a girl. But my neighbors call me a boy. I feel like both. People see me as both. I feel happy I am both. If my mother had not told anybody, nobody would know. I say I am Naweed to those who don't know."

It is a name that means "good news."

"What do you want us to call you?"

She shrugs. It would be impolite to ask anything of visitors.

Zahra has a very clear idea of what sets boys and girls apart. More than anything, she explains, it is in how they live their lives: "Girls dress up. They wear makeup. Boys are more simple. I like that. I hate the long hair that girls have. I wouldn't have the patience to brush it, to clean it. . . . And girls talk too much. They gossip, you know? Men talk, but not as much as women. Women are always sitting between four walls and talk. Talk, talk. That is what they do. Because they have no freedom. They can't go outside and do things. So they just keep talking."

After a pause, she adds, "I hate the scarf. I hate to put it on. And the long shirts. And the bra. I refuse to wear it." Her cheeks blush a little again, and the hair falls into her eyes as she turns her head away.

"Girls like to have beautiful houses, to color them inside and outside," she continues. "The boys don't care about houses or discussing how to decorate them. Men leave the home anyway, and go for work. There are things that women like to do: to cook, to clean, to make themselves beautiful. To go to weddings. Fashion. Men are not interested in any of that."

Men, on the other hand, like to race cars, hang out with their friends, and fight. Zahra describes the ultimate man as Kabul's current favorite character on television: Jack Bauer on 24. To her and the other boys in the neighborhood, the American action hero symbolizes a real Afghan. A true warrior. The payoff is in every episode: When the hero is beaten half to death, he will rise again and protect his honor. Just like an Afghan, in Zahra's view, he never fears death. And he never stops fighting.

I try something cheap: "So are boys better than girls?"

Zahra shakes her head. Absolutely not.

"Girls are more intelligent than boys, because they work more in the house and they can do more things. Men are suited for different kinds of work. They are intelligent, too, but they can do fewer things. All the work that boys can do, women can do, too. I know it, because I do it. The work that women do, men cannot do."

The conservative older brother turned somewhat progressive teenage girl has a self-perfected logic: "You know, *women can be men, too*. Like me."

Hard to argue with that.

WE APPROACH A sand pit where some young men have gathered around a three-wheeled motorbike for rent. Zahra wants to go for a ride. She strolls over to the man in charge and presses some coins into his palm. On the bike, she begins to loop around us at high speed. She breaks out in a large smile when she feels the wind on her face. As she passes us, her hair sprayed in every direction, she stands up on the bike, for effect. When I take her picture, a neighborhood boy yells at Setareh: "Tell her not to think she's a boy. She's a girl."

Climbing off the bike, Zahra says that the boy is her friend and we need not worry. He knows her secret, but he treats her like a fellow boy. "If someone beats me, he protects me."

"Have you been attacked?"

"It happens."

In reality, Zahra's freedom of movement has become more limited in the past few years. She is feeling increasingly isolated. Girls have begun to shy away from her, and young boys like to challenge her. She is not entirely safe in her own neighborhood anymore, where more people seem to have an issue with how she looks. What used to be freedom in disguise is now a slight provocation to those who know. And lately, more seem to know. Zahra suspects her mother has a part in that—the family used to protect her secret, but in the last few years, her mother has tried a variety of urging, begging, and demanding that Zahra look more feminine. It is time, her mother argues, for Zahra to become a girl and develop into the woman inside of her. But Zahra still resists. Her small freedoms have become curtailed but in her mind it still beats being a woman. The idea that she would go on to repeat the life of her mother, with a husband and a long line of children, seems absurd and horrifying to her.

As we sit down under a tree in a park, Zahra suddenly goes quiet when her Pashto teacher walks by and gives her a long stare. The female teachers in Zahra's school have never commented on her appearance. They have seen her putting on a head scarf that is a required part of her uniform as she walks up the steps, only to rip it off the minute she walks out of class. But recently her Pashto teacher told her that what she is doing is wrong, and that it is shameful for her not to look like a girl and cover her head at all times.

As with many social issues and rules on how people should live their lives, mullahs in Afghanistan take different views on whether God has anything at all to say about *bacha posh*. It's not a crime to dress as the other gender, but it could possibly be viewed as a sin. According to one Islamic hadith, the prophet Muhammad "damned those men who look like women and those women who look like men and stated 'expel them from homes.'"

Moses reportedly said something similar in Deuteronomy 22:5. "A woman must not wear men's clothing, nor a man wear women's clothing, for the Lord your God detests anyone who does this." Still, the interpretation of both of these passages, which could be condemnations of cross-dressing, are not agreed upon by religious scholars. God and the prophets may, in fact, have had no real problem at all with cross-dressers of either sex. It is important to note as well that these writings speak of "men" and "women"—not boys and girls.

But in Afghanistan, references to Islam can be made by anyone, at any time, for any purpose. No matter the issue, a person may cite an appropriately vague hadith, said to represent the thousands of (often contradictory) opinions and life events of the prophet Muhammad, or a recollection of what a mullah has once said. Such determinations—and they are usually exclaimed with absolute certainty—of what is Islamic or not are liberally distributed by Afghans both young and old, by those who hold university degrees and by those who use only their thumbprints to sign documents. The constant references to religion lead many Afghans to believe that any new rule imposed on them is indeed mandatory for being "a good Muslim."

The crippling catch-22 in Afghanistan is that as soon as someone refers to God, the prophet Muhammad, the Koran, or anything Islamic at all, anyone who questions that statement is also potentially questioning God. And in that, he or she could be suspected or accused of blasphemy. To avoid that potential danger, most contradictory and at times confusing interpretations of Islam remain unchallenged in Afghanistan. The Koran can be read in many ways, even by those who can read, and there are thousands of hadiths used to express different rules. So the scope for interpreting Islamic law and putting it into context is immense, according to scholars.

As there is no strictly organized clergy, the very title of mullah is open to anyone who is viewed as having some religious credentials. The mullah can be an illiterate farmer who doubles as a religious leader for the village. Considering that a mullah can be the one to declare a newborn girl a son in order to help out a son-less family, some religious leaders not only condone *bacha posh* but also encourage and accept it when deemed necessary.

Zahra is not aware of any specific Islamic rules on the issue of what to wear; nor does she know of one interpretation or another of them. But she is an observant Muslim who prays, and she told her Pashto teacher what made sense to her: "It is my body and you should leave me alone."

As the teacher muttered and walked away, several girls at school were astonished that Zahra had spoken back to a male teacher on a religious issue. Some were told by their parents to stay away from her after that.

Still, Zahra has gained some popularity for one reason: She is the closest many of the students in the all-girls school will come to conversing with a boy of the same age. At times, they let Zahra stand in for their movie-star fantasy, pinching her cheeks, joking to one another that she is "such a cute boy." Sometimes, a giggly girl will want to take the play further, asking Zahra to hold her hand and declare that they are engaged.

Zahra doesn't really like any of those games, but she plays along, so as not to alienate anyone further.

WHEN WE CLIMB out of the car on another day, Zahra greets us on her bicycle. Smiling and waving, she runs up to the car and opens the door on my side. When she leans in, I instinctively do the same and kiss her three times on the cheeks, in a classic Afghan greeting, before I realize my mistake. It's used mostly as a greeting for people of the same gender. Three boys are standing behind another car looking at us. I apologize to Zahra, who is very polite: It's not a problem. I had completely forgotten the routine we had almost perfected last time: a firm handshake, followed by the American high five that Zahra always seems to execute more smoothly than I do.

At the house, Zahra's mother, Asma, has prepared an overwhelming lunch. She and Zahra's father, Samir, want to thank us for our interest in their daughter. For this occasion, Asma has been cooking for two days, and on the table is a big serving plate of fried rice with slices of carrot and onion, chunks of meat and raisins, and the special dried herbs sent from Andkhoy hidden inside the rice, Uzbek-style. The *quorma* is luxurious: a whole chicken cooked in tomato sauce. *Manto* are carefully folded dumplings with minced meat inside, steamed in a cooker with onions. There is a large plate of minced tomato, cucumber, and onions that have been tossed with thick mayonnaise. All food is prepared with the expensive vegetable oil used for special occasions, marked "USA" and "Vitamin A fortified." It is a World Food Program item openly sold at one of the bazaars, and considered to be better than the Pakistani versions. The dessert has already been set out; it's *firiny,* a creamy version of rice pudding with a shivering poison-green Jell-O on top. Pepsi cans are lined up next to drying oranges and darkened bananas. The fruit is a rare treat from Pakistan.

Samir, in a great mood and still wearing his well-worn khaki flight uniform, has been dismissed early from his work piloting helicopters for the Afghan air force. He balances his youngest, a fourteen-month-old girl, on one knee. The baby is wearing a red jumpsuit and has little hair; without the announcement of her gender, no observer would know for sure. Dressing little boys and girls in blue or pink was a marketing gimmick invented in the United States in the forties. Before then, all children were mostly dressed in white, with lace and ruffles. Pink was actually regarded as the more masculine, fiery color before it came to be the signifying color for a baby girl.

A three-year-old boy tries to climb up onto his father's other knee, only to be gently brushed away. The other siblings move around the table; they are too young to be invited to sit with the grown-ups and too old to earn a place in someone's lap. Still, Samir gives everyone a good chunk of attention. He beams when speaking of his children. "I am so happy I have a big family. The dream of every parent is for their children to give them grandchildren. And if they don't have children, it's a big problem. I was lucky."

Samir smiles at Asma. Nine children puts her above Afghan women's national average of six surviving children. Zahra, at fifteen, is number three, with four sisters and four brothers.

Asma and Samir are first cousins in an arranged marriage. According to Samir: "It was both our parents' choice. And Asma's choice."

Asma shouts in protest. "*Neee neeee!* It was you who came to my home a hundred times and told me you wanted to marry me."

Samir chuckles. "*You* wanted to marry *me*—I still have your love letters." He turns to me: Asma found him irresistible; is that so hard to imagine? "I will show you a picture from my youth, and you will see I was very handsome."

He corrects himself: They were lucky, too, in what their parents decided for them. Most marriages are not like theirs. The big family, however, was Asma's doing. "It was your fault," Samir throws out in the direction of his wife, grinning. "Maybe you want another one?"

She grins back at him. There are four sons in the family already and her work is more than done. "I have told you the factory is closed. I have put a lock on it!" Their youngest was unplanned. When Asma went to the doctor for a sore throat, she learned that she was three months pregnant.

Samir roars with laughter as he is reminded of her surprise, and starts to shovel up rice with a fork over to his own plate. Another child would be hard. They have almost outgrown the apartment already and cannot afford to go anywhere else. They rented it from a wealthier relative when they returned from Peshawar after the Taliban years. Their time in Pakistan was not bad—the family ran a small carpet business there. But during those years Samir was unable to fly, and it was almost unbearable for him. He was never quite a carpet dealer, like his relatives.

Asma worries about her overgrown *bacha posh* daughter: "At first, I only had two daughters, and when Zahra wanted to wear boys' clothing, I was pleased. I liked it, since we didn't have a boy then." She hesitates before continuing: "Now, we don't really know."

Samir agrees it's time for Zahra to change: "I have told her one thousand times that she needs to cover herself in long coats and let her hair grow out. But she says it's her own choice. She's even taller than her older sisters now. She refuses. Maybe she has some of me in her." He says it with a father's sense of pride.

Asma is not amused by her husband's relenting on Zahra's appearance, and she is eager to convince Samir that something is not right any longer in how their daughter looks.

I have told her that we have met many girls like Zahra, although so far, all have been younger. But what is it like in the West? Asma wonders, urging me to explain what the universal rules are for what women should look like. "If you walk in the street in your country and a girl had short hair and looked like a boy, do you think it's shameful?"

I weigh my words carefully, noting that Zahra is listening intently.

"It's very common for girls to have short hair and pants, and it's not considered shameful."

Asma is not satisfied. "But what do *you* think?"

"I have met many girls who live like boys here," I say, trying to turn it back to her. "It is a choice within each family. But I am not sure if it is a good thing for the girls, or if it is a problem. Perhaps it can be both?"

But Asma is not interested in psychological consequences. She is more concerned with the social ones. "It could maybe be a shame in Afghan culture, now that Zahra is older." She pauses. It's something she has been thinking a lot about lately. But there is no manual for this; Zahra certainly doesn't look like a woman just yet. For some reason, she has not developed as quickly as her sisters, although she is physically normal, Asma explains: "She has what other girls have."

Zahra looks at her mother in astonishment. "Why are you telling them? It is personal business!"

Asma rolls her eyes. It's the truth that she is a woman; why would that be shameful?

"In my view, it's not too bad," Asma continues, almost to herself. "It's not like she has shaved her head or anything. She wears pants and she has short hair. But she is not too masculine. Zahra is something . . . in between, I think."

Her father just shakes his head. He doesn't actually condone Zahra's choice of clothes and haircut, but as he is away during the day, it's hard to control. Today his daughter is in her usual outfit of pants and a baggy shirt. Her father does not seem to mind. But with one eye on Asma, he declares that Zahra does not respect her mother the way she should. And they do not allow her to go out in the evening anymore. Samir has always considered it a privilege to have an extra boy, even though Zahra is a little older now. There are still advantages; she can help with errands and other heavier tasks, he points out, in both his own and Zahra's defense.

His opinions about marriage and family extend to all of his daughters, including Zahra—every Afghan should get married and have children. It's the natural course of life. It will happen, sooner or later. But right now, he admits he can get confused by her appearance. "All the time I am reminding myself that she is really my daughter. But she has made herself into so much of a boy, I can't help it that I forget."

He laughs again. His daughter is just a little bit of a rebel, just like he is. Zahra smiles down on her plate of *manto*.

LATER, ASMA BRINGS out a picture of herself as a glamorous, made-up young married woman. Looking serious before the camera, she is in a pale blue dress, with a tiny Zahra next to her on the sofa.

In the photo, Zahra is barely two years old, in jeans and a tight little denim vest, with a short haircut—all by her own choice, Asma exclaims. Since Zahra had no older brothers at the time, the outfit must have been bought for her. I say that as far as I know, every *bacha posh* has been the result of the parents' desire to have a son in the family.

As Asma reveals her pregnancy history, the truth slowly comes out. After she had Zahra, her next pregnancy ended with a late-term miscarriage. It would have been a boy. The next year, she gave birth prematurely to a son who died. After having three surviving daughters but two sons who had died, Asma felt increasingly desperate. "Please, please God, give me a son," she prayed. She needed some good luck to boost her prayer. Her relatives were prodding Asma to get pregnant again, and Zahra was being cared for by her cousins—one of whom had been turned into a *bacha posh* to ensure her mother's next-born would be a son.

Asma's relatives urged her to try the same tactic. And what harm could it be? she thought. It had worked for others. It was also easier to have Zahra dressed as a boy, so she could move around with her cousins. If it had magical benefits beyond that, it would be a bonus. So before she turned two, Zahra became the family's son.

By the time she turned six, she would attempt to cut her own hair—or, rather, try to shave her head—and refuse to play with other girls. Zahra's older cousin who had been a *bacha posh* moved to Europe, where she now lives with her husband and three children. She warned Asma that her path back to womanhood was very difficult. But Asma gave birth to four living sons after Zahra, so to her, no one can dispute the power of magic in *bacha posh*.

THERE IS FURTHER, empirical evidence of benefits in the family, too. Turning girls into boys is a practice that has given them many sons through the generations, according to Samir's white-haired mother, who shows up at the family's apartment one day. The family has a long history of powerful women who took on the role of men, both in looks and tasks. In the grandmother's view, there is no down-side to Zahra remaining a *bacha posh* until she gets married. Zahra's great-great-grandmother also dressed like a boy and lived as a young man for years.

The great-great-grandmother rode horses just like the famous warrior Malalai of Maiwand, an Afghan equivalent to Joan of Arc who helped drive the British army out of Afghanistan in the 1880s. Zahra's foremother held the prestigious male position of a land in-spector during King Ḥabībullāh's time, when the female guards in Nancy Duprée's photo also dressed as men. She married at age thirty-eight and bore four children. She had switched over to wom-en's dress by then, after holding out as a man longer than most. But it certainly did not do her any harm to live as a boy for a few years, says Zahra's grandmother.

Finding a suitable husband for a *bacha posh* was never an issue, ei-ther, as far as she knows. Living as a man a little longer is nothing unusual in the family; there will be plenty of time to get married later on. Afghans of an Uzbek heritage are liberal, independent people who don't care what people think of them, the grandmother says. She supports her son in not strictly enforcing Zahra's transition right now, and she can't see why Asma fusses over it. Eventually, Zahra will marry, like everyone else. She is certain of it.

To the grandmother, there is something distinctly Afghan about *bacha posh*: "It is our tradition from a long time ago. Afghan girls dressed as boys when there were no weapons, only bows and arrows."

She has never read it in a book, but everybody has heard tales of girls who grew up as boys and later lead brave and unusual lives as women. And, she adds, it was not just the fearless Malalai who drove out invaders. Other Afghan women warriors came both before and after Malalai; the grandmother heard their stories many times grow-ing up.

Different tricks have always been employed, too, for producing sons, according to the grandmother. "Our mothers would tell us about the *bacha posh* and then we told our own families," she says. "It was before Islam even came to Afghanistan. We always knew about it."

"Before Islam" would be sometime before the seventh century and more than 1,400 years ago. Islam is just the latest religion to take hold in Afghanistan, where Louis Duprée's excavations revealed settlements as old as 35,000 years, and where modern oil and gas explorations regularly uncover evidence of ancient civilizations. As conquerors came in over the mountains from different directions, they brought with them new religions, practices, and beliefs. Some were erased by those who came after, and others have stuck to this day. Afghanistan, believed by anthropologists to be one of the original historical meeting places between the East and the West, has in fact seen and often tolerated most known religions as well as an influx of believers in such faiths as Buddhism, Hinduism, Judaism, and Christianity. Even with the advent and dominance of Islam, other religions were still practiced freely by minorities in Kabul up until the 1980s.

But through decades of war and with every wave of refugees, the most educated Afghans have usually been the first ones to leave, and with every shift of villagers into urban areas, more conservative elements have crept into society, bringing with them stricter rules and far-flung tribal customs and rules from isolated provinces.

I finally understand that Zahra's grandmother is trying to steer me in the same direction as Dr. Fareiba's gathering of health workers, without saying it out loud. They speak of an entirely different time. The old woman just cannot spell it out to me: Beliefs and practices for producing sons from a time predating Islam are still very much alive in one of the most conservative Muslim countries on earth. It means that the trail of Afghan *bacha posh* could go much further back than to the Taliban, or even to Zahra's great-great-grandmother.

CHAPTER NINE
THE CANDIDATE

Azita

SHE TRIES ON a few different faces in the mirror: A furrowed brow and a clenched jaw read as *resolute*. Lips pressed together: *wise, serious*. The slippery silk head scarf needs another pin; it keeps sliding down into the pasty foundation on her forehead.

She is having her picture taken today.

Azita's living room has become the campaign headquarters for "the Lioness of Badghis"—the name she was given by supporters in the previous election and which she has now adopted for her posters as she lobbies for her 2010 reelection. Her campaign moniker is a not-so-subtle reference to the legendary Ahmad Shah Massoud, "the Lion of Panjshir," a mujahideen warrior who fought the Soviets. He also later stood against the Taliban's rule with the Northern Alliance before he was assassinated.

When Azita emerges from the bathroom, she is met by an appeal for a puppy; the girls have just seen one in a cartoon. She tells them she is not sure what the neighbors would think—keeping a domesticated dog is a Western thing. Here, dogs are wild. But she promises to think about it, if they will all go and play in their own room. A small argument over who gets to use Azita's laptop has already broken out between Mehran and one of her sisters. When Mehran slaps her sister in the face, she gets a threat in return: "If you do that again," Mehrangis says, glancing toward the photographer and then back again at Mehran, "I won't call you my brother anymore."

With that, Mehran stalks off as her mother sighs behind her. Azita smiles apologetically to the photographer and his assistant, who are setting up a large theatrical-looking light on a metal tripod in the living room. Azita's husband, dressed in all white, tries hard to be a good host, serving tea and then struggling to move a large plastic fan back and forth on the floor. Each guest gets a few moments of fan air straight in the face.

"He is my house husband," Azita jokes with the young photographer. He looks back at her with a blank expression.

She poses by the yellow-painted cement wall and the photographer snaps his camera a few times. It takes only seconds, and suddenly he is finished and pulls up the images on his laptop. Most are out of focus or overexposed, leaving Azita's face flat. But that's a good thing—so long as the scarf is in place and her face betrays no happiness, it works. The best shot has her showing a hint of a smile, but that one is wasted: A smiling woman translates as frivolous and lightweight.

Azita picks one where she has on a hand-embroidered Tajik coat, another where she is wearing a red striped Turkoman jacket. She needs to play to all sides of the complicated ethnic patchwork of her province, while still maintaining her own Aimaq heritage on her father's side, which is a Sunni Persian tribe with a Hazara dialect. Lineage is always determined by the father's ethnicity, but as a minority that has been both ignored and persecuted over time, the Aimaq have traditionally been lumped together with the Tajiks in Azita's home province. That determination is to her benefit, as Tajiks have formed an alliance with many of the Pashtuns in Badghis. To Azita, ethnicity is mostly a reminder of war and of Afghan infighting. To anyone who asks about her ethnicity, she usually says that she's *Afghan*.

Her tagline on the posters is "I am fighting for *your* best life." The message is expanded on the audiocassettes she plans to distribute: "I don't want power and I don't want money in my pocket. I only want to represent you and bring your problems to our central government. I want to raise your voice to Kabul."

It builds on her first campaign. What Badghis lacked, she would try to snare from Kabul. That means—in the most basic sense— almost everything. Life in Badghis is much the same as it was when she lived there as a teenager. Except for those in the few Badghis towns with wells, most residents collect snow and rainwater in a hole as their supply of drinking water. In the summer, they walk long distances to collect water, and hope that government tank trucks filled with drinking water will reach them. Azita now takes credit for a few of those trucks reaching Badghis. And she has mediated between those who make their livelihood off the pistachio forests and those who keep chopping them down to heat their houses.

Azita tries to get the message out that she operates with a campaign budget of only $40,000 and is not from a rich family, but that she is running as an independent and is not beholden to many people. Her wealthier competition is backed by several powerful businessmen in Badghis, but Azita has secured only a few pistachio farmers on her side. She has also accepted office supplies and smaller monetary contributions from an Afghan defense contractor in Herat and an Afghan pharmaceutical company, both of which support the other candidates too. Most of her campaign contributions go toward food for a few hundred people each day at her house in Qala-e-Naw. Good hospitality, which must include good cooking, is as important for the campaign as her political message.

The photographer suggests they do a little something extra with one of her images. It's special, and it has been popular with some of the other candidates he has worked with, he explains. He pulls up a photo of an empty podium with lots of press microphones attached to it. The image of her could be Photoshopped in there, to make her look important. He would throw it in for free. Azita hesitates—she has plenty of authentic images of herself in front of microphones. But why not? If it's something the others have done . . . She decides she needs all the help she can get.

AFTER PAYING THE photographer one hundred dollars in cash—just as in many other unstable countries, the U.S. dollar is the currency that buys most things—Azita puts out fresh tea and cookies in preparation for her next visitor. The UN office called earlier in the day; their gender unit has offered to coach her on campaigning. It's not the first time Azita has heard from them, but every house call has been canceled in the course of her five years in parliament. Azita knows the UN rotation schedule better than most: Each time they call, it's a new articulate woman on the phone, saying she wants to "reach out," offering to teach Azita the basics of the parliamentary system, the importance of female participation in the election process, and how women can gain more self-confidence to do so.

A few hours later, when the official has yet to show up, there is another call. The United Nations is under "lockdown" and its staff have a strict curfew after a drive-by shooting in another part of Kabul. No "internationals" are allowed to exit the fortified compounds as long as the "White City" status is in effect. But a local employee, an assistant, will be available to come over the next day, the caller says.

"Because it doesn't matter if Afghans are shot," Azita mutters as she hangs up, showing a flash of temper toward those whom she usually welcomes. "They all say they want to help women politicians, but they never say how. And I never hear back from them."

Or, rather, she feels there is little follow-through.

At one point, Azita imagined she would have more power and perhaps be recognized as a real player on the political stage in Kabul. But Badghis, with its Pashtun minority, never held much interest for the national stage. The reality is that she represents a small province and she lacks a powerful lineage and a personal fortune: the two most important ingredients for getting things done in Kabul. And she is a woman—a provocation to many of her colleagues, who would rather she not be there at all. Still, she sometimes fantasizes about being the minister of the interior.

A female minister does run the Ministry of Women's Affairs,

which foreign delegations often ask to tour. But those involved in Afghan politics pay little attention to it. The Ministry of Interior Affairs, on the other hand, is what aims to hold the country together, as it controls security for the government, as well as the national police and their counternarcotics division. The problem with any man—and it is always a man—holding the post, in Azita's view, is that he inevitably owes someone favors. The Taliban may not be openly represented in Afghanistan's top leadership, but unofficially, many politicians are well connected to the Taliban as well as organized crime through their business dealings. Lucrative arrangements have made it possible for multiple well-known officials and elected politicians to secure both capital and visas for an escape to Dubai or to Europe, for vacations or more permanent stays. That is considered by many politicians to be a reasonable safety precaution and a necessary privilege, should the government be as short-lived as those in previous decades.

It frustrates Azita that foreigners call on her to discuss "women's issues," but when it comes to other topics that matter as much to women as to men, such as how the state is actually run, neither Afghans nor foreigners show much interest in her opinions.

"The foreigners think they are helping women in Afghanistan, but it is so corrupt," she blurts out. "All this money coming in, but we still suffer. They think it's all about the burka. I'm ready to wear two burkas if my government can provide security and rule of law. That's okay with me. If that is the only freedom I have to give up, I am ready."

THE NEXT CALL is a threat, but not of the usual death variety. Instead, the anonymous caller warns that he intends to make sure everyone in Badghis knows that she's a Communist, unless she withdraws from the race. Azita cuts him off and makes a quick call to her father, giving him the caller's cell phone number as shown on her display.

Being likened to or called a Communist is as grave an insult in

Afghanistan as it once was, and may still be, in U.S. politics. The label "Communist" still today translates as "traitor," from the war that killed one million Afghans. In current-day Afghanistan it also has a few added twists: "Communist" is a slur indicating someone is not a proper Muslim, but rather a suspicious, Westernized character who drinks wine and fails to pray. For a politician to be branded a Communist or rumored to have Communist sympathies must be avoided, even though several known former Afghan Communists sit in the current parliament. Their legacy is such that other powerful liaisons have the effect of declaring void the former Communist label.

The default Communist-bashing has its contradictions, of course. In the occasional angry rants about Americans—"the new occupiers"—Afghans in Kabul can sometimes speak longingly of the Soviet era, when they say there was order, infrastructure improvements, and social programs that seemed to work better than those put in place by *Amrican,* which includes all foreign countries that make up the coalition. Also, the Russians may have been occupiers, but they are often described by Kabulis as the lesser evil compared to the destruction and mayhem that arrived with the mujahideen infighting. That same reluctant praise is rarely bestowed on the Taliban rule that followed, however, whom those in the capital almost uniformly seem to have detested when they were in government.

Over the phone, Azita's father assures her he will find out who the caller is and prevent any rumor from taking root. He has taken on the role of her adviser and stand-in campaign manager, mostly for his own sake. He enjoys his unofficial and self-imposed status as Azita's local spokesperson, and having a daughter in parliament boosts his reputation as a wise old man who can give advice and resolve conflicts.

It was Mourtaza who convinced Azita's husband to let her run again. He was reluctant at first. Life in Kabul was stressful, he had complained to his father-in-law, and the constant stream of visitors had become taxing. He would prefer to support his own family back home in Badghis, rather than be what increasingly felt like a servant to his powerful wife in Kabul. But eventually he conceded to his father-in-law's arguments that his and Azita's standard of living in Kabul and the educational opportunities available to their children far surpassed what was offered in the province.

Azita is grateful for her father's support. She thinks of it as his way of compensating for the marriage he forced her into. He is a strict man, she says, and rarely shows any feelings toward her, but she hopes he is proud of her. Fortunately, people cannot complain his daughter is imperfect these days, with Mehran representing the requisite grandson in the family.

Azita does not speak of it, but she is deeply anxious about the risk of not being reelected. She does not fear only her competitors' larger, more costly campaigns, or the gossip attacks she knows will be launched. She also fears the system itself: The ballots have already been printed, and her name has been smudged onto another candidate's number, which will add another layer of complexity for her mostly illiterate voters. She is particularly nervous about the counting of those ballots: It will take days for the boxes to travel back to Kabul, and they will pass through many hands on the way. But she absolutely *needs* to win—so that her life does not slide backward again.

"I THOUGHT OF dying. But I never thought of divorce," Azita says of her darkest years in the village. "If I had separated from my husband, I would have lost my children, and they would have had no rights. I am not one to quit."

In the Taliban years, both Azita and her parents could have been arrested had she left her husband. But instead, on three different occasions, her father called for a form of family counseling performed by older men. It was done according to tribal custom, and Azita was allowed to make her case only through her father, by standing outside the door where negotiations took place among the men. Each time, Azita brought up the abuse by her husband and her mother-in-law. And each time, her husband promised the elders and her father that he would do better.

She could hardly hide the fighting with her husband from the children during the village years, either; they have all seen much more than Azita would have wished. But almost five years have passed since the family moved to Kabul, and she describes it as though something in their dynamic shifted, as her husband has not laid a hand on her since. Azita doesn't think of herself as very forgiving—just that it is necessary to forgive for life to work: "My husband's family is very poor. They do not think of a woman as an individual. He was under the control of his mother. He did not know better," she explains.

So did her status as a parliamentarian put him on a new track? Can a woman's increased power and status also quell domestic violence?

She laughs at my idealized suggestion. Perhaps. But she likes to take a more profound view of how she believes her husband has actually changed and become a better person: He realized he was wrong. Several factors contributed, she believes. In Kabul, his status as her husband improved. With his children growing up in a more urban context, where they were learning to read and write, he wanted to present an image of himself as a more modern man. Azita had always hoped that, with time, she and her husband would grow more alike and could become partners instead of adversaries. She prefers not to dwell on thoughts of what may happen if she loses the reelection. But she concedes that she has several reasons for wanting to stay in parliament. The opportunity to somewhat affect her country is only one of them.

Azita glances over to her husband, who is transfixed by a wrestling game on cable television. "Some people tell him to take a third wife."

The family's youngest daughter is important in Azita's fragile house of cards. With Mehran playing the role of a son, her husband has stopped pushing her to get pregnant again and, at least not out loud, thinking of taking another wife. The prophet Muhammad had several wives; in Afghanistan, a man is allowed up to four wives, whereas a woman can have only one husband. It is a display of wealth and prestige for a man in Afghanistan to have several wives; he is seen as someone who can afford to multiply his chances of male offspring. Many of Azita's male colleagues in parliament, especially those with extravagant security arrangements and many guns, have more than one wife. In her own family, it is hard enough that there are two already.

During Azita's first year in parliament, the first wife—as Azita always refers to her—lived with them in Kabul with her daughter. Inside the family's small apartment and with the designation as the family's breadwinner with a high official status, Azita set many of the rules, and their relationship deteriorated from an initial friendship to loud fights. Eventually, the first wife moved back to Badghis. Now Azita's husband travels to Badghis every other month to stay with his first wife and daughter. It is a bit of an embarrassment for him, as he can be suspected of having left one wife behind. He frequently complains to Azita that they should all be reunited as a family soon. But for now, with Mehran, Azita exerts some influence over the household as the mother of its only son. Just as in politics, she is a pragmatist at home: "We are fighting for human rights and democracy here. But I cannot change my husband."

As AZITA WINDS down one evening and is soon to begin her nightly ritual of covering her face in cold cream, I challenge her on Mehran. I tell her about Zahra, and how hard she seems to resist her birth sex. What will time do to Mehran as she grows older? When will you change her? I ask. And what if that just *won't work*?

"I don't think it will be a problem," Azita responds. "I don't think that society will give her any problems. I have seen this many times, and I have so much experience from seeing it. These girls are just normal girls when they change back. I have not seen any bad examples."

"How can it not be difficult for her when, later on, she has to become more limited, as a woman? How can you be so sure?"

Azita leans forward, smiling. "Should I share something with you, honestly? For some years, I have also been a boy."

Of course. I should have guessed it.

In Azita's case, it was a practical matter. During her childhood in Kabul, she was the eldest daughter in a family of all girls for several years before a baby brother arrived. Business had picked up in the family's small store and her father needed help in the afternoons. Who could be more trusted than family?

But it needed to be a boy.

Azita's parents approached her together to ask if she would be willing to do it. They already called her "the little manager" at home and wondered if she would take on some more work. How could she say no? The way ten-year-old Azita saw it, this was the chance to be her parents' "best son and best daughter" in one. She put on pants, a shirt, and a pair of sneakers and went to work.

Her two long, dark braids had been her pride, but as soon as they were gone, she did not miss them. Her new short hair was mostly hidden under a baseball cap in the afternoons. She wore it with the brim in the back; that seemed cooler and resembled characters in Western films she had seen. In the store, she became the assistant runner, fetching goods and assisting customers. There was no name for her; Mourtaza just referred to her as the *bacha,* or his boy, while ordering her around before the customers. The store stayed open until one in the morning, since most people shopped in the evenings. Among the big sellers were her mother's homemade yogurt, bread, pastry, cheese, and imported tea.

Azita likes to think her time in the store built character. In school, she had been told she was beautiful and was maybe a little bit too proud, but working taught her resilience. Already chosen to be captain of the girls' volleyball team at school, she was strong and tall, which worked well, both in the store and when she joined the boys outside on the street.

She enjoyed feeling less monitored; there was no need to watch how she dressed or spoke at all times. It was relaxing not to be defined by her body. While there was moderate progress for urban women during "the Russian time," girls still needed to closely watch their behavior and dress in public, as social codes remained the same.

Above all, masquerading as a boy gave Azita *access*. She could approach any situation or group of men or boys without being scrutinized or considering how to behave appropriately. Her clothing, her very being, was never a hindrance. It seemed as though she was a more natural fit everywhere in society, and she was always welcome. She felt special, and she didn't need to avoid anyone. Women and girls would shy away on the street, giving way to her. It was a magical high.

She once observed a boy her own age, about thirteen, lurking around the store and then suddenly tucking a biscuit under his shirt. As the male guardian of the store, Azita reacted instinctively—launching herself at him, grabbing him by the arm, and pulling him out of the store, onto the street outside. With a firm grip still around his arm, she punched him in the stomach. The boy folded and sunk to his knees. Out of the corner of her eye, Azita saw another group of boys running toward her, and knew she must quickly retreat. She leaned in and whispered to the boy: "I am a girl. But I think I'm stronger than you are. And I will beat you even more when you come back." Then she let go of her grip and ran back into the store, feeling a rush she would never forget. She saw the boy a few times after that, always on his bicycle, but he never attempted to come into the store again.

Her stint on the other side came to an end when her father dismissed her early one afternoon when she was almost fourteen. Azita had begun to grow quickly; she was up two sizes in clothing in just a matter of months, and the day came when she complained of stomach pains. Too afraid to ask her mother, she learned the next day from a classmate what had happened. Neither of her parents said anything, but it was apparent that they knew of the event that had turned her into a woman of childbearing age. Her father made it clear that she would no longer work at the store and that it was not a good idea for her to run around outside anymore, either.

Azita protested her father's decision, but it was firm. To encourage his daughter to think positively about womanhood, he brought home a full-length bright blue dress for her. Azita remembers it as a "beautiful, expensive and pretty kind of fairy-tale dress." She hated it. At first, she struggled to walk in it. She fell twice when the heavy fabric snarled in her long legs, but she soon learned to take shorter strides. She wasn't walking very far anyway, since she was now mostly confined to the house in the afternoons, like other proper Afghan girls. The improvised volleyball tournament she had set up with a few friends went on without her. She would watch the other children play from her window in the evenings. She would not wear her baseball cap again, or her jeans.

"DO YOU EVER wish you had been born a boy?" I ask, as we sit in a corner on the floor, with the silence of a thick Kabul night outside only occasionally interrupted by distant bursts of gunfire.

"Never. It's the men who create all our conflicts here."

But she is sure of this: It certainly did her no harm to spend some time as one among them. The way she sees it, her boy years have helped her all her life: They made her more energetic. They made her strong. For almost five years, she could sit and talk to men openly. "I was not afraid of them," she says. And she never feared them much after that. Those short years are some of the best she can remember. "I have had their experience, too, so I am never embarrassed to speak to men. Now no men will ignore my power. Nobody will ignore my talent."

"Are you saying this is an experience for Mehran that you want her to have?"

"Yes. An experience."

"Or is it more of an experiment?"

Her eyes dart back and forth a few times, and she nods, slowly.

"I don't disagree with you. I will prepare my daughter very carefully for turning back to a girl. I was a boy part-time, and she is a boy full-time. It's different. I know."

Her voice fades slightly.

"Is it necessary to do this or not? I don't know. I couldn't tell you. We have tried it now for more than a year, and the gossip has stopped. Most people believe I have a son. So now, at least for me, it has become better. I am giving my youngest a taste of the whole life, you know? I have seen her change. She is much more active now, much more alive. She is not afraid of anything. And my guests now respect my family and my husband."

"So what do you know that other Afghan women do not?"

That's an easy one. "Most of my voters are men. Society is dominated by men. All the leaders are men. And I have to talk and communicate with them. Of course, I talk to women, too, at gatherings and in families. But all the decisions are still in the hands of men. Of the elders. With the male *shura* councils, in the villages. So I have to talk more to them. Even when I want to talk to women, I have to go through the men to get their permission. And I know their language; I know how to approach them and how to get them to listen to me. Even when I make speeches to voters, I know I have to speak the men's language even when I talk about women, so they will tell their wives to vote for me."

The language of men, she says, is calm, direct, and uncompromising. Not too many words, never too much of an explanation. Whatever she says needs to exude authority and ideally lack emotion. Female communication, on the other hand, is all nuance and detail. To men, that can be confusing, she has found.

"What if Mehran came to you tomorrow and said she wanted to be a girl?"

Azita looks up to the ceiling in a silent inshallah: Whatever God wants.

"I would not force her. We asked her if she wanted to be a boy, and she said 'Wow, let's go.' But if she said, 'I would like to be a girl again,' I would accept it."

To Azita, *bacha posh* is less about a preference for sons and more a symptom of how poorly her society works. But, as in politics, she works with the reality she's been dealt. And sometimes, she argues, you have to think of temporary solutions while you try to slowly change something bigger. She resents the fact that boys are the preferred children here. But she has a long way to go before she can make the argument in a convincing way that girls are of equal value in Afghanistan. She believes her decision for Mehran, at its core, is also deeply subversive, since it will make her daughter into another kind of woman one day—one who can push society even further. It seems a slightly idealized version of reality, but her best argument lies in her own journey from Badghis back to Kabul.

Azita is fully aware that others may disagree with her mothering choices. At the same time she is defiant: "Yes, this is not normal for you. And I know it's very hard for you to believe why one mother is doing these things to her youngest daughter. But I want to say to you, some things are happening in Afghanistan that really are not imaginable for you as a Western people."

CHAPTER TEN

THE PASHTUN TEA PARTY

O N THE OTHER side of town, in a more upscale neighborhood, a regal-looking woman in an emerald-green Punjabi-style dress, her arms heavy with gold bangles, fully agrees. Being a *bacha posh* should not be seen as anything other than a useful and character-strengthening education.

Sakina has done the *hajj*—the pilgrimage to Mecca—and proudly describes her journey as her daughters bring in glass plates of ripe, sugary melon and apple slices. Dark red curtains with heavy tassels give everything a pink glow as we sit on lush carpets, leaning back against brocade cushions lining the walls. Sakina is the daughter of a Pashtun general from one of the eastern provinces, and she has no regrets about growing up as the son her family called Najibullah.

Sakina insists that many Afghan parents know *bacha posh* as good life training for daughters, as well as having magical benefits. It was the capacity she served in: Her own father took a wife who birthed only girls. He took another one, but the unfortunate streak of girls continued. A neighbor saw the family's dilemma and recommended that Sakina's mother, who was wife number two and pregnant with Sakina, present the child as a son the day she was born. The good luck arrived—a little brother was indeed born as the family's next child.

Still, her parents kept Sakina as Najibullah for many years.

Her father, the general, taught her how to shoot a gun and how to ride a horse—to him, there was nothing young Najibullah was too weak, or too fragile, to master.

The change came at a big party at the family estate on her twelfth birthday. The occasion was not celebrated for her birthday, but for her becoming a woman. She had not yet menstruated, but her parents wanted to make sure she changed back well in time for the onset of puberty. All their relatives had been invited. Food and bakery-made biscuits were brought out to a garden table crowned with a big pastel-colored cake. It was a day of eating and celebration: A lamb was slaughtered and burned in sacrifice, and there was dancing. Sakina's ankle bracelet, just like the one her younger brother wore, was taken from her and a dress was prepared. She was dispatched to her mother's quarters for the transition and stepped out in the yellow dress before the guests. She was prompted to parade around so everyone could get a good look at her. They applauded and congratulated her.

"Were you happy to become a woman?"

Sakina, now in her forties, ponders it for a moment. She was not *un*happy. The right word might be *confused*.

"I felt all right. It was my parents' decision. I did not go outside anymore when I became a girl. *That* was the thing I was sad about. I stayed inside. By sixteen, I was married, so it was only three years that I really was a girl before I became a wife."

She laughs at the experience. "I was not an expert on the women's things, like cooking and cleaning. But I was taught by my husband's family."

Her father did not adapt as quickly. "I was his son; that's how he's always seen me. I am still the boy to him." They still discuss politics and warfare, and Sakina even weighs in on money and finances; they are, she says, the kind of conversations that she will rarely have with her husband and never with her mother. Sakina has no lingering thoughts about difficulties in becoming a woman; it's not like she had a choice. She has excelled at motherhood, she points out, with her seven children, both boys and girls. Her husband does lucrative business with the Americans, so the family leads a comfortable life.

Sakina repeats that she considers herself lucky, as she nods to her four daughters peeking through the doorway.

A SASSY RUNWAY parade of color and clothing dripping with rhinestones and sequins fills the room. The girls' wide pants and long sheer tunics range from purple to red to lavender, and there is the sound of tinkling as they move around. These outfits are strictly for at-home use. Their eyes are lined with kohl to enhance perfectly chiseled features, with straight noses, impossibly long eyelashes, and sharp, elegant cheekbones. Sakina's family lived as refugees in Pakistan for several years under the Taliban rule in Afghanistan, and the girls picked up some beauty tricks there. They are well aware that their looks are a bargaining tool when it comes time for their parents to negotiate good husbands for them. The girls seem excited; foreign visitors are few and far between, and almost always for their father. Almost in a chorus, they invite Setareh and me to stay for their afternoon tea party, with its teen agenda: gossip and beautification.

A girl with large earrings and bushy eyebrows takes my nonwriting left hand and places it on her knee. With a slim paintbrush dipped in henna, she outlines delicate flowering loops along each finger, quickly growing on my hand, up, onto my forearm. The girls are around the same age as Zahra, but while she prefers to discuss martial arts movies and wrestling matches, the topics here are very different.

Setareh and I soon realize that the only interviewing taking place is directed at us. When a few neighbor girls also drop in to join the party, they total eight. They all lob questions at me:

How old am I? Over thirty, indeed? What cream do I use on my face? How many children do I have? Really—none? They offer condolences and smack their lips over my bad luck. My husband's family must be very upset—I am married, of course? No? Again, they offer their regrets: a great shame that nobody wanted me. They understand—it is known to happen to some girls. Usually the very ugly or poor ones. Their concern extends to my parents: They must be unhappy, ashamed even, to have an old, unmarried daughter. And the relatives, horribly embarrassed, certainly?

By now, I try to insist it may not be a complete disaster to be unmarried, but Setareh feels the need to intervene and freestyle the translation a little. She explains to the girls that, in her personal view, it is indeed a little tragic for my family. That concession renders sympathetic faces all around.

When Sakina steps out of the room, questions become juicier: In the West, do I walk around almost naked in the streets? And have I "had relations" with *a thousand men*? Their Koran teacher has discreetly let it be known that every Western woman easily reaches that number. Setareh, too, looks relieved when I deny it being true with some emphasis.

Just as I am warming to their prompts for an actual number, a young, skinny James Dean in low-slung jeans and a short-sleeved shirt walks in, flashing a smile at us before slumping down into a corner. It is Sakina's youngest daughter, with the slouch and hip bones of an aspiring rock star. She is fourteen, and almost identical to her older sister, who also lived as a boy until a few years ago. She has pleaded with her parents to let her stay a boy for a little longer. There are sons in the family, but their mother wants to instill some strength in the girls by raising them as boys at first. That is the official reason. A little magical luck for the son making did not hurt either, a proud Sakina has let slip.

I ask the youngest jean-clad sister if she will get married one day. She shrugs. Probably. She does not seem upset by the prospect, and if she is, this is not the place to show it. Her female cousins are either engaged or married by now. She is a top student at school, and if it were up to her, she would like to study to become a children's doctor. But that will be in God's hands. Or rather, her future husband's. She politely explains how she hopes he will allow her to work.

The features of her sister are strikingly similar, but the sister, three years older and now turned into a woman, is distinctly feminine, with a nose ring, a long braid down her back, and a red Punjabi dress. She already has a future husband picked out for her, someone whom she has never met and knows little about.

As Sakina reenters the room, she admits that they are "a little late" with their youngest daughter. Her father and brothers have already begun to demand she wear a head scarf more often. And her body is just at the beginning of becoming a woman, so she does not have much time left now. But as long as she is turned back before puberty, no harm will have been done. She will follow a long tradition of girls in her family who have become excellent wives and mothers. As a bonus, she will have spent her youth cultivating an assertive, confident kind of womanhood.

The young rock star in the corner listens to her mother but says nothing. She just looks at her hands resting in her lap. Her rough hands have not been offered any henna painting, and her nails are chewed down to the quick.

WHEN I INSIST to Setareh that we splurge on an actual lunch break between visiting families, we are soon reminded it is not what women do in this residential part of Kabul. We settle on the only option—a hole-in-the-wall where kebabs are grilled over whitening coal outside in the sun—and try to look confident as we enter and endure the stares from the all-male clientele. A nervous waiter ushers us into the back of the restaurant, into a room that doubles as a storage space. As we sink into an overused leather sofa covered in plastic, we are surprised to discover that two other women are already there, seated by the opposite wall. They seem to be in their twenties, and one of them immediately looks down before our eyes can meet. The other, well covered with a black scarf conservatively tucked and pinned around her face, looks straight back at me.

I recognize the steady gaze.

But Setareh has strong opinions about the way I frequently strike up conversations with strangers, so I study the kebab options in Dari on my greasy menu some more. When I look up again, the young woman is smiling at me.

"You are American, yes?" she asks. "I like to practice speaking English when I meet foreigners."

"I'm Swedish, actually," I say, returning her smile. "But we can practice together if you want."

Setareh gently touches my hand in warning. The chatty American is the side of me she likes the least. It is both impolite and potentially dangerous, she has let me know several times. But I go on, telling our lunch companions that we are working on a little project where we are meeting girls who grow up as boys. In fact, we have interviewed a few dozen by now. The shy girl looks up at her confident friend in bewilderment. Setareh almost chokes. The conservative-looking girl just laughs.

"Yes. Yes. I am one of them. I was a boy."

"I had a feeling."

We grin widely at each other.

Her nickname is Spoz, and she is the youngest of six sisters in her family. They have just one brother, who arrived as number three. Before he was born, the family needed some magic, and once he was born, he needed a friend to play with. So the three younger sisters took turns, each playing the role of a boy for the first decade of their respective lives. Spoz says she had fun under the Taliban, roaming around outside and playing football, with her hair cut short. She learned to challenge boys in sports, fights, and conversation. Right before her tenth birthday, she was turned back. Now she is nineteen, and sees nothing but opportunity beyond her studies at Kabul University.

It makes her a very unusual young woman, as she is one of a few thousand female university students in the entire country. Many fathers do not allow their daughters to be educated beyond the ages of ten or twelve. Economic and security factors are most often cited, but some also say that it's just not "necessary" to educate a girl who will be married anyway. Too much education can potentially make a girl less attractive as a spouse, as she may develop plans to work or simply become too opinionated.

But Spoz's father, just as Azita's once did with his daughter, has taught her to dream big for herself: "I am happy God made me a girl, so I can become a mother. In my heart I am still a boy, but it is my choice to wear women's clothing now. It's only important to be a *bacha posh* in the head, to know you can do anything."

Now that she is a woman, she would never want to be anywhere other than in this part of the world, she says. Why? Women in the West "have relations" with thousands of men, and that is just wrong, she believes—a woman should be with only one man.

Setareh is mortified again, and I hasten to mention that I don't think that is true where I come from, or most anywhere for that matter. The pious former *bacha posh* interrupts me, offering a reassuring compliment of my all-black styling by Setareh: "No, no. I can see you are different from how you dress."

She aspires to become an engineer, and says her deep faith has strengthened her grasp of women's rights. But a *bacha posh* upbringing does not necessarily lead to liberal views on all things gender. Spoz is only one example of how an Afghan girl who is very religious and from a conservative family can have a firm grasp of women's rights while still advocating strict rules for them. She believes girls approaching puberty should absolutely not look like boys, and that women absolutely need to be well covered in Afghanistan.

"We are two kinds of humans," she explains this belief. "We are too different. But only in the body. Nothing else. A woman is a very beautiful thing. In order to protect something beautiful, you should cover it. Like a diamond. You cannot just put it on the street, because everyone would just come and take it."

At the same time, she is sure that if Afghanistan would become more modern, clothing would matter less. "I'm a Muslim, and I hate this kind of clothing," she says, pointing to her black coverage. She would wear the head scarf anywhere to respect and demonstrate her faith, but she wears the full covering only because it is necessary in her conservative country. "We have been in war for thirty years. We are not very developed here. This is not the time to experiment with clothing."

WE MEET AT the cramped offices of the Afghanistan Independent Human Rights Commission, of which Dr. Sima Samar is the chairwoman.

A former minister for women's affairs, Dr. Samar walks in wearing a white *peran tonban* and flat sandals, set off by white pearl-drop earrings peeking out from under her thick gray hair. The muted colors of her clothes match her office. Plush leather chairs are draped in Indian paisley throws. Her latest-model BlackBerry rattles on vibrate mode on a side table.

Sima Samar's longtime work as a doctor and as an advocate has taken her around the world to accept awards and speak as an authority on some of the worst human rights crimes in Afghanistan: domestic violence, self-mutilation, rape, and child marriage. She is the country's perhaps most respected advocate for women and children, and I am eager to talk with her about my research.

By now, I have arrived at the conclusion that it can in fact be an empowering experience for a girl to live like a boy for a few years, as more such examples of successful women, resembling the stories of Azita, Sakina, and Spoz have surfaced: In the northern Balkh province, a female official says that spending a few years as a boy child later helped her make the decision to go into politics. The female principal of a Kabul boarding school described how it was a way for her to get an education under the Taliban and allowed her to go to university once they were gone. For those whose lives are not solely devoted to survival, where creating a *bacha posh* is primarily a way of adding to the family income, it seems clear that some time on the other side can benefit both ambition and self-confidence.

However, no one can agree on when the boy years should precisely end before a girl is at risk of becoming "strange in the head," when the charade may have gone too far. So are there any risks at all? And is anyone looking out for these children, or are they always at the mercy of their parents' arbitrary judgment?

There are few universally recognized rights for children on gender. The word itself is not mentioned once in the UN Convention on the Rights of the Child, which lists other rights, such as those to education and freedom of expression. The concept of a "childhood," and what it should entail, is a fairly new one, even in the Western world. And gender is rarely discussed in the context of customary law or in international conventions; it is one of those seemingly untouchable issues, since religion and culture vastly differ among countries and conservatives lobby hard against anything that could potentially question heterosexuality as the norm. The right to live and present as a specific gender, at any given time, is nowhere specified. And perhaps it shouldn't be.

When I have probed those with knowledge of the area, including several Afghans working with women and children for the United Nations and international NGOs, about how *bacha posh* can exist right under the surface in Kabul, they have told me that they would never dream of advancing the issue on their organizations' agendas. Not only is it the private business of Afghans, but it would also potentially be too confusing to the foreign aid workers who love to help little girls—who look like girls.

"The foreigners like to teach *us* about gender," one longtime local Afghan UN employee put it when I inquired as to why she had never mentioned this practice in her work, which is focused on women and children. The UN official even had personal experience: Her own daughter has asked to wear pants and get a short haircut so she can play outside more with some other boys and *bacha posh* in the neighborhood. So far, her mother has not allowed it.

My hope in meeting Dr. Samar is to finally learn whether Afghanistan's *bacha posh* are of any concern to those protecting the human rights of women and children. Or if they ought to be.

But like most other Afghans I have asked, Sima Samar is certain: There is nothing strange about girls pretending to be boys. Probably nothing harmful either. Her own childhood friend from Helmand lived as a boy for many years before immigrating to the United

States. Samar's colleague at the commission also had a *bacha posh* who was turned back to a girl at age sixteen, and who now, a few years later, thrives at Kabul University. Much like Carol le Duc also suggested, *bacha posh* is logical in Afghanistan, Samar declares. To her, it is not a human rights issue of any sort. Ideally, of course, children should choose what they wear, she says, although few do in Afghanistan. She hedges her comment by adding that if cross-dressing had the potential to confuse a girl she would discourage it, since, in her words, "girls are confused enough in this country."

Still, *bacha posh* was never part of that confusion, to her knowledge.

"Are you interested in this?" I ask, at last.

Ever the diplomat, Dr. Samar smiles. "Why are *you* interested in this?"

I pause, considering that the last thing I want to do is to inspire a new human rights issue where there is none or draw government attention to *bacha posh*. Or any of their parents. Instead, using a recent argument from Azita, I suggest that the fact that girls live in disguise is perhaps another symptom of a deeply dysfunctional society. Maybe it is also a little troubling that nobody knows what consequences it may have for the minds of children. And doesn't the need to hide your birth sex have everything to do with a person's rights?

Sima Samar raises her eyebrows a little when I have finished.

"Well. That is interesting. To this, I wasn't paying attention, to be honest."

She smiles again, as if to mark that she does not have much more to say.

As I leave, after what can only be described as a demonstrable lack of interest by one of the country's most prominent activists, I wonder if the complexities of *bacha posh* may simply be too controversial for a politically savvy Afghan to touch. That may explain why it has remained under the surface for so long, and is still denied even by the expatriate Afghans I have approached. As with sexuality here, gender determines everything. But one is never supposed to talk about it, or pretend it exists.

CHAPTER ELEVEN

THE FUTURE BRIDE

Zahra

I T WAS JUST a small blink, and she wanted to take it back.

The world could not be let in. Especially not the bloody, intrusive woman part of it. Zahra lay motionless in the hospital bed, breathing slowly, trying to make herself go back to sleep again. Maybe she could wake up somewhere else. As someone else.

Anywhere but here in the bright, white children's ward.

When it first began, soon-to-be sixteen-year-old Zahra hid in the bathroom several times a day, frantically washing her underwear, praying for the bleeding to stop. It came from down there, so she did not tell anyone. August had been scorching hot, and Ramadan did not help with the mess her body was making. No eating or drinking—or, for some Afghans, at least not in public—during the day made most everyone sleepy and tired and gastric problems were expected.

At first, the family did not notice Zahra's increased bathroom presence. But then Asma found a pair of stained underpants.

"It is nothing to worry about," she told her daughter as she appeared from the bathroom. "It already happened to your sisters, and it's normal. All women have it."

Zahra quietly looked at her mother. Then she said: "No. No. No."

"You do not have to be afraid," Asma tried to comfort her by saying. "It makes you a real woman. It means you can have children."

With that, Zahra turned around and went into the sitting room. When Asma followed, Zahra fainted to the floor.

She came to quickly, but was rushed to the hospital by her mother. When the very upset Asma arrived with a child the doctor at first took to be her son, it took a few minutes before he understood the reason for their visit. The doctor told both Asma and Samir, who came as soon as he could get out from work, that their daughter had lost a lot of blood. She was slightly anemic, he explained, as she had likely been bleeding for a few days. But Zahra just needed to rest, he advised.

Zahra had seemed numb, refusing to speak to the hospital staff and shrinking from their touch. She really should have been referred to the women's department, the doctor said, but due to the initial mixup she had been put with the other, younger, children. But now that her birth sex and her condition had been clarified, Zahra should probably be taken to a "lady doctor" to make sure everything was in order for the future, the doctor concluded.

There was another concern, though. He believed Zahra was likely suffering from shock. The doctor had seen such cases before: Once puberty had commenced for a *bacha posh,* her acceptance of the future as a woman was not always immediate. Zahra had been something else for a long time—and now nature would have her revenge.

Asma and Samir felt a little embarrassed upon hearing the doctor's theory. They quickly assured him things soon would be set right with their daughter.

On the way home, Zahra refused to speak. Since then, she has only menstruated every two or three months. Asma has found herself wondering if the law of nature has just given in to Zahra's persistent mind: "She does not want to be a girl. So much so that maybe God has granted her wish in some part, and that is why she is not bleeding like she should?"

ASMA HAS HER sewing machine out on the living room floor. There are three orders for new girls' dresses from neighbors and friends to fill. Samir's air force salary isn't much, and feeding eleven costs at least two hundred afghanis per day. It is the equivalent of four U.S. dollars, which is what we pay our driver as the standard foreigner fare for a fifteen-minute ride to Zahra's house. Plus a dollar in tip.

Fabric snares in the hand-cranked sewing machine every few minutes, and Asma mutters as she frees it. She is hoping a cousin will bring an electric machine from Pakistan soon so she can make zigzag patterns, and maybe something for herself, too. She wistfully looks at Setareh, whose Pakistani creation hints of her slim frame after she has removed her coat. "When I was young, I, too, had a figure. I was always wearing something beautiful."

Zahra brings juice and cookies from the kitchen, but Asma prompts her to bring the other cookies—"the better ones." Her daughter grumblingly obeys.

"You are so different from my other children," Asma yells after her. "You are always angry, never in a good mood. You don't smile. You don't speak friendly to me."

Zahra says nothing as she puts the better cookies on the table and sits down. They are in little white plastic wrappings, with the WFP logo. The World Food Program's iron-fortified biscuits are made for malnourished children and meant to be given away for free to the hungry, but somehow make their way to bazaars. They are a favorite snack of Setareh's and many other Kabulis who can afford them. Zahra arranges five biscuits for me on a napkin. Abundance is a sign of hospitality. Then she sits in one of the big chairs, legs apart, hands on armrests, her body taking up more space in the room than any of ours do.

One of her younger sisters enters, modeling one of Asma's new designs, a shiny purple dress with a wide skirt and short sleeves. She takes a swirl in front of us, before Asma grabs her to pin the back a little tighter. It is on order for a teenager who is to wear it at a wedding. Her mouth full of pins, Asma calls Zahra's attention:

"Your sister will wear a dress. Look at her—she is beautiful. She is a girl. You look like a monkey compared to her."

Zahra's face turns into a grimace. "Stop it! Don't say that!"

She fires back by apologizing to us, her guests: "My mother is just jealous. One time I rode a horse, and she yelled at me. I know it is just because she will never do that in this life. Look at her—she will just stay in the house all her life."

It may be less that Zahra desires to be a boy, and more that, like so many other *bacha posh,* she merely wants to escape the fate of womanhood in Afghanistan. Over the past months, tensions between Zahra and her mother have simmered and inched closer to a showdown, as Asma has tried to make the case for Zahra to accept her birth sex and live like a woman. Zahra, in turn, has insisted that is impossible. Because she is no girl. Nor is she a woman.

There is really no in-between period for a young woman here, who can never live on her own before marriage, since she must always officially be under the guardianship of a man. Her few legal rights are socially curtailed, and as a practical matter, she could not easily rent an apartment, hold most jobs, or even get a passport without the explicit permission of a father or husband.

"We have a common saying here," Asma says in a matter-of-fact tone. "When your luck shows up, nothing can stop it. I will not let Zahra be single her whole life."

She barely gets to finish the sentence before Zahra interrupts.

"No! I will not get married. I will not get married for as long as I am alive."

"So what will you do?" her mother asks, rocking her head back and forth, to mock her daughter. "You are a girl and this is a fact. You will have to get married."

"It's my choice," Zahra shoots back. "Will you force me?"

Asma just looks at her daughter.

As Zahra defiantly stares back, tears begin to stream down her face. Finally, she gets up and leaves. She begins to scream from the other room instead: "There is a girl in Pakistan I know about! She changed herself through an operation. I will find money, too, and change myself into a man. I know it can be done, and I will be rid of this body."

Asma looks at the wall separating her from her daughter. It pains her every time Zahra brings this up. Why would her child not want the body she has been given? It would appear to be an act of defiance against both her parents and God.

From the other room, Zahra throws out what by now has become another one of her common threats: She will run away. Or: "When our relatives from America come and visit, I will force them to invite me. I want to study, and work."

"You are dreaming," Asma says in a low voice, almost as though she were speaking to herself. "No one will invite you."

Options for getting out of Afghanistan would seem bleak for Zahra. Holders of Afghan passports have little chance of obtaining visas to most countries. Student visas for particular talents are available, but competition is fierce for the Fulbright and other scholarships. Zahra is ranked in the lower half of her class and does her best to avoid reading books. As for sex-change operations, the nearest option is Iran, where they have become more common due to the strict ban on homosexuality. To change gender is, for some, the only way to have a same-sex partner without risking the death penalty.

"So what do you want?" Asma repeats to Zahra, as she reappears in the doorway. "You cannot live at home with me. Do you want to marry another girl? Should I find you a wife instead? You need to have children."

Asma throws out a random number that seems reasonable to her: "Five."

It sends Zahra over the edge. "No! *You are crazy*. I wish you would leave me alone!"

And she is gone again.

Asma looks tired as she slowly unfolds a low ironing board on the floor and begins to press her husband's long white shirts. She wants to complete this chore before the electricity goes out. The stroking movement causes her some pain after carrying her youngest on her hip all day.

Zahra's resistance has also begun to wear her down. It has come to the point that they can hardly speak without ending up yelling at each other, when Zahra will taunt Asma for having too many children and for rarely leaving the house. As if she could, Asma will retort. And since when did a woman have to defend having many children?

Asma worries about Zahra. She is seeing signs that the outside world will come down much, much harder on Zahra than she ever has, in trying to get her to adopt a female identity. Neighborhood harassment of Zahra has increased, too: "The girls are the worst," Asma says. "Sometimes they ask her to prove she is a girl—they ask her to take her clothes off." Devastated by the humiliation, Zahra will then run home and hole herself up in one of the bedrooms.

Asma, too, is frequently challenged by neighbors: "People ask me if she is a third gender, something between a boy and a girl. I tell them absolutely not. She is totally a girl. I tell everyone—there is nothing wrong with her! She is normal and she has all the things girls have." Asma makes a gesture toward her own body. "But they scream '*izak*' after her. I have heard it."

Izak is a colloquial term familiar to most Afghans, as a derogatory slur for someone who is *without* a distinct gender. The actual meaning is "hermaphrodite," but it is used for anyone who appears different.

Even Zahra's little brother, who is only six, urges his sister to put on a head scarf, accusing her of embarrassing her family. Sometimes he pleads with her—he is teased by his friends at school for having an *izak* sister. Zahra usually responds by slapping him in the face.

IT IS THE responsibility of Afghan parents to gauge the timing of when something that is silently accepted for children becomes an outright provocation. A few days earlier, in another house, I had been told the story of how a thirteen-year-old *bacha posh* was found out by one of her former neighbors. A member of her football team heard a rumor she was actually a girl. Not long after, the boys on the team locked her inside a circle and demanded she prove her gender. As she tried to break out, onlookers gathered. Her father ran out to defend her, striking down some of the young boys for getting too close to his daughter. The neighbors were infuriated—but not with the young harassers. They had done nothing wrong. Instead, blame came down hard on the girl's father. He had allowed his daughter to play football with teenage boys, and that made him alone responsible for the street fight. And what kind of man was he?

The problem Afghan society has with a *bacha posh* who approaches puberty lies less in the rejection of gender and more in the rules, social control, and expectations that surround a *proper* young Afghan girl. As soon as she can conceive, she must be shielded from all men until she meets her husband for the first time. That responsibility, to keep a young girl pure in a culture of honor, is entrusted to the male members of her family. If they fail, the entire family will be disgraced. Just as an adult, a married woman must carefully avoid being likened to a whore at all times, a younger woman must demonstrate absolute purity. Her virginity is capital belonging to her father, and it is his to be traded. The more sheltered, demure, and quiet parents can demonstrate a daughter to be, the higher the value of her virginity. If a girl is discovered alone anywhere near a man who is not a blood relative, rumors can spread. Judgment is always in the eye of the beholder. And the Afghan beholder's imagination can run wild.

Since neither a groom nor a groom's parents will usually speak to a bride before the deal is made, everything hinges on her reputation. That reputation is perpetuated by the opinion and observation of everyone who has been in contact with her, and information is usually obtained through rumors. Thus, a woman's honorability depends only to a very small degree on her own chastity. It has much more to do with "gossip" and what the neighbors conclude based on observing her. A wife or a daughter who is allowed to move around too much risks turning her husband or father into a *begherat,* or a coward, who cannot protect his women, in the eyes of others.

Much like in the historical culture of honor and guns in the American South and Southwest, an Afghan man must be able to protect and control both his property and his women at all times. An Afghan man needs to demonstrate readiness to use force against any threat.

The three pillars of Pashtunwali, the Pashtun code of conduct to live by, are *revenge, refuge,* and *hospitality.* (A favorite phrase of gun owners in the United States may as well be used by the ever-polite and always gun-carrying Afghans: "An armed society is a polite society.") Should an Afghan man fail at this, his most fundamental task of protection, he can no longer function in society, since his honor capital will be depleted.

A young unmarried woman is, in other words, under a bigger threat from within her own family than the outside world, should she even be suspected of not behaving properly. That's why it is called "honor killing"—justifying the murder of a young daughter by her own family to preserve and protect their own reputation.

At almost sixteen, Zahra no longer feels like "both" a man and a woman, as she described it when I first met her. At this point, more than a year later, she dismisses her physical sex and views her female body as something that must change.

Neuroscientists agree with Dr. Fareiba's observation that puberty is "a dangerous time for the mind"—or rather, that puberty is when the human brain expands and takes a huge leap forward, fueled by hormones, which help grow a personality and form a gender identity.

As Zahra's situation shows, the experience of a *bacha posh* also begins to leave a more permanent mark when a girl goes through puberty as a boy. As I encounter more adult women who have grown up as *bacha posh,* I note that those who herald their boy years usually experienced them only as children. Any potential empowering effects of living on the other side seem to be preserved in an adult woman only if her time as a boy was brief, and ended before puberty. After that, just as in the case with Zahra, it quickly becomes far more complicated.

In another country, Zahra would perhaps by now be suspected of having what the World Health Organization terms *gender identity disorder.* It is defined as "persistent and intense distress about being a girl, and a stated desire to be a boy." Resistance to growing breasts and to menstruating are two other things cited in such a determination.

In order to qualify for an adult diagnosis of the disorder, there should also be distancing from one's own body. The definition of adult *transsexualism* is "a desire to live and be accepted as a member of the opposite sex, usually accompanied by a sense of discomfort with, or inappropriateness of, one's anatomic sex, and a wish to have surgery and hormonal treatment to make one's body as congruent as possible with one's preferred sex."

But what Zahra is or has, or what she might be afflicted by, cannot be directly compared to any Western version of a child or young adult who is uncomfortable with his or her gender, and upon which existing research in the field has been made.

According to Dr. Ivanka Savic Berglund, a neuroscientist at Karolinska Institutet's Center for Gender Medicine in Stockholm, who studies the formation of gender identity in the brain, a person's diet, personal experiences, and environment all affect hormone levels. So even if Zahra were to be examined by doctors, her blood drawn, and psychological evaluations made, she could still not be placed side by side with most Europeans or Americans in similar studies. Growing up in war, living as a refugee, and eating a different diet, Zahra may have a physical and psychological makeup that is too different to compare.

What also makes Zahra distinctly different from other children or young adults in the Western world with a possible gender identity disorder is that she was picked *at random* to be a boy. As with other *bacha posh,* the choice was made for her. For that reason, it would be hard to argue that she was *born* with a gender identity issue. Instead, it seems as though she has *developed* one. That, in turn, could mean that a gender identity problem in a person can be *created*.

IN A WESTERN context what may constitute such a disorder is not far from clear-cut, either.

The children brought to Dr. Robert Garofalo, director of the Center for Gender, Sexuality and HIV Prevention at Lurie Children's Hospital of Chicago, can be as young as three or four when expressing a feeling of having been born in the wrong body. Among those at the forefront in the world of understanding how gender is formed in children, Dr. Garofalo receives one or two referrals per week, often from parents who have at times lived in fear and shame because their children do not fall into expected gender roles.

In 2013, the American Psychiatric Association removed "gender identity disorder" from its list of mental health illnesses. Dr. Garofalo prefers not to pin a specific term on the children he works with, as he tries not to get stuck on a binary view of gender and the idea that a person always needs to be one or the other and possess absolute feminine or masculine traits only. In his view, what goes on with these children is "part of a natural spectrum of the human being— not an -ism or thing or condition that requires fixing."

No one knows today exactly why some children identify with a gender that is different from their anatomic sex. Multiple factors such as genetics, hormones, and social structures are all thought to play a role. Treatments for advancing one gender or the other in children who fall in the middle of the gender spectrum are currently still experimental and controversial.

"There is plasticity in children," says Dr. Garofalo, who believes that what he calls a nonconforming gender identity could probably be created in a child over time, such as the case with Zahra seems to be.

But one would also need to consider what part of Zahra's desire to be a boy is directly related to the experience of being a woman in Afghanistan. Would she really want to be a man in another environment, where most people did not care whether she wore a head scarf or a pair of pants, and where women had more opportunities?

Maybe Zahra could be seen as healthier than most. Or does the desire to wear pants and not to get married actually need a cure? Maybe it is something else that should be defined as sick. Zahra's situation could even prompt a whole new category in the World Health Organization's index: "Gender identity disorder due to severe and longtime segregation."

When one gender is so unwanted, so despised, and so suppressed, in a place where daughters are expressly unwanted, perhaps both the body and the mind of a growing human can be expected to revolt against becoming a woman. And thus, perhaps, alter someone for good.

ZAHRA SITS CROSS-LEGGED on a carpet, her eyes fixed on the small television set on the floor. The title of the Indian drama translates as "story of love," and Zahra has been following it for a while. It is a Bollywood take on the *Twilight* series: The main character is from a vampire family, but one day he falls for a non-vampire girl. From that, a complicated romance unfolds.

I ask if she's ever been in love. She smiles faintly. "No. I don't want to be. I'm not crazy like that."

"What will you do if they force you to get married?"

"I will refuse to get married. My *no* is a no! When I grow up, I will go to the West, where nobody gets involved in your business. My will is very strong, and I will refuse my parents. Nobody can force me to do anything."

"Would you dress like 'a woman' in the West?"

She shakes her head at me in disbelief. "Don't you understand? I am not a girl."

I hand her our parting gift from one of the Kabul stores that sells torn T-shirts and jeans, supplying the trash-rock look popular among the city's teenage boys. It is a gray felt fedora. I explain that I have seen both men and women wear it in New York. Zahra beams with excitement and jumps up to try it on in the mirror, adjusting the brim to give it the perfect angle, casting a shadow over her eyes.

"It's beautiful," she says.

CHAPTER TWELVE

THE SISTERHOOD

THE BRIDE COULD be crying because she is only a year older than Zahra. Or because the husband her parents have chosen is twice her age. Or because she does not know him at all. She could be crying because her husband asked for the hand of her sister, known by reputation to be the more beautiful of the two. And because her parents then decided that her sister could probably do better than this older man of moderate means; so for her, it would be wise to hold out for a bigger offer.

None of that matters. Tears are both expected and required here.

To look happy would be disrespectful to her parents. There should always be some histrionics about leaving the family home. This event is where only a proper girl ends up, and this is what Zahra fears. The bride executes her performance with precision.

It has taken about five hours at one of Kabul's many beauty parlors to have the virgin bride's hair perfected into stiff, sprayed curls, her nails painted red, and her face a white-powdered death mask with crimson lips. Her thick, dark eyebrows have been threaded off entirely and replaced by thin blackbird wings. They are the proud mark of a married woman, signaling that she is now taken. Her husband-to-be's family has spent more than a hundred dollars on this important preparation for the wedding. Beauty parlors were closed under the Taliban, and the stories of their reopenings filled American women's magazines after 2001, as evidence of how liberty had finally reached Afghan women.

It is a relative of Setareh's who is getting married this evening, in what stands to be a rather low-key affair for Kabul. If it had been a ceremony for one of the city's wealthier families, a Las Vegas–style wedding hall would have been taken over, with thousands invited and fed for an entire day, at a cost of tens of thousands of dollars to the husband's family. A wedding is an event of a lifetime, often paid for with borrowed money that will be paid back over that same lifetime. Afghans often complain about the money, but everyone knows that a lavish wedding display is an important way for families to demonstrate as much power and prestige as they can muster.

As explained by Carol le Duc, this is the moment when daughters are most visibly the cards played by Afghan fathers: "Men make alliances, and not necessarily in the best interests of their daughters. These alliances are related to the social prestige and honor of the family. But it may also be opportunism. They want to marry up to create more security—financial or physical—for the family in a time of need. Freedom of choice is a modern thing, relatively speaking. That is not always practical in terms of how Afghan families measure assets for survival."

Marriage is a core component of the patriarchal system.

According to Gerda Lerner's research on ancient societies, a woman could achieve at least some status, and with that, better treatment and privileges, through preserving her only capital—her virginity—and eventually offering it to just one man. That idea evolved into the marriage contract, where a woman vowed to remain sexually exclusive to one man, with the expectation that it would bring him heirs to preserve a lineage of land and capital. Any woman suspected of not being a virgin posed the risk of carrying someone else's child, which disqualified her as a potential bride.

No group can be truly suppressed until its members are trained and convinced to suppress *one another*. To hold the system of patriarchy in place, a woman could always further prove herself a chaste and proper person by shaming those who fell short of the mark, Lerner explained. In other words, by calling out other women as suspected whores, as women commonly do to this day.

In Afghanistan, young women are largely removed from this major event of their own lives. Through the *khastegari* process, one family will court another for their daughter. It revolves mainly around money, when the equivalent of a bride price, the *toyana,* is determined. Negotiations between parents take into account how much "wedding gold" will be hung on the bride at the wedding ceremony as literal proof of the wealth of her marriage. The actual ceremony, or *nekah,* is often performed in a small setting with just a mullah and two witnesses. They will visit the bride and ask who she has chosen to speak for her, as she herself is expected to remain mute. Seated or standing behind a piece of fabric that is held up for discretion's sake, she will designate a brother or her father as her intermediary. The groom then accepts the marriage by uttering the words "I accept it in the present and I accept it in the future" to the mullah, and then when the bride's male representative agrees three times, the verbal contract is sealed. Rarely will there be a written document of a marriage. By law, the bride should also receive a *mahr* as security, an amount of money or property for her personal use, from her husband. But that detail is usually ignored.

At this wedding, the *nekah* has been completed and the bride is placed on a chair atop a foil-clad stage, homecoming queen–style, so the guests—all females—can take a good look at her dark green, richly embroidered gown and frozen face.

Her dress exhibits a plunging neckline on a flat chest, and her thin, bare arms are covered in gold bangles, stacked so high she cannot even raise her arm to pluck a drink off the many soda-can pyramids on the tables. The female guests sit packed next to one another on the floor as plates of rice and chicken are passed around. The men are next door celebrating in a larger space. The windows are closed and the stale air has little oxygen. If there was a fire, we would likely not all get out safely through the one small door. But any such perceived risk is less of a concern than that of having men peek in from the outside and catch a glimpse of any dark hair flowing as the guests dance wildly in circles, always with one woman in the middle and the others around her. The makeup is heavy, and everyone is in their best outfits. Even the small children are decked out in tulle and sequins. They fall asleep, one after the other, on the floor. One teenage girl is wrapped in Kermit-like green, like a small elf, with matching green nail polish, eye shadow, and high heels. The gold is on full display, too. Those with the heaviest load on their chests and arms sit a little more regally overlooking the others, knowing they qualify as the richest, most prominent guests with a proven record of fertility, as proved by the gifts from their pleased husbands.

SMALL GROUPS OF girls form alongside one wall. These are the proper girls, on the track that Zahra is veering away from. Tonight, they are giddy.

They know gossip is deadly, but their voices are drenched in music and they don't care. This is a rare opportunity to sit out of earshot of their mothers, who otherwise guard their movements carefully to ensure they are never alone with boys. Which is exactly what their conversation revolves around tonight.

The teenage years leading up to marriage can be some of the most romantic these girls will ever have—not knowing what awaits and who their parents will pick for them. It affords plenty of time for daydreaming of romance. All the girls keep diaries, where they sometimes write down fantasies fueled by saucy, often thinly veiled homoerotic Persian poetry, with its tales of doomed lovers prepared to die violent deaths for each other. And just as fast-drawing heroes of American Western films usually fall for pure and innocent women, the girls' favorite Bollywood dramas feature dark, passionate, and often violent strangers who abduct coy Indian actresses. In a common narrative, the stranger hardly needs to utter a word before the female decides she is madly in love with him and delighted to go against her family's wishes. The film *Titanic* is the perfect Afghan tale, where impossible love ends with death. All the girls have seen grainy, pirated versions of it more than once.

It's the universally efficient concept of unrequited romance: Never actually speaking to boys makes for endless musings on what they are really like and how to get closer to them. At this wedding, tricks and tips are shared. One girl admits she's locked eyes with a boy twice, and now they have a bond. Another is more daring: She has accepted a postcard with an Indian actor on it from an admirer. Nothing is written on the card, but the act of delivery, through a wall outside school, sealed the romance. Girls with cell phones or laptops at home or in school have an advantage, as secret Facebook profiles adorned with pictures of flowers and rainbows in place of a headshot can be used for exchanging messages.

As in any largely illiterate country, cell phones sold in Afghanistan feature a variety of animals and cartoon avatars as an option to typing a name on the speed-dial function. Still, the girls routinely erase messages and call lists, as mothers tend to check cell phones at least once a day. To actually meet a boy in person is the gutsiest move of all, since it carries the highest risk. Their imagined boyfriends are perfect, bold, heroic, and willing to die for impossible love. But the greatest crime an Afghan girl can commit is to actually fall in love and act on it. The girls all know a tale of a distant someone who has gone mad from love and tried to kill herself, or who was actually killed by her family. Fantasies about boys are as far as these girls dare take it. At least they can glimpse one another in the city—in the villages, tales of romances will have to be spun from under burkas and by just looking out the window.

Their future marriages consume much psychic energy, as there is so much to ponder: Who is the most beautiful of them? Who among them will marry first? What will they wear? They all agree that the bride onstage is only of average beauty—that is why she has been matched with such an old husband. Every girl is highly aware of her own ranking, and in this group, those with crooked teeth or scars from cooking oil speak less often than the more obviously stunning girls who know they will bring a big reward for their fathers. Still, they all share the dream of being the center of attention, of sitting on the tinfoil-clad stage, made up like a movie star. Leaving the isolation of a house with parents and siblings for a new family is for now spun like a romantic adventure.

Some of the girls have career ambitions; others do not. What they all know is that it takes more than looks to marry, and that reputation is key. Without that, no prince will appear. Hopefully that future husband will at least have some of his hair left, they joke, as they take turns on the dance floor, generating even more heat in the shuttered room.

The dancing looks like a joyous celebration of womanhood in explosive color, but it has a distinct purpose. A wedding is actually no time to relax among friends—it is a pivotal event, and one's performance must be flawless. A secondary purpose of a wedding is to generate more weddings in the future. The girls are even filmed on cell phones for discreet distribution to families who get to see them without scarves. Those who take the floor are well aware that they are dancing on a stage before judges in a very serious, high-stakes auction.

ON THE OPPOSITE wall of the crowded room, the older women sit in a line, one next to another, wearing more demure dresses in darker colors. Some have kept their head scarves on. They observe the dancing mostly in silence, sometimes exchanging a few words with serious expressions. Chinese whisper games will start, where one woman will nod at a young dancing girl, asking a question that is passed down the row from one woman to another, before a response comes back up the line in the same manner. These women are in the business of finding wives for their sons and they offer up occasional commentary on the performance before them.

"Not so pretty. Her sister is better."

"That poor one will have a hard time, yes. The dark skin—she is already an old woman. She will have to wait, yes."

Information about the girl's family's honor, purity, and place in society is also exchanged:

"Her mother works, you know."

"Really?"

Translation: Too progressive. The girl could become a problem.

It all comes down to whether the subject of their observation really is a *proper* girl: "She seems made of fire, that one. Look at her dancing."

"Yes. Best to be careful. And too much cake in that belly!"

Another woman disagrees: "A little more on the bones will give her husband many children."

Every now and then, a teenage girl is called forward, always through an intermediary, for a more thorough interview.

"Do you pray?"

"How often?"

"What dishes can you cook?"

It can be a life-changing exchange. This version of Miss Universe takes place every day in Afghanistan, where a girl's looks, character, and body fat percentage are assessed in short, determined sentences, as women enforce and perpetuate their own subjugation.

To Setareh, who like any other unmarried girl has often been scrutinized by other women, it is a familiar routine. "They spy on us and look at how we dress and how we move. The other women will tell her all the gossip about you—if you have a bad reputation or if you are proper. If it is not a relative, they will ask someone for your address. Then they will spy around the house, and maybe the boy will go to get a look at the girl. If he likes her, his parents go to the girl's father. But the boy will not be allowed to choose if the mother and father have already found a good girl and decided for him."

Once these young girls are picked for marriage, their mothers-in-law will control them in their new homes, just as Azita's once controlled her. In Afghanistan, as in so many other places, abuse teaches abuse, and older women pass on their own horrors to those who come after. Stories of torture or an honor killing will regularly surface from around the country, and commonly, perpetrators are not the men in the family, but the women. Mothers-in-law do not just condone but also commit acts of violence against daughters-in-law who do not obey. Afghan women have very little tolerance for acts of transgression by other women, particularly those who are younger. As in any suppressed group, one person's attempt at freedom can be a grave affront to the suffering of others.

Still, both men and women sometimes cultivate the idea that there is a sisterhood among women—a loyalty that exists between those who belong to the softer, kinder, and warmer gender. That they look out for one another in some sort of universal solidarity. Yet Afghan prosecutor Maria Bashir, who has been heralded as a women's rights champion by international NGOs as well as the U.S. Department of State, has a long record of relentlessly prosecuting women who flee from abusive husbands or parents who want to force them into a marriage. Those women are often prosecuted on adultery charges, to clearly mark them as whores in society.

WHAT WILL TAKE place later on this particular evening, after the bride and groom finally meet in the presence of their families and have spoken their very first words to each other, is shrouded in mystery for the teenage wedding guests.

Most mothers will share nothing; they don't want to risk tarnishing the mind of an unwed daughter. Instead, creative explanations on the origins of life are traded among the young girls. One has been told that as a baby, she was purchased by her parents from the market; another, that there is a man who distributes babies from a donkey. Those with married sisters have a clearer idea, since highly subjective information has been shared, of what the bodies of men look like and what the wedding night may entail. The idea of taking clothes off in front of a man, as one girl has been told she may need to do, is the first horror to process. Beyond that, no girl can risk starting a rumor that she is well-informed, so very few details—and often flawed ones—are what get around. Knowing too much can be detrimental for the wedding night, girls are cautioned. The husband may think she has experience. A telltale sign is also if she should express anything other than discomfort and pain in bed. If that should happen—and ideally, it should never—a new bride must make sure not to let it be known to her husband.

Disaster stories are more generously shared, about newlyweds who have ended up at the hospital the next day, due to missteps when trying to consummate the marriage. But if the groom has a previous wife, or if he has taken a trip to visit prostitutes in Tajikistan (a popular weekend destination for wealthier Kabul men) or has had access to online pornography, the situation may be slightly improved, a few of the unmarried girls have been told.

Shortly after the wedding, if no pregnancy occurs, discretion is no longer called for. By then, relatives can begin asking detailed questions about a couple's frequency and mode of intercourse and disburse advice. If still nothing happens, Dr. Fareiba and her magic-making colleagues may be called in to produce results. Of the right sort, that is.

WHEN I RETURN to my guesthouse where I rent a spare room, my legs numb after many hours of modestly sitting on my feet on the floor, I find two aid-worker friends cooing together in front of a Soviet-era television set. On the grainy screen, Kate Middleton's white veil—a symbol of virginity—is being lifted as she is passed from her father to her husband-to-be, England's royal prince. As the choir sings, they are joined in matrimony, blessed by the archbishop.

As of that moment, when the future Duchess of Cambridge enters into marriage in Westminster Abbey, only one major thing is required of her: to bear a child. It will be another five months after the wedding before the rules of succession are changed by Queen

Elizabeth II to allow a potential baby girl to inherit the throne. But the issue will remain unresolved throughout the Commonwealth, who may or may not recognize a female heir. And the demand for procreation is nonnegotiable. From this point onward, Kate Middleton's body owes payment to entities and a tradition more important than herself and her husband.

The dress, the virginal veil, and the modest expression on the future queen consort's face delight millions of viewers all over the world. She is so thin, so beautiful, so dreamily perfect. It's a fairy tale to aspire to for many of the two billion witnesses around the world watching on television. The bride has passed many levels of vetting as a very, *very* proper girl, whose womb will ensure the perpetuation of the British Empire.

It's very romantic.

PART THREE
MEN

All oppression creates a state of war. And this is no exception.

—SIMONE DE BEAUVOIR, *THE SECOND SEX*

Courtesy of the author

SHUKRIA

CHAPTER THIRTEEN

THE BODYGUARD

Shukria

I N THE END, the act itself was not as bad as she had been told. Her colleague, a married woman at the hospital, had warned her of something so painful and dehumanizing that she had begun to stutter as she described it. On the wedding night, she told Shukria, a bride did not only suffer excruciating pain—there was also a risk of permanent injury.

"Where?" Shukria, who was soon to marry, asked. "Where will I be injured?" Her friend pursed her lips and closed her eyes. The unspeakable area. Of course.

Twenty-year-old Shukria was embarrassed. She was to be married in only a week and she knew how babies were born, but she really had no specifics on how they were conceived. Indeed, she would be lucky not to end up at the hospital, her colleague continued. Shukria's new husband would need medical care, too, if things went awry.

"It made me so worried," Shukria remembers. "I lost weight. What to do? I thought about it all the time. She told me such strange things that I did not understand."

But when the consummation of her marriage finally took place, Shukria escaped unharmed. It was a little weird, certainly. But "more okay" than what she had been told. It was the other thing that worried her more—that she ought perhaps to have been the one with a penis. Up until a month before her wedding night, Shukria had lived as a man.

DR. FAREIBA HAD heard that her old classmate got married in the end, after having been a man for longer than most. After wondering for a while if there were women in Kabul who could shed light on what might be in store for Zahra—on what might happen on the other side of a forced marriage for an almost-grown-up *bacha posh,* I had convinced the elusive doctor to introduce me to her old friend from school. As always, there is no phone number, but together and on foot, we finally locate Shukria at one of Kabul's busy hospitals.

It is in a small garden behind the hospital that the story of Shukria's former self is told for the first time. No one ever asked her about it before. She describes a cocky young man in jeans and a leather jacket, who always carried a knife in his back pocket in case he needed to defend his honor—or that of a girl. Shukria thinks of him in the past tense. *Shukur.* He is dead now.

Now thirty-five, or maybe a few years older—like many Afghans, she only estimates her age and shaves off a few years to her advantage—Shukria dresses in a full-length brown robe, or abaya, six mornings out of seven and puts on her small tinted eyeglasses. She carefully applies a thick beige foundation on her weathered face and draws a dark red lipstick over her lips, trying not to smudge it too much. It helps get her into the right state of mind. She even dabs on a little perfume from a small vial she treated herself to at the bazaar. The fragrance, named Royal After Shave, was "Made in the Kingdom of Saudi Arabia." It is a dark, woodsy scent. She could not bear any of the more flowery options. Shukria told the vendor it was for her husband.

Her dark curly hair is entirely tucked under a silk scarf. She owns several, in patterned silk, and she feels good putting one on. The scarf shows everybody which side of society she belongs to. She is with the women now. She needs to know it, *feel* it, herself.

The mother of three then rides the bus to work at one of Kabul's busiest hospitals, where she changes again, into her roomy light blue scrubs and a little cap. One style fits all; her male colleagues wear the same. The female nurses usually wear longer tunics, but Shukria always opts for the male shirt. She keeps the gold studs in her earlobes, a sole marker of femininity.

In this outfit, for thirteen hours a day, she supports her children and her unemployed husband by working as an anesthesiology nurse. The hours are longer when the sparsely equipped surgical wing fills up with the injured from a blast somewhere around Kabul.

They appreciate Shukria at the hospital, where she has been employed for more than a decade. At least she thinks so. They know she works fast and with little instruction. She rarely gets emotional, either, like some of the other nurses. It makes her useful.

The jolt of adrenaline still happens, though. Especially when she feels the shock wave of a bomb from not far away. But moments later, she clicks right into the familiar routine of walking behind a doctor doing triage, noting how close to life or death each patient is and where he or she will go next—straight into surgery or onto one of the plastic-sheeted beds. Plastic, so the blood can be more easily hosed away later. After a blast, they can arrive by the dozens, on stretchers or carried by others. It happens that a parent and a child will share a stretcher.

Shukria never studied trauma medicine, but she has seen the human body destroyed in multiple ways, each a snapshot cataloged in her brain. The sharpest images are of small bodies without legs or arms, or gaping holes on thin torsos. She can still call up the faces of surprised children looking up at her. There is often screaming and crying, but later, there is no sound in her slide show. It is silent, but in color. In the operating theater, Shukria's job is to make them silent.

There's never a "debrief," or even much of a conversation after a day like that. The staff just carries on, and no one takes a break until the flow of victims begins to ebb. Shukria will wash off and take the bus back home again. In Kabul, everyone has experienced their own horrors, and most have seen a violent death.

She keeps a few pictures of herself as a young man with big, curly hair and a serious mien. Never smiling. She smiles when she looks at the photos now, remembering what she now considers her "best time." She sometimes gets angry with herself for not having enjoyed it more—never knowing, or perhaps acknowledging, that it would end so abruptly.

WHEN SHUKRIA ARRIVED in the family, her parents were taking no more chances. Her training began the day she was born. It would have been ideal, of course, had she actually been born a boy. But it really did not matter for the task she had been assigned at birth: to protect her older brother.

Her mother had been married at age thirteen to a man thirty years her senior. She was his second wife. His first wife had failed to conceive, but Shukria's mother quickly became pregnant, to the joy of everyone except the childless first wife: Her shame was underscored and worsened by the newly arrived teenage bride's fertility. But the new wife's baby died after just a few months of life. So did the next one, the following year. When a third infant son fell ill, suspicion fell on the first wife that she had tried to poison him and had killed the two sons who had come before, since she had helped bottle-feed them formula.

Shukria's mother, the teenager, gradually settled upon wife number one as the culprit. One day a fight broke out, and each wife took aim at the other's face with kitchen tools. When their husband entered and tore his bloodied first wife away, she dropped to the floor and cried uncontrollably, begging him to divorce her. "I will never give you a divorce," he responded. Then he beat her with his fists until she lay silent and unconscious on the floor.

It was never spoken of again in the family, but it was decided that day that the next child born should be given the task of safeguarding the remaining son, should he survive. Whether he had been poisoned or not, no one would ever know.

That next child, arriving later in the year, happened to be a girl.

She was given the formal name Shukria but introduced to the world as Shukur.

Growing up, Shukur always knew her special role, and she felt proud to be her brother's companion. Together, they became the two princes of the household, distinctly set apart from the five sisters who followed. Shukur shared a separate bedroom with her brother, while her mother, father, and six sisters all slept together in another room. It is common in an Afghan family to assign older siblings to take care of the younger ones, but Shukur had an even more specific task.

She was to follow the family's most precious asset—their son—at all times, as his guardian. They did everything together: They slept in the same bed. They prayed. They attended school. What she first ate, he then ate. What she first drank, he then drank. If there was a threat from another child, Shukur would shield his body with hers. She never questioned it; she was told it was an honor for her.

Besides, it gave her an opportunity to explore life beyond the confinement her sisters endured. Not that she had much idea what they did with their days. Shukur and her brother never spent a minute more than necessary inside the house. There, they would always eat first, speak first, and never be bothered with any of the mundane things that were expected of the sisters, such as washing, cleaning, and cooking. That was not for boys.

Together, they owned the world outside, climbing trees and exploring the hillsides around Kabul. Shukur's friends of both sexes always knew she had been born a girl. So did the rest of her extended family and most of the neighbors. But it was not out of the ordinary— one of her female classmates was also passing as a boy. It was another family, with its own reasons; no one would pry further.

As the brothers grew into teenagers, they would have even less contact with girls as they learned that mingling too much with the fairer sex would appear unmanly and invite weakness into their hearts. The brothers joined a gang of eight young men who roamed the town in Fonzie-style short leather jackets and tight jeans, their hair groomed to look Western.

To impress one another, and to cultivate their honor, they would pick fights with opposing gangs. What she lacked in raw strength Shukur made up for by being quick on her feet. Never once did she consider presenting herself as a girl when she was challenged. That would have meant immediate defeat—and shame.

At prayer hours, she prayed in the men's section at the mosque with the others, placing her hands on her stomach like the men, instead of on her chest, the way women are supposed to do. To her friends she was accepted and respected as an honorary young man. On the bus once, Shukur pulled a knife on a boy who sat down and attempted to harass a female student. It wasn't something she needed to consider; it was a reflex. Women should be protected from men by other men; she knew it was how society was arranged and it was for the best.

At times, Shukur's little gang was guilty of mild harassment, too. More than once, they roamed dangerously close to girls, who pleaded with them to stay away so that their parents would not be upset. The gang did not care so much about the girls; the point was to provoke the girls' brothers.

The boys knew about love, but it was not something they liked to spend their time thinking about. They knew girls did, though, and the boys would play along sometimes, just to see how far the girls would go—how much they were willing to risk. Shukria learned early that love was something that could distort one's head and that should be left to the weaker sex. The minds of women were especially susceptible to being led astray by poetry and books. The minds of men, on the other hand, were more focused and better equipped for solving important problems and building things. Or so she was taught.

With the privileges attached to being her father's second son came responsibility. Running to the bazaar, buying food and supplies, hauling heavy bags of flour and cans of cooking oil—it all fell upon her. The eldest son was spared—he always enjoyed a higher status than the family's *bacha posh*—but Shukur was made to do hard physical labor. It was especially onerous when she got her period. Mentioning the event to her father was unthinkable: It would paint her as a woman, and worse, the bleeding would mark her as impure and weak. So beginning in the late summer and early fall of her fifteenth year, Shukur contended with stomach cramps as she filled a wheelbarrow full of mud at a nearby pit and ran it to the house to prepare the roof for winter. During the summer, the mud roof usually dried and cracked, so in the months leading up to each icy, cruel winter, it had to be patched up again. Between the mud runs, Shukur would squat down and hug her legs, trying to block out the pain and warm her stomach. Her mother never asked, and her father could never know. Shukur loved her father and wanted to do anything she could to please him by being a perfect son.

She is grateful her period came late; her younger sisters started their menses far earlier, in their early teens. But when Shukur turned thirteen, just like Zahra, her hips did not round out below her waist. She forced her voice to take a turn for the deeper, just like those of the other boys. Her chest remained flat.

She had learned from her mother that a child comes from a woman's body. The actual birth seemed disturbing to her. Her mother, like many other Afghan mothers, told her that the baby would suddenly burst out from a hole in a woman's stomach. It was just one of the reasons Shukur was relieved to think that she would never get married—confident that she was needed more by her family. Shukur imagined she would take over from her father the task of providing for them all. Her father, a security officer at the airport, retired when she was barely fourteen, and Shukur decided to pursue an education to become a nurse. She had really wanted to become a doctor, but it required several more years of study and would be costlier. She would need to work and earn an income so she could remain a son to her father and a brother to her sisters.

That was the plan.

SOON DANGERS BEGAN to present themselves. As Azita's life radically changed around this time, in the early 1990s, so did Shukur's. But her family remained in Kabul throughout the civil war that followed the Communist rule. Shukur was seventeen on the day three mujahideen arrived at the door. Stricter dress codes for women had just been instituted in Kabul, with mandatory head coverings. The fighters had heard stories of a woman who dressed like a man and they had set out to correct the abomination. Shukur was at home in the Darulaman neighborhood where she had grown up, in jeans, a slouchy shirt, and the Afro-like hairstyle she had cultivated. The fighters stood by the door and demanded to see the cross-dressing criminal they had been told lived at the house. At first, her father would not budge. But Shukur stepped forward and plainly said she was likely who they were looking for. The two men studied her and exchanged looks before one spoke up, in an authoritative tone: "Okay. You look like a boy and you are completely like a boy. So we will call you a boy."

With that, Shukur had been mujahideen-approved as a credible male. The fighters left and never returned. But they were harbingers of darker days ahead. Her parents began thinking it might be impossible for Shukur to stay a man, especially since their relatives constantly complained—they, too, were turning more conservative and scared. Some argued it was inappropriate to have an adolescent girl in the family who passed as a boy. As always, reputation and honor were at stake.

So when her three-years-older cousin one day blurted out "You are engaged," Shukur reacted the way she normally did to an insult: She punched him in the face. As he howled, his hands went to his nose. He knew better than to hit back at his cousin.

And he had told the truth.

Shukur's uncle had made the winning argument to her parents: It was now too dangerous for their daughter to carry on living like a man. As the Taliban rode in, instituting full-on gender segregation in Kabul, cross-dressing was officially banned. As a rule, women were not to go outside at all, and if they did, they needed to be completely covered so as to not inspire lust in men and contribute to the downfall of society. The family had to protect Shukur—as well as itself—

the uncle had told her parents. The best way was to marry her off. And there was the money, of course, that the husband's family would provide for getting Shukur as a bride, he reminded them. Why say no to a decent bride price in these uncertain times?

As Shukur could not speak directly to her father about the issue— that would have been disrespectful and inappropriate—she made her case to her mother: "Please. I am not causing you any trouble. I do not demand anything of you, like other daughters. I never ask for new clothes, even for Eid. I am no burden. I am just trying to help."

Shukur's mother listened to about half of what her daughter tried to say. Then she cut her off. She herself had been married at thirteen. Surely, Shukur could handle it, especially after so many years of roaming around like no other women could. She had had a long run of it, too. Shukur should be grateful. It was possible her future husband would let her continue working at the hospital, but her duties as a wife would take priority. Her tenure as the useful son was over. She could now either comply or lose her entire family. There was no real choice to be had.

A few days later, Shukria's aunt brought her a floor-length skirt, a burka, and a pair of impossibly small pointy shoes. Putting on a woman's dress may feel strange at first, but she would get used to it, the aunt assured Shukria. She remembers thinking her aunt was lying.

At the engagement party, a small, Taliban-era gathering of seventy-five people, Shukria recognized her husband-to-be as they met for the first time. She had seen him sneaking around the hospital several times, looking directly at her. Staring, even. She had not thought much of it then; the hospital was constantly in various stages of chaos, overflowing with patients and their families. But she remembered his face, observing her as she scurried between operating rooms, always at a distance. He had been there to take a look at her, at the insistence of his family.

Shukria would make a good wife, he had concluded from observing her. He had been told that under those scrubs she was a woman like all the others. Even better, she already supported her family by working at the hospital. It would provide a safety net for him, too, he figured, if his construction company did not do well. Later, Shukria understood how it all had happened: "Some colleagues knew my female name, and his mother found out I was a woman. She was warned that I was a *bacha posh,* and that I would probably beat him up if his family dared approach mine for marriage. But he liked my style."

The man Shukria married recognized that she was new at being a woman and said he would give her time to adapt. He, too, had a *bacha posh* in his extended family. In this case, he just happened to be her destiny and the one who would bring her back to proper womanhood.

As a concession when they first married, he encouraged her to wear trousers at home. He knew it cheered her up.

IN HER NEW domestic life, the sudden restrictions on movement bothered Shukria—as a newlywed, it took time to grasp the fact that she could not leave the house when she wanted to. Several times, she just walked right out the door on her own, only to be quickly brought back inside and reprimanded. Her husband's family told her she was a little "silly in the head," and she agreed something was not right with her. Several times, she promised to listen better and remember things.

Even more disturbing, to herself and the family, was her inability to perform the most basic female tasks. She was told such skills came naturally to women. But she seemed to lack any innate female gift for creating order, beauty, and peace around her. Yes, something was clearly wrong with her, Shukria concluded. Dinner was served raw or burned. Laundered clothes were not clean, even though her hands itched after soaking in water for hours. When she tried to mend a lapel on her husband's jacket, her fingers seemed too large, and the needle would escape. When her mother-in-law tried to teach her how to clean floors, Shukria knocked over the buckets of water and created such a mess that she was sent to her room.

She worked on her exterior, trying to arrange her hair in ways that would look more feminine. With much time and effort in front of a mirror, she found that at least sometimes her curly hair could be flattened and made to behave. As it grew longer, it would hang down her back instead of stand straight out from her head, the way she had always liked it. But when she met other women, they still told her she looked odd.

But these were her new friends, with whom she was mostly confined to the dark indoors, with curtains drawn and windows painted black. When she did brave Kabul's thick dust outside, always with the required male escort, she could never go exactly where she wanted. She could hardly see anything through the burka's small grid, either. Taliban rule was perhaps the worst time to become a woman, and Shukria's life came to consist of a lot more sitting quietly in dimly lit rooms. But an invitation to take tea with other women in the neighborhood or even her husband's female relatives always made her extremely nervous.

Trouble would begin at the greeting.

The three cheek kisses exchanged between women seemed overly intimate. Shukria had never been that close to another woman and it was strange to feel their skin against hers and to smell them. It made her embarrassed. Their skin was softer, too. Some had offered to share their face cream but Shukria decided she could not stand its sweet smell.

The all-female gatherings presented more challenges: Proper women sit on their feet, with their legs neatly tucked underneath them, having been taught to do so since childhood. Shukria, who was used to spreading her legs wide as soon as she sat down, tried hard to endure the pain that invariably ensued in the new position. It took time before she mastered the proper mode of speech, too: She was too loud, and her voice too deep for a group of only women. To this day, she sometimes mistakenly answers the phone with her "throat voice," as she calls it, before quickly correcting herself.

Worst of all was the socializing itself: She just did not know what to say. The women spoke a language she did not understand, of food, clothing, children, husbands. They exchanged tips and tricks on how to get pregnant with a son. Shukria had no expertise in either area and found it hard to describe most events in her own life with an equally dramatic touch. It seemed she simply could not make friends. The women readily accepted her as someone's wife, but they did not bother to engage her much, as she was mostly awkward and fell silent when asked a question.

It took time before she noted one particular way the women seemed to connect: gossip. After swearing herself to secrecy, one woman would pry a small secret, perhaps about a romantic fantasy or something equally forbidden, from another. She would then pass on her friend's secret, often followed by a degrading remark, as a kind of bait to connect with a third woman. Establishing intimacy based on violating another woman's secret was a way of socializing for the women, Shukria understood. Accuracy did not count for much— opinions, observations, and suspicions about others were equally valid currency. Those who had collected the most secrets had the most friends, it seemed.

Shukria, too, tried to mimic how women played one another, to increase their own influence in isolated groups where information travels only by word of mouth and is easily obscured. But most often she mixed up secrets and instead lost potential acquaintances. After a while she also realized—through trial and error—that women were seldom direct with one another, but preferred to express opinions and ask in roundabout ways for what they wanted. From her band of brothers, Shukria was not used to that approach, but with time, she learned to at least sense an unspoken request or gentle criticism.

The thing she never quite mastered, however, is what she calls "flirting," where women giggle and court new friends during what looks like a mating game, flattering each other and expressing joy about one being better or more beautiful than the other. Even with practice, that kind of giggling and charm never quite worked for Shukria. Now, with fifteen years of being a woman under her belt and having borne the requisite number of children, she no longer tries anymore. At times, she even goes as far as to cut gossipers off when she cannot stand to listen anymore.

Still, she wishes she were more like other women. It gets lonely. Shukria finds it hard to express herself. To her, it seems women tell the same handful of repetitive stories from their lives, often riddled with emotion-laden complaints about their own suffering. Shukria could never imagine sharing the details of her confusing and anxiety-filled male-to-female journey with any of them. She would not want anybody to feel sorry for her—the thought of being seen as a victim makes her cringe. She may not be one anymore, but inside, she likes to think there is a soul of a brave man. To be pitied would be the worst of all fates and ruin one's honor.

Slowly, painstakingly, Shukria continued to model her new female persona on the women around her, just as in her life as a *bacha posh* she took cues from her older brother. Eventually she prided herself on at least getting the makeup almost right. She would tiptoe around in her burka with what she had worked out was a suitably ladylike gait that replaced the way she swung her arms by her sides or put her hands in her pockets while taking long strides and moving along quickly. When a burka was no longer required, she continued walking in her new, more feminine way. Often, she forgot the most important part—to keep her head submissively bent—but she was constantly reminded to do so by those around her. No woman should walk with a straight back and a raised neck, she learned. Instead, she trained herself to hunch over as soon as she stood up, and she is careful to inhabit a far smaller physical space than she used to, by keeping all her extremities close.

By observing and imitating women's behavior, Shukria now has arrived at very distinct ideas of the differences in male and female behavior.

"I had to change my thoughts and everything inside my mind," is how she puts it.

She explains the way she became a woman in much the same

way American philosopher and gender theorist Judith Butler has described it. Shukria's gender—both the male and the female—was experienced as a social and cultural construct, where repetition of certain acts formed her identity on each side. According to Butler, just as little children learn to speak a language by repeating the same words and actions over and over, gender behaviors are learned. A person's *sex* is determined at birth, but *gender* is not: It is trained and adopted through performance.

But just as learning a new language, with its own sounds and melodies, is often more challenging to an adult, for Shukria to retrain herself to be a woman remains a work in progress and a language in which she may never be entirely fluent. The male side of her "stuck" in a way that she describes as "natural." It was her first spoken language and her first body language, and boys were her first friends. Everything else—everything female—she has to constantly correct and remind herself of.

BUT WHAT MADE Shukur? And who is Shukria? Where is Zahra headed, and who or what will Mehran become, depending on how long she remains in the disguise of a boy? It would be hard to argue they were born this way, as each of them was chosen to grow up like a boy. But can nurture alone really be responsible for forming a gender identity in a person?

Most people would say that men and women are different—that each perhaps has certain behaviors and traits, and maybe even certain preferences, that are specific to that gender. At least we like it to be that way, as we have organized our entire society according to two distinct versions of gender—one male, and one female.

It helps us perform our own roles, it provides security and comfort, and guides how we should interact with one another. So much revolves around perceived differences between men and women in our daily lives, and without constantly using gender as a touchstone, we may lose our bearings altogether. Gender is one of the ways we try to understand the mystery of being alive. My brother once described his joy at finding out that his partner was pregnant with a girl: "That you have created another human being is incredibly hard to grasp to begin with. When you find out whether it's a boy or a girl—well, at least then you know that one thing about them."

Gender holds beauty, romance, and magic for us. Men and women are "different" because we often *enjoy* those differences, and because we like to enhance and play with those notions. Gender is an unknown that we are able to explore—although too much experimentation with the binary definition of two distinct genders makes many people uncomfortable.

But as soon as the conversation turns to *how* we become different—by nature or nurture—gender becomes less a fact and more a subject of controversy.

The "nature" line—that we were each born with a certain set of skills, and that any gender-specific behavior or traits are programmed in our DNA—supports the idea that each gender is biologically suitable for different things from birth. That thinking has historically been used to propose that women lack certain traits, are incapable of some tasks, and should therefore not have certain rights. Women and girls have traditionally been described as "naturally" softer, gentler, and overall more domestically talented than men. Following that historical view, any logic, decision making, or even much *thinking,* was best left to men, whose minds were more sharp and analytical.

Over time and with varying results, science, medicine, and psychology have all tried to prove these theories, perhaps most notably in research on women by male doctors. For instance, a central argument in nineteenth-century Europe was that a woman's brain is directly linked to her uterus. The uterus, heavily burdened by menstruating and childbearing, ruled the brain and caused a woman's innate and erratic behavior. Those same arguments are used by many educated Afghan men and women still today, as a way of justifying the lack of women's rights. It took a long time for that type of pseudoscience about women's "naturally" weak brains to be debunked in the Western world, although remnants can still be heard among conservative and religious politicians in lauding the value of the traditional family.

But where the legacy of determining inherent differences and traits in humans based on skin color has been thoroughly dismissed by now, the idea that baby boys and baby girls are born with entirely different brains that determine behavior as they grow up has dragged far into our time. There is however little scientific validation today for discrimination based on birth sex or gender, as no simple way to separate individuals by gender exists. To strictly group individuals by traditional "male" or "female" traits, skills, or behavior from birth is no longer considered valid or acceptable in many educated societies, as research has shown that two people of the *same* sex are actually likely to be *more different* than a random man put next to a random woman.

The answer to the nature versus nurture question is less controversial than what some may want: What makes a person and a personality is in fact a *combination* of nature and nurture, in the brain's development in the womb and life experiences that follow.

There is also a perfect twist: What is "natural," in the sense of presumably being innate, is not the same as what might *feel* natural. Acts or behavior can feel "natural" to us after many years of performing them, because the brain has physically adjusted or developed in one particular direction.

In other words: With time, nurture can *become* nature.

This is where science meets Shukria's experience. For her, the male gender stuck to some degree, when her mind and body grew and those experiences formed her personality. She doesn't need a neurologist or a psychologist to tell her what she already knows: "Becoming a man is simple. The outside is easy to change. Going back is hard. There is a feeling inside that will never change."

Where she works, doctors exist for purposes of immediate survival. There are few mental health professionals in the country. Although Afghans commonly confess they suffer from anxiety from living through near-constant war, few have had access to or have sought professional help. That would be shameful, and the few doctors who specialize in matters of the mind are busy taking care of those who have lost theirs entirely. Psychology is associated with rundown asylums where the *really* crazy people are kept, so they do not pose a danger to others. Just like other adult women with a history of *bacha posh* that may have gone too far who live as married women silently around Afghanistan, Shukria has so far only had herself to consult on her own psyche.

Her own opinion is clear: Her parents should never have made her a boy, since she ultimately had to become a woman. As a parent, Shukria takes great care to raise her daughter as a traditional girl and her two sons as boys. She would never allow her own daughter to switch.

SHUKRIA BELIEVES THE clear rules on exactly what constitutes masculinity and femininity in Afghanistan are the reason it was hard, but not impossible, for her to learn how to become a woman. She offers some of her own observations—none of which has any basis in science but that nonetheless helped her train herself: Men begin to walk with the right foot; women with the left. A man breathes from the abdomen. A woman from the chest. A male voice comes from the throat: "You have to go deeper to the right sound." A female voice comes from just under the chin, with a lighter breath.

She stands up, demonstrating her manly walk: shoulders pulled back, taking big steps with arms swinging by her sides. She used to put her hand inside the pocket of her coat as she walked—a chest pocket, kind of. Like Napoléon.

"Do you think gender is all in your head, then?" I ask.

"I know it. It's about how we grow up."

"But are we not born with some things that set us apart? Other than the body?"

"No." Shukria shakes her head insistently and points to herself.

"I have experienced this myself. You learn everything. It's all in the mind and in the environment. How could you explain me, otherwise?"

Setareh turns to me, waiting for an answer to translate for Shukria. I shake my head. I don't have one.

On this day, we are in a small, foul-smelling windowless room at the back of the restaurant where by now we have spent dozens of afternoons with Shukria. We are separated from the men, who are lying on thick carpets smoking hookahs and eating chicken kebabs on the other side of a thin wall.

Women rarely visit the restaurant, the nervous owner has explained. Once again, a storage room next to the men's bathroom—there is none for women—has been made available to us. If a few black-covered guests were found in too close proximity to the men, it might ruin the entire establishment. But it is on Shukria's way home from the hospital, and its "security" is excellent, she believes. She does not know, and neither do we, that a few months later, the air outside will be filled with mortars and rocket-propelled grenades directed at the neighboring U.S. Embassy.

The menu is in both Dari and English, possibly inspired by the embassy next door, and offers various choices of pizza: *"cispy," "spaisee," "tike," "teen," "soft,"* or, simply, *"amrican style."* On most days, we stick to tea and cardamom cake.

I rise from the floor, to stand opposite Shukria.

"Okay, so make me into a man, then," I say. "If you think a person can switch. Show me how it's done. Teach me."

Shukria looks at me for several seconds. Then she turns to Setareh. A stream of words come out; Setareh can hardly keep up with Shukria's explanation.

She has watched me several times, she explains, in the hospital garden. Although I have been styled and persistently trained in discreet, womanly behavior by Setareh, people still stare at me as I stride by, taking big steps in my all-black coverage. They watch me not only because I am obviously a Westerner, Shukria points out. They look at

me because I walk around as though I "am the owner of everything."
I arrive everywhere without a husband or a father. And when we
speak, Shukria has noted, I look her in the eyes, seeming neither shy
nor emotional. I do not giggle—my laugh is more of a hoarse kind.
And like a child, my face has no makeup and my wrists and hands
carry no jewelry. Shukria looks at me again, quickly, before she turns
back to Setareh, striking an apologetic tone. She asks that her exact
words not be translated, as they may be too insulting.

But Setareh has already burst out in low laughter, gently passing
the message along: "She says you are a man already. There is nothing
she can teach you."

CHAPTER FOURTEEN

THE ROMANTIC

Shukria

IT WAS THE most painful moment Shukria can recall. It was also the moment when she felt love for the first time. She knew then, at least to some degree, that she was a woman.

Giving birth made her certain there was something female in her, a confirmation that she did indeed have the body, and hopefully something more, of a woman. It came as a relief that she had perhaps not destroyed it altogether by being a man.

With all that she had tried to learn and observe—how to dress, how to behave, and how to speak—she finally would not have to worry that the other women would catch her slipping up.

She had the proof now: She was a mother. One of them. In all, she would have two sons and one daughter.

As for how children were created, it was not discussed much among her friends. No one wants to be known for knowing too much or seeming too willing to discuss anything to do with "the secret parts," which is only one of the many ways Afghan women refer to their reproductive organs.

Sex is, by definition, illegal in Afghanistan: The marriage contract is what finally turns it into a permissible act between husband and wife. At times Shukria's female friends joked about the unfortunate "chore" of being in bed with their husbands. About how everyone knows "what men are like." Some husbands wanted to do it more often; others insisted only on Afghanistan's Thursday-night conjugal tradition, when the workweek is over and both men and women take extra care to wash and groom in advance of Friday prayers. But Shukria did not dare ask any of her friends about what was normal and how anything related to the secret parts was supposed to feel or function. None of her friends ever mentioned enjoying sex, either, though they had all been told there were women who did: whores, with unnatural and obscene desires. And of course foreign women— more or less the same category.

Shukria's own particular issue always seemed much too strange to bring up as well. None of her women friends grew up as boys, and she could not exactly ask her old male friends, either, why it is that sex makes her feel like "a nothing." She laughs nervously when she tries to describe it: "I cannot give my husband love as a woman. I tried, but I think I got a very low score in this. When he touches me, I don't feel comfortable. I just don't feel anything. I want to ignore him. When he gets excited, I cannot respond. My whole body reacts negatively."

What actually makes her cringe is not the physical contact, but shame: It is not right for her to be in bed with a man, even though she is his wife. "I don't have those feelings other women have for men. I don't know how to explain this to you. . . ."

She looks at us and hesitates: "Sometimes it is very hard for me to be in bed with my husband because he is a man. I think I am also a man. I feel like a man myself, on the inside. And then I feel it is wrong, for two men to be together."

So perhaps she is gay?

Shukria is not the least bit offended or embarrassed when after dancing around it for a while I finally just ask the question. She is almost sad to admit she feels no attraction to women, either. Avoiding them and cultivating a deep belief that they are the weaker sex brought no romantic allure for her. Being intimate with a woman would be wrong, too.

She is actually quite sure she prefers men over women in general:

"Men are strong, strict. Women are very sensitive. I understand men. I feel them very easily."

MY QUESTION OF whether Shukria, or other *bacha posh,* may automatically develop homosexual preferences by living as boys turns out to have been entirely misguided.

First of all, as Dr. Robert Garofalo, the expert in Chicago on development of gender, explains, growing up as a gender different from one's birth sex does *not* by default translate to homosexuality in adult age. But perhaps most important, whether *bacha posh* become homosexual presupposes that women who live in Afghanistan have an opportunity to embrace, develop, or practice sexuality of *any* kind.

They do not.

In Afghanistan, sex is a means to an end, of adding sons to the family. But nowhere in that equation is a sexual orientation or preference a factor for women. Having sex with a husband in a forced marriage is an obligation—one fulfilled in order to have children. But when, or how, to have it is not a question of lust, willingness, or even conscious choice. To identify as either *heterosexual* or *homosexual,* and define what that means, can be very difficult for an Afghan woman, who is not even supposed to be at all *sexual*.

That any woman, anywhere in the world, is capable of being sexual is a fairly recent idea. Not until the 1950s, with the help of research by Dr. Alfred Kinsey and others, did the idea that women's sexuality is in many ways similar to that of men's begin to take hold. Before that, a healthy woman, in Western literature and science, was an *asexual* woman.

A woman who showed tendencies of being at all interested in sex was often subject to treatment to cure this bothersome and dangerous predilection. The reproductive organs of women were thought to be at the root of trouble: In nineteenth-century Europe, contemporary literature documented how a woman's uterus could be surgically removed in order to stem any unruly and exaggerated sexual behavior. This sentiment still forms the modern-day argument for female genital mutilation around the world: An asexual wife is always preferable in order to promote a stable family.

There is a contradiction, of course, in the fact that medical experts in nineteenth-century Europe, as well as many Afghan men and women today, insist that a woman can and should feel nothing sexually since she exists only for procreation. At the same time, they fear and suspect an underlying, explosive sexuality in women that must be contained. Once it is ignited, a woman's sexuality might be impossible to control, so best not to encourage it in any way. Most discreet if convoluted conversations in Afghanistan about sex usually end there: Men are sexual; women, not so much—unless there is something horribly wrong with them, making it difficult, or even unlikely, for many Afghan women to explore their sexuality or develop any sort of preference.

Still, women's sexuality, and sexual feelings, of course do exist in Afghanistan. But as with gender, they are convoluted and often do not correlate to how we have learned to describe them. Interestingly, the sexual feelings described by several young unmarried Kabul women I privately pressed on the forbidden topic were abstract and in soft focus. It is the opposite of porn: Their fantasies are not directed at men and do not include visualizations of sexual acts, but are described as more meditative; a fantasy while masturbating may include something about "heaven," "beauty," or just a sense of calm and pleasure. But the act of masturbating is not only hindered by shame and fear—in small quarters where children and parents often sleep together, a moment of privacy is often very hard to come by. A young woman is also often told that touching oneself too much below the waist in any way may endanger her virginity.

For a married woman, having recognized some sexuality of her own and having figured out how to touch herself may not translate to enjoying sex with her husband. On the male side, a Pashtun doctor in his thirties confirms that he, just like Dr. Fareiba, is often asked by men for advice on how to make sons, which is a pretext for discussing sex. The conversations follow a similar pattern: While some men are interested in making their women "happy," there is a fear that if women are made "too happy" they will fantasize about, or even turn to, men other than their husbands; they may develop an interest in sex and become uncontrollable. As for his own marriage, he states with confidence: "According to my opinion, how should I put this . . . before I come to the end, my wife should come to the end. It's better if she can come to the end twice."

But the response from one Kabul woman was typical of several other married women's view of sex: "If it were up to me, my husband would never touch me again."

WHERE SEXUALITY IN general is suppressed and the idea that women can be sexual at all is a matter of indifference or fear, *homosexuality* is at the next level of taboo. If sex barely exists, homosexuality absolutely does not—and certainly not in the case of women. An attempt to speak of homosexuality with Afghans will most often render nervous laughter or an outright refusal to engage in conversation.

Even among educated Afghans, the idea that women could be sexual with other women is both ridiculous and mysterious, since, as was explained to me, it challenges the very definition of what a sexual act is. As one man said: Without a penis involved, sex just seemed physically pointless for both parties.

Comparative sociologist Stephen O. Murray and historian and anthropologist Will Roscoe, who have scoured history and literature for definitions of homosexuality in the Muslim and Arab worlds, found only "paltry" references to lesbianism throughout time:

> Within most present-day Islamic states, where representation of even married heterosexual conduct is heavily censored, woman-woman sexuality remains thoroughly submerged.

In their book *Islamic Homosexualities,* they also quote a passage from Muslim geographer and cartographer Sharif al-Idrisi, who lived in the twelfth century. This rare writing acknowledged the early existence of women who preferred women; it even offered an intriguing explanation of why they did—while at the same time explaining how they posed a danger to society:

> There are also women who are more intelligent than the others. They possess many of the ways of men so that they resemble them even in their movements, the manner in which they talk, and their voice. Such women would like to be the active partner, and they would like to be superior to the man who makes this possible for them. Such a woman does not shame herself, either, if she seduces whom she desires. If she has no inclination, he cannot force her to make love. This makes it difficult for her to submit to the wishes of men and brings her to lesbian love. Most of the women with these characteristics are to be found among the educated and elegant women, the scribes, Koran readers and female scholars.

Note how he underscores that this occurrence is due solely to the lack of suitable male partners—so-called situational homosexuality. Also, he suggests that an *educated* woman may become more sexual and therefore choose women over men as sexual partners. The implicit conclusion remains a concern to this day with many in Afghanistan: Education for women can be detrimental for society, and ultimately the end of mankind. It is best to keep women's intellects in the dark, or they may get strange ideas, such as choosing to abandon men in favor of women, with the added consequence of no more babies being born.

Moving to the other gender, *male* homosexuality is referenced only in a range between ridicule and disgust by most Afghan men; such acts are committed by the lowest of people. Male homosexuality officially does not exist in Afghanistan, either, nor in neighboring Iran or most other Islamic societies. At most, it is viewed as a sin, a crime, or both.

This includes some stark contradictions, however.

In Afghanistan, as well as in the historical context of male homosexuality, a man may well engage in homosexual *activity*. That, however, does not automatically turn him into a *homosexual*. A distinction is made between the active and the passive role in the sexual act, between "taking" pleasure and submitting to someone. The penetrator is the manly man, whereas the penetrated is the weaker party, likened to how a woman submits to a man. The receiver may not be a homosexual, either, unless he shows signs of liking it too much, in which case he may actually be denounced as a homosexual person, or a *bedagh*: a word for the passive homosexual.

Male homosexual behavior, in the active role, is traditionally explained in Afghanistan by the lack of available women. Women should also primarily be used to create children, not necessarily used for pleasure.

Pederasty can be justified similarly. Since men's sexuality is a force of nature that must be released, exactly how that occurs is of lesser importance. A younger, weaker boy may even be preferable, since he cannot be dishonored the way a woman can be. There is also less risk of retaliation by an infuriated family: Raping a boy is a lesser offense than raping a woman. As a bonus, the perpetrator is considered macho and as far from "homosexual" as one can possibly be.

When children's rights organizations have attempted to explore the abusive practice of *bacha bazi,* or "boy play," in Afghanistan, in which young boys are traded as dancing child entertainers and also kept as sex slaves by military commanders and other powerful men, they are often met with a wall of silence; many Afghans confirm its existence, but few will admit it happens in their own communities.

Radhika Coomaraswamy, the UN special representative on children and armed conflict, came right out and said it in 2011: "Very powerful warlords and regional commanders from all the security forces as well as anti-government forces have young boys who are taught to dance."

The United Nations Children's Fund (UNICEF) also warned in 2010 that the number of boys sexually abused through this traditional activity is likely small in proportion to the more commonplace sexual abuse of "ordinary" boys by "ordinary" men. So despite legal and religious censure of homosexual behavior, research indicates that man-boy sexual relationships are considered neither exceptional nor criminal in the traditional or modern cultures of Afghanistan.

Afghan men are often equally careful with their phrasing; they will never speak in the first person, but sometimes say they "know someone" who as a young boy was subjected to a violent assault by another, older man. In his study on Pashtuns during the 1980s, anthropologist Charles Lindholm reported: "The first sexual experiences of many, if not most, boys is with one of their passively inclined peers, or with an older man who is a confirmed *bedagh*. Older men still may cultivate a handsome young protégé who will accompany them everywhere, though the practice is hardly universal."

These underage victims of sexualized violence, who have been assaulted by other men and are too ashamed to ever speak of it, are also expected to eventually grow up to function sexually with women in marriage, in order to have children.

What we may think of as homosexuality, involving two consenting parties, had not been much documented in Afghanistan until an Afghan refugee to Canada wrote about his experiences.

Author Hamid Zaher recounts how he began feeling attracted to other boys in the eighth grade. He states that whereas sexualized abuse of young boys is widely accepted in Afghanistan, it is "absolutely impossible" for two adult men to have an equal, consensual sexual relationship there. For that reason, his road to discovering and exploring his own sexual orientation was a painful one, which included a diagnosis of mental illness and culminated in his fleeing his country.

Just as female homosexuality took much longer than male homosexuality to be recognized in most of the West, it may take decades before an Afghan woman is able to define her sexual orientation as lesbian or bisexual. Or anything else. In a distant future, each human may not need to be defined as *either* heterosexual or homosexual in a lifetime, but with the recognition that a person's sexuality can be more fluid and situational.

BUT IN A place where marriages are arranged and sex is about reproduction, shreds of romance still endure, as demonstrated by the giddy female wedding guests who find allure in what is most forbidden. Even though marriages for love are rare in Afghanistan, tales of them abound, and both women and men harbor fantasies of unions inspired by the appearance of adventurous and often tortured but passionate relationships in literature and poetry. The rush of a high school crush may have to last a lifetime here.

Like many Afghan women, Shukria wears no wedding ring. But there is an intriguing bulky silver ring on a right-hand finger that she initially refuses to address. Until I dare suggest she may be the object of a secret crush by whoever gave her the ring. She denies it: No, no, it's not like that.

"I had a very good friend who was close to me. The ring is from him. But I have never been in love."

There are two identical rings. When her friend gave her the ring, he kept the other one. He, too, has worn it ever since.

It sounds very romantic. I look to Setareh for support. She keeps her game face. To her, I'm the one who knows nothing of love. We have had a disagreement in the car. She has asked me to cover for her when she meets up with "a friend" from the university. Should her father call, I am to say that she's with me. I tell her it's much too dangerous. What if there is a blast, and I can't tell her parents where she is? When I am responsible for her, we should be together, I insist. In turn, she has let me know I am a cold-hearted machine.

I know Setareh will eventually just gamble and tell her father she is with me anyway, and I can only pray she doesn't get caught or get too close to a suicide bomber. I know she fears neither.

Shukria does not waver on the ring. There is no romance. Only the eight men she counts as friends. Her gang from childhood. They still stick together. When she gets sick, they come to visit, and they all check in regularly. Shukria is especially close to one of them—they went to school and later worked at the hospital together. His parents love her like their own child. He still calls her Shukur. To demonstrate how their bond has been misinterpreted before, Shukria recalls how his mother once thought that she was in love with him and arrived at Shukria's parents' house to make a marriage proposal on behalf of her son.

"I was so upset. I went to his mother and said, you have misunderstood everything. We are not in love; I am a man and if I was together with your son we would be in fights all the time—is that what you want? I was very angry. And she said, 'But I thought you were in love.'"

Shukria laughs. The idea is too ridiculous. They were brothers! Not some sappy romantic couple. He eventually married, too, as she knew he would.

Shukria is not entirely sure how love is defined.

"He is my best friend, and sometimes I think that if something happened to him, how could I live? Maybe that is love."

She has tried to have civil conversations with God on the topic. But too often, they turn into silent, one-sided arguments. Perhaps she should be grateful; God made her both a man and a woman in one person. Yet she feels completely alone most of the time. The noise inside her head is painful, and only occasionally can she shut it down. It works best when she is at work, in her scrubs. It also feels good when she gets to be protective of other women, just as Shukur always was. Whenever she sees a woman being harassed by a man, she will jump in and forget all her womanly manners. She doesn't pull a knife anymore, but she will not hesitate to shame any man by getting too close, waving her arms, and threatening to beat him up.

Shukria has seen this dynamic played out in pirated American DVDs. There is always a hero and the woman he rescues. Even when the main character is a woman, she will fall in love with a man, who is always stronger. It gives Shukria a great deal of satisfaction to watch the men scoop up women in distress. And like every other woman with a television in Kabul seems to do, Shukria follows the soap operas from India and Turkey.

"When you see stories of love, can you relate to the feeling?"

"No. But I feel love for my children, my parents, my friends, and my coworkers. Love is not just for a partner, I think."

Perhaps the notion of romantic *love* is another social construct. Do we actually learn how to fall in love and expect certain behavior from those we fall for? If it's reciprocated, we call it chemistry. Just as giddy Afghan teenage girls speak dreamily of marriage as presented in Bollywood movies, perhaps we, too, have read books and watched many movies to learn what romance looks like and how it should feel. We perform certain rituals we have been taught are romantic. Then we go about piecing together our own romantic comedy script in the best way possible, with the material we have already collected.

Biological anthropologist Helen Fisher at Stanford University has defined three different forms of love: *Lust,* which is mainly sexual attraction. *Romantic attraction,* defined by an intense yearning for another person, not unlike a substance addiction, where the affected craves someone or something. The wanting is the key feeling, just as a heroin addict needs a fix. Finally *attachment,* signified by a calm feeling of deep union with another person.

Shukria has no answers as to why romance never appealed to her. But she knows why she enjoys her television so much. Even though the concept of romance between the protagonists feels foreign to her, it still excites her to follow a love-struck couple for a very specific reason: "I like happy endings."

That may be what is truly universal.

CHAPTER FIFTEEN

THE DRIVER

Nader

B Y LAW, WOMEN are allowed to drive in Afghanistan. Just as they are formally allowed to inherit property and divorce their husbands. They just don't, most of the time.

Nader wore a head scarf while driving once, just to please her brothers and to humor what they insist God requires from her. It nearly got several people killed, herself included. At the sight of a covered head behind the wheel at one of Kabul's many checkpoints, there ensued a traffic jam, with other drivers honking their horns, yelling, and throwing their fists in the air. They hollered out from their windows and thrust their cars toward her. Others pulled ahead, hitting the brakes in front of her, trying to trap her like a little mouse.

"You shameful woman, you should not drive!"

"A car is not for you. You will destroy it!"

"Your husband should beat you!"

"Stop the car! Or we will force you!"

When she did not yield to any of their warnings, it made them angrier. She did not feel defiant so much as scared. She had to focus hard to shut out their loud words and just stare ahead, to keep her wobbling Toyota Corolla away from the curb as she drove away. By the time she finally reached Jalalabad Road, most other cars had scattered in other directions. But one car seemed determined to race her, driving up next to her, roaring his engine for effect. As the others had failed to stop her or run her off the road, he would at least teach her a lesson by showing he was faster.

So fragile apparently is the power they hold in this country where men are born to almost all the privileges society confers, that this one felt a need to immediately rebuff a woman out of place and demonstrate strength and superiority before her. By getting into a car by herself, Nader had reached for a privilege that was not hers to be had.

She did not want to race him, but she did not slow down, either. She just kept her eyes on the road and drove faster than she really was comfortable with. When her challenger gave up after a while, she tore off the head scarf and threw it on the passenger's seat. *Nadia* was not meant to be a driver.

Nader looked at herself in the rearview mirror. Her short, curly hair had been flattened by the scarf, and she ran a hand through it. Then she put her sunglasses back on and drove back to the house, without any more drama. Her brothers could yell at her all they wanted. It was her car. After all, she had fixed the engine herself. She had lived as a man for all of her thirty years.

LIKE SO MANY of the other girls, Nader was designated her family's *bacha posh* at birth, to ensure that sons would follow. Her two older brothers had just joined the army, so the need for more sons had become acute, for her parents feared their older children would be killed in their dangerous jobs. For the parents to be left with only girls was a risk they did not want to take. They also needed a helper at home, to run errands and help shuttle the younger ones around. Nader's mother had been told by several neighbors it was guaranteed to work—dressing her newborn daughter as a son would render magical results.

The magic arrived when two more boys were born, in addition to another four girls. The older brothers soon argued that Nader should go back to being a girl before she came of age as a woman, so as not to embarrass them before friends and relatives.

But Nader's life, where she was a Mehran, and later a Zahra, never took the turn of Shukria's: Nader did not marry. She did not become a woman. In the circle of life of a *bacha posh,* Nader is one of the exceptions. Her life veered in a different direction.

Her father had watched her grow up, and had seen his girl be her happiest in pants and a turban. He thought she should decide for herself what she wanted to wear: "Do what you feel good about and what you are comfortable with. It is your own choice in this life," he kept telling her when she was a teenager and throughout her twenties.

There was another reason to maintain the status quo: Under the Taliban, women were mostly confined to the house. But Nader would tool around town on a bike avoiding the checkpoints. Her father often laughed at the stories she brought home—of how she had fooled everyone as she went to the bazaar or even to pray with other boys. Like most everyone else in Kabul, her father had only disgust for the Taliban, and Nader's cat-and-mouse game was their private little resistance movement. Sometimes she exaggerated the drama of how close she had come to getting caught, just to entertain him.

The entire family was ecstatic when the Taliban left. But as the Americans moved in, Nader's aging father fell ill. With his passing, power over the family and Nader's future was passed to her brothers. They did not marry her off, but she had a few close calls: Several proposals for marriage from relatives aimed at setting her straight were turned down.

After a few heated family arguments, Nader found her salvation: The family does not lack money, and her mother has not wanted to remarry. Since her brothers have adjacent houses of their own, Nader made a case for herself as the useful male companion to their elderly mother. Now the brothers will not have to worry about their mother, since Nader is there to protect her honor and that of the two youngest sisters. She does all the work around the house and runs errands for her other sisters' families, too.

So far, that role has allowed her to stay in pants, a T-shirt, and the bulky pinstripe sports coat she prefers on most days. She has perfected a slightly bow-legged walk, and speaks in a low voice. When she leaves the family's big, carpeted house in one of the better parts of Kabul where houses are surrounded by thick walls, she keeps her head down for fear the neighbors might see her. Gossip is everywhere, and she does not want to unnecessarily provoke anyone. Many know her just as a man who lives with his mother and sisters.

Now, as she approaches thirty-five, she is hoping to be out of the marriage market for good as she is simply too old for anyone to want her. And, she hopes, infertile. Watching how her brothers treat their wives and her younger sisters, she cannot imagine being ruled by a man. She went through university as a young man and holds a part-time office job at a software firm in Kabul, making some money of her own.

The power of prayer has worked well for her, too. As her four sisters developed breasts and hips, Nader's early teenage pleadings with God revolved around staying flat-chested, bony-hipped, and premenstrual. She vowed to give anything in return for those things. God listened, and although she did bleed at fifteen, it was two full years after her younger sisters had their first menstruations. She has never let anyone touch her thick eyebrows, and she has taken every chance to let the sun burn her skin to make it a little darker and rougher. She prayed for a full beard, too, but got only a smidge of black hair above her upper lip. A sports bra one size too small keeps her chest safely minimized. Just to make sure, she slumps a little, her shoulders turned inward. There is no better compliment than when her brothers tell her she looks too much like a man. She has heard them speak among themselves, too, about how Nader may have turned into a man for good. It's the way it should be, she reasons: "I am free now. I don't want to go to prison."

There is an expression sometimes used for *bacha posh* who have aged themselves out of the marriage market. She is *mardan kheslat*: "like a man." It can be either a condemnation or a compliment, an expression of admiration and respect for a woman who has the mind and the strength of a man.

For a woman to live as a man is especially controversial as she comes of childbearing age and lives through her fertile years, the way Zahra is experiencing. But when she becomes too old to have children, she is no longer a sexual threat to society, and she may earn a grudging acknowledgment or at least tolerance from a wider circle as an honorary man, just as Carol le Duc described the woman called "Uncle" she once met. By then, she is of no use as a woman anyway. Only then—when her body is no longer fit to be appropriated by others for childbirth, does it become more her own. An infertile Afghan woman is considered less of a woman, and that is exactly the point: She is a woman who has renounced the feminine.

Nader is not the only *bacha posh* who has refused womanhood and now lives as a man in Afghanistan. Forty-five-year-old Amir Bibi in Khost, the violent province bordering on Waziristan, carries a gun and sits on the local *shura,* where she is seen as a village elder and her opinions have bearing. Meeting Swedish correspondent Terese Cristiansson in 2010, she explained that she had been given permission not to marry by her father, who brought her up as his son among seven brothers.

Another woman who holds the role of an honorary man in her community is fifty-year-old Hukmina. She, too, lives in Khost, in the small village of Sharaf Kali, with both the Pakistani Taliban and unmanned drones above as everyday threats. There, she is a member of the local provincial council, rides horses, and carries a gun with her at all times. She fought the Russians during the war, and she certainly does not fear the Taliban. Having been brought up as a companion to her brother, she tells us she "never had the thoughts of a woman. If I felt like a woman I would not be able to do these things."

She says she is supported by a whole group of women in her province who live like men. There used to be ten, but two died.

BOTH WESTERN AND Eastern history is filled with Hukminas and Amir Bibis and Naders. In almost every era, there have been women who took on the role of men when being a woman was made impossible. Many of those whose existences are remembered are preserved were warriors, since wars are a manly business deemed worthy of recording.

In the first century, Triaria of Rome joined her emperor husband in war, wearing men's armor. Zenobia was a third-century queen in Syria who grew up as a boy and went on to fight the Roman Empire on horseback. Around the same time in China, Hua Mulan took her father's place in battle, wearing his clothes. Joan of Arc was famously said to have seen an archangel in 1424, causing her to adopt the look of a male soldier and help fight France's war against England.

The Catholic Church seemed to not only accept women dressing as men but also to admire and reward those who showed bravery and displayed other male traits. In a study of medieval Europe, professor Valerie Hotchkiss of the University of Illinois at Urbana-Champaign described the phenomenon of cross-dressing women as revolving around avoiding marriage, renouncing sexuality, and forever remaining virgins. Both *Scívias,* a twelfth-century collection of religious texts by Hildegard von Bingen, and *Summa Theologica* by Thomas Aquinas mention how women dressing in male clothing may be permitted in circumstances of necessity. In other words: war.

Dutch historians Lotte C. van de Pol and Rudolf M. Dekker also documented more than a hundred women who lived as men between the sixteenth and nineteenth centuries. Many were discovered to be women only when their bodies were carried off the battlefield. These women "existed throughout Europe," mostly as sailors and soldiers, and likely there were many more who will never be known.

They took on a male identity for reasons similar to the *bacha posh* in Afghanistan today: Some needed to support themselves and their families. Others needed to disguise themselves to travel or to escape a forced marriage. Some managed to disguise themselves to study, since higher education was closed to women. A few who were found out faced prosecution, but there is evidence indicating some leniency was given to those who had fought for their countries.

In the 1600s, orphan Ulrika Eleonora Stålhammar supported herself and five sisters in Sweden by enlisting in the army, eventually attaining the rank of corporal and fighting the Russians. She was only one of several Swedish women known to have fought alongside men in male dress to escape a forced marriage. Briton Hannah Snell famously served with the marines in India in the mid-1700s as James Gray, and several dozen Englishwomen have been recorded as having served as men in the British Royal Navy, initially unbeknownst to their commanding officers. German women were also found on the battlefield in the guise of men, as was Geneviève Prémoy of France, who was eventually knighted by King Louis XIV. Women living as men were among the conquistadors in South America, and in North America women clandestinely took part in the Civil War.

By the nineteenth century in Europe, the frequency of women who dressed as men seemed to diminish. Historians attribute it to an increasingly organized society where various forms of civil registration such as border controls and mandatory medical examinations for soldiers made it more difficult for women to pass as men. A more dysfunctional, primitive society works in favor of those who want to disguise themselves; the less papers or checks of any kind, the better—circumstances still true for much of Afghanistan today.

But women who live like men can be found in Europe to this day.

IN NORTHERN ALBANIA and Montenegro, the centuries-old practice of "sworn virgins" has been documented for a little over a century. There, British anthropologist Antonia Young tracked down women still living their lives as men in the early 2000s. Similar to Afghanistan, Albania has a tribal society with its ancient customs still preserved. Society is traditionally strictly patriarchal and patrilineal, where children are thought to stem directly from the blood of the father, and the woman is considered merely a carrier.

The family structure is focused on producing sons, and exterior markers such as dress determine a person's rights. Young girls move in with their husbands' families when they marry. The men protect the family, ensure its status, and take care of elderly parents—even holding their souls after death, according to old beliefs. A man can also inherit property and avenge and settle blood feuds.

But every family needs a leader, and women are sometimes allowed to assume that role in Albania. In some documented cases, women took on the role when all the other men in the family had died, but most often, they were designated boys at a young age, or even at birth, when parents were unfortunate enough to have only daughters. At the core of the sworn virgin construct was an absolute requirement to remain a virgin and never marry. They would be dressed like boys, with their names tweaked to male versions, and taught to shoot and hunt. As they entered puberty, they would master most exterior male traits and use them to compensate for anything girlish in their physical appearances.

Similar to Zahra, Shukria, and Nader, in adolescence and young adulthood, the Albanian sworn virgins, called *burrneshas,* would develop fully realized male identities, in both mind and behavior—even physically. With late and irregular periods, small, shrunken chests, and deep voices, the sworn virgins would display traditionally male traits, smoke tobacco, swear, fight, and frequently dismiss women as the weaker gender.

As Albania has become more modern and open to the outside world, the tradition of sworn virgins still exists but has diminished in recent years.

Perhaps this decline speaks to how much women pretending to be men really is one of the clearest symptoms of a segregated society so dysfunctional that it inevitably must change. As the practical and financial need to be a man in Albania has lessened, with women able to inherit property and gaining rights to take part in everyday life outside the home, there is now a lesser need for women to disguise themselves as men. Albania's centuries-old tradition of coping with suppression is now almost extinct, and the speed of its decline is indicative of how Afghanistan may change, too, if it were allowed a reprieve from constant war and was able to move out of the most severe poverty.

The question of when and how the practice of sworn virgins in Albania first developed is debated among scholars. Albanian laws stemming from the fifteenth century mention sworn virgins, which would indicate that the tradition is at least that old. Some suggest that it is perhaps even older, predating Islamo-Christian civilization.

Serbian historian and ethnologist Tatomir Vukanovic proposed that women who lived like men—and presumably boys who grew up as girls—may have been a worldwide phenomenon. That a very similar practice to *bacha posh,* where adult women live as socialized males, exists in current-day Albania—many countries away from Afghanistan—speaks to the universal and historical need for it in patriarchal societies.

It also indicates that turning daughters into *bacha posh* may have been both practiced and well hidden throughout the history of women in other places, too.

CHAPTER SIXTEEN
THE WARRIOR

Shahed

SETAREH IS CALLING for me. "Come! Now! Hurry."

As I half-sprint from the house across the courtyard from my guesthouse toward the outer gate, I see her blocking the guards with her body. Behind her stands another figure, much taller, all dressed in white.

The guards look at Setareh in amazement as she waves her arms around in a most unfeminine manner and explains to them: Yes, she knows about the no-gun rule in the compound and yes, she is aware that all male visitors must be body-searched. It's just that this guest is actually a woman and for that reason, they should not touch her. Must she say it again?

Setareh holds out her arms to halt them from advancing on the guest in white. The guards look to me for confirmation; is it true what Setareh is saying? That this one is not really a man?

They nod toward Shahed.

"Yes, just let her go. She's a woman. I guarantee it."

Shahed is a friend of Nader's, and to the uninitiated, she looks like just another broad-shouldered, athletic male. She has arrived early for our lunch.

The bearded guards do not move away, but turn toward each

other. Finally one guard, the shorter of the two, turns around and disappears into the hut by the entrance. The other silently follows. Before the door closes some muted chuckles dribble out. It will be a story retold for weeks to come.

Setareh enters Shahed's name in the visitors' log on the small table to spare her more embarrassment, since she does not read or write. Shahed appears unmoved, giving me a brief nod by way of greeting. It's our compromise between a handshake and the cheek kissing I have learned not to try again. I nod with my head down and touch the left side of my chest in return, in a respectful greeting between men. She brushes off my apologies about the guards; I should not worry. It happens. As a member of an elite paramilitary police force, she knows better than to get worked up over small disputes that could lead to bigger ones.

Shahed is usually undercover in more ways than one.

The ID issued by her unit spells out her full name: *Shaheda*. And her birth date. Her mother could not even remember under which government Shahed had arrived, usually the most reliable calendar to determine age here. After unsuccessfully trying to determine her age, Shahed decided she was twenty-eight when she enrolled and that she had been born in winter. Over thirty seemed too old; too close to death. She could be older; the deep lines around her mouth indicate this is perhaps the case. But she has not always eaten so well, either.

The Americans who arrived in Kabul to train her never asked too many probing questions on age or gender. They were really good people, actually. Shahed knew it when she saw their women. The female instructors looked a lot like she did. With their broad shoulders, weathered skin, and baseball hats, they were no-nonsense. Not a single female trainer came in wearing a head scarf or skirt. They never brought up any of the usual woman talk either, about marriage or romance. They just taught Shahed how to shoot properly and how to run faster and longer than she thought she was capable of.

She admired their sunglasses and their shiny tracksuits and appreciated how they would joke, too, sometimes using a few words of

Dari for encouragement, patting her on the back when she did well at training. The men shied away from the back patting by female trainers, but it made Shahed feel good. One time, she got to borrow a pair of Oakley sunglasses from one of them, and another snapped a picture of her wearing them. It was the sharpest she had ever looked—even better than when her entire team got thick, oversize sweatshirts with the letters "DEA," just like the ones some of the Americans wore. Shahed keeps hers stashed away at home, next to a box of photos where she's posing with foreigners in uniform, at lunch, with arms around each other's shoulders. Always grinning, always holding up fingers in a "V" for victory.

The Americans did not probe, either, on why she had chosen to be in the paramilitary unit; a job far more demanding than regular police duty. Female officers were usually placed as security guards at the ministries to search female visitors. There was a constant need for that type of service, but the work seemed far too uninteresting to Shahed, with little chance of advancement. But mostly, it was about the money.

When she first enrolled in the Afghan national police force, she was picked to train on the foreigner compound for an antinarcotics unit. It meant another $70 per month, in addition to her regular $250. Shahed was grateful; it seemed like a plum job with which to feed her extended family of twelve. It was maybe even enough for an after-prayer picnic some Friday, she imagined—a luxury her family had often talked about for a future where things would get better. Bread, chicken, and sodas for all of them in a garden. Years into her employment, she is still hoping for the picnic. It symbolizes the ultimate treat to her—something that the rich can afford. But the money doesn't stretch that far yet.

The promotion, and a higher salary, could still happen, she imagines. If God allows her to live. Her way with the Glock, the Makarov, and the Kalashnikov has earned her a designation of number two sharpshooter in the unit. She knows how to use a knife, too. Out in the field, she keeps one tucked into her belt and another strapped to her leg, just above the desert boots, over camouflage pants. Her helmet and goggles cover her face almost entirely, and when they gear up as a unit, there is no way to distinguish her from the other, male, members. In height, Shahed falls somewhere in the middle when they all line up, and the contours of her muscles match those of the others.

When her eyes are hidden behind those goggles, people listen when she speaks, in her low, dark voice. They even move out of the way for her. Some raise their hands in the air to signal defeat. They almost never run. Most just kneel down when she asks, their hands behind their backs, accepting the plastic cuffs.

Shahed's unit always arrives unannounced, often in the dark. A man cried at her feet once, pleading with her not to kill him. It made her uncomfortable. She asked him to stand up, so he could be a man again.

She knows how humiliation feels. She knows it from the days when her salary is spent and she cannot afford bus fare and must walk home by foot—a journey of an hour and a half alongside one of the mountains that surround Kabul, where mud houses are scattered on the steep slopes and threaten to slide down at every heavy rainfall. No electricity, no heat, and very little cell phone coverage exist up here, and every horizontal layer of earth delineates a division of class. The higher up, the more unattractive the land and the poorer its residents. It is where the first snow lands in the winter and where the most unrelenting heat of summer lingers longest.

Whoever settles that high above the city makes their own roads, finds their own water, and—if they can afford it—makes their own power from Soviet-era rechargeable batteries. It is just a few steps above the permanent refugee camps on the outskirts of Kabul, where a decade into one of the greatest foreign aid efforts of a generation, children still freeze to death in the winters.

FOR OUR LUNCH, we unpack three large bags of foil-wrapped kebabs and minced-meat-filled *manto* from the restaurant next door to the guesthouse after learning that Nader will join us much later. Shahed grows slightly laconic sitting on the shimmering-green chintz couch. Only after we move to the floor where we sit cross-legged and I am instructed by Setareh to for once shut up ("With Afghans, you either talk or you eat") does a hint of softness appear around Shahed's eyes. She eats quietly. Then she asks for a cigarette. Any kind will do, but she likes the American brands Kabul vendors call "Smoking Kills" as the cartons dictate. She smells it and then licks it sideways before lighting it, to make it burn slower, then inspects it after each drag to see how much remains to be had. Ashes form slowly at the end, which she flicks down into the thick rug from Pakistan.

Meeting at a restaurant would be more complicated for her than coming to my small rented room. The guard incident earlier could escalate to the point at which she may not have been able to keep her cool. She likes to carry a little something with her—usually a knife— for protection at all times. Men with guns are a given everywhere, but women with guns are a provocation and both a public and social danger. It doesn't matter that she is a police officer—it only adds to the insult. For her to bear arms confuses the entire concept of honor, where it is women who require protecting.

But Shahed knows what one of the Swedish diplomats has already taught me: The best way to enter any Kabul establishment armed is to just pass through the metal detector. When the beep sounds, one acts appropriately surprised and apologetic, and immediately hands over a gun, knife, or cell phone. After a nod of appreciation and understanding from the guard, one then walks away with a second weapon stashed somewhere on the body. Very rarely is a visitor asked to walk back through the arch again or to submit to a manual pat-down. Even then, a small knife is easily tucked inside the pants in the small of one's back, as the hands of security guards—male or female—usually do not go there.

By the time Nader arrives to join us for tea, Shahed has gone through the entire tutorial, using the small army knife in my wash bag. Her own knives—the one at her back, the other strapped to a hairy leg—she rarely removes.

Unlike Zahra and Shukria, who are both isolated in their respective environments as somewhat male in female bodies, Nader and Shahed have navigated much of their adulthood together in the past few years. It has helped them figure out who they are. Both devout Muslims, they each sought advice from a religious leader on how to relate to God, worrying that God was angry with them for living as men. But the religious man told them each in turn that God was on their side and that there was hardly anything unusual about it. To prove his point, he introduced them to each other.

Before that, Nader and Shahed had both wavered on faith. But now, together, they decided that at least in God's eyes, they are not outcasts, but rather, his creation. Nader, who has just arrived to our gathering, agrees when Shahed explains what they have both come to believe: "It was God who decided our destiny. It's his decision we are like this. He did not create us as men, but he gave us all the abilities and strengths of men."

It makes sense to them both: God is practical and generous, and he wants someone to take care of the family. When there are no suitable men around, God may leave that responsibility to a woman. Nader, who has a degree in Islamic studies from Kabul University, concludes: "We can never make ourselves into complete men, or complete women. But we try the best we can to be good humans before God."

THEIR FRIENDSHIP IS an unlikely one: Nader is upper class, and Shahed, although she holds a job, is closer to the bottom of society. Neither initially chose to be a man, but now it is all they know. As a child, Shahed volunteered to work with her father, who took day jobs painting people's houses. The Taliban was in control, and it was simpler and certainly less life threatening if she accompanied her father as a son. But she rarely made any friends. For poor children there are not many opportunities to play outside or roam. For Shahed, being a boy was mostly about work. As she became a teenager, boys came to fear her and girls shied away from her. She has spent most of her adult life sharing a house with her mother and sisters. Her brothers abandoned the family long ago, unable to find work or being able to afford to marry anyone. "Poverty made me like this," she says, running her hands down from her cheeks and over her body.

As a woman, as a man, her looks display an androgynous beauty that defies a traditional gender, with unlikely green eyes and the occasional smile. When she curls her upper lip slightly Shahed looks as though she can hear what I am thinking: "If my family had been rich, I would have been a woman," she says. "With five or six children." She pauses and looks at Nader, who immediately gets the joke. "Or maybe more like ten or twelve."

They both laugh at the idea. Children are not for them. If womanhood culminates with becoming a mother, they are very removed from it. Nader, too, used to be asked when she would change back. She always gave the same one-word response: *Never.*

Those around her used to argue that biology would overtake her one day, when she married and had children. She would agree, just to make them stop talking, knowing it would not happen. Both Nader and Shahed believe what others, too, have expressed: Once you have gone through the early teenage years as a man there is no turning back. When you go against nature, nature will follow, adjusting the body to the mind. They are slightly unsure about what they are, and they do not define themselves as one definitive gender.

It was a survival strategy that with time grew into an identity. Shahed offers an idea of what she has become, echoing a long history of women before her: "They say men are braver, stronger, and more powerful than women. But some women are braver and stronger than men. I am a *warrior.*"

She measures herself against other warriors, in both endurance and strength, during all the weightlifting and the explosive runs they practice. When thoughts of fatigue take hold in her mind, she fails sooner. When she pushes them away, she can keep going for longer. The Americans who trained her said a soldier needs a good mind more than a strong body. Her mother will sometimes worry, telling her it is not good for a woman to use her body in the ways she does. But Shahed ignores her. Showing fatigue should be avoided. A warrior must keep her focus and, beyond that, it doesn't matter if the warrior has the body of a woman. Shahed looks to me for confirmation: In the West, everyone knows this, right?

MAYBE. THE TRADITIONAL narrative of war and gender is present throughout Western societies as well, even though the idea that women possess something inherently good and peaceful has proven to be flawed many times. And despite a legacy of female warriors, women are still traditionally seen as those who should be protected. Just like the range for acceptable sexual behavior shrunk in the past centuries, the definition of how a woman should act and what she is capable of has also narrowed. Dead or wounded soldiers were always a potential political problem. Dead or wounded women—mothers and daughters—are even harder to explain and justify. In the past few hundred years, leaders of many societies have demanded women stay behind as men fight the battles. Excluding women from battle has even been brought forward as a measure of a country's degree of civilization—presuming, of course, that war is at all part of a civilized society.

Men may also need to keep war to themselves for other reasons.

While females endure rites of passage on the way to womanhood, including menstruating and later maybe motherhood, manhood does not automatically occur in such a distinct way. When anthropologist David D. Gilmore researched concepts of masculinity for his 1990 study *Manhood in the Making,* he found the pressure on men to demonstrate their gender was far greater than that on women in most societies. Going to war to protect the honor of a country and its women was always a certain way for a man to define himself. To then include women in warfare is to threaten one of the most effective ways men prove themselves in society. By cultivating what we may think of as a "natural" aggression in sons from an early age, we are raising future warriors, suggests international relations professor Joshua Goldstein in his book *War and Gender*.

Still, women today make up 15 percent of troops on active duty in the U.S. military. They have been shot down, killed, and maimed in the hundreds in Iraq and Afghanistan. Despite that, women have not been officially allowed in "combat positions." A third of positions in the U.S. Marine Corps as well as the army have been closed to women; the Pentagon made a decision to revisit the ban on women only recently, in 2012. The idea of women serving in some specialized units is still expected to be met with great resistance, with the familiar arguments: Women in the field are not as physically or mentally strong as men. It could also be too distracting for men to serve in close proximity to women. The biggest hesitation around allowing women in battle, however, as openly expressed by several male American military officials, may be that it changes the honor narrative of war, in which men are supposed to act as the protectors of women and home. And that may be the most dangerous thing of all to the military—if they cannot explain why we must fight.

Presenting a convincing threat to loved ones is vital in selling any war, with the underlying idea that war is absolutely necessary to preserve peace. In Western society, and particularly in the American political story, women are still the bearers of honor for their family and their country, and the very reason to *defend freedom;* the most often cited reason for going to war in our time.

FREEDOM IS AN interesting concept. When I asked Afghans to describe to me the difference between men and women, over the years interesting responses came back. While Afghan men often begin to describe women as more sensitive, caring, and less physically capable than men, Afghan women tend to offer up only one difference, which had never entered my mind before.

Want to take a second and guess what that one difference may be? Here is the answer: Regardless of who they are, whether they are rich or poor, educated or illiterate, Afghan women often describe the difference between men and women in just one word: *freedom*.

As in: Men have it, women do not.

Shahed says the same thing, when I ask her. "When no one is the boss of your life," is how she goes on to define it.

"So in the West, there is less difference between men and women?"

Shahed and Nader look at each other again and then back at me. They don't know. Perhaps I am supposed to tell them? But then Nader changes her mind, telling me not to bother. She doesn't want to hear it. "We are nothing. We would be nothing in the West, too."

Shahed is more hopeful, inspired by snippets of information from her American trainers: "I have heard that people don't care what you are or how you look in the West."

Not exactly true. But our definition of "freedom" may be different, and it changes with each generation. The current war in Afghanistan, for instance, is named "Operation Enduring Freedom" to indicate something worth fighting a thirteen-year war over. But freedom as we know it today is yet another evolutionary luxury, American author Robin Morgan says, when I later tell her about Shahed and Nader. "[Birth] sex is a *reality*; gender and freedom are *ideas*."

And it's all in how we choose to define those ideas.

The Afghan women I have met, sometimes with little education but a lifetime of experience of being counted as less than a full human being, have a distinct view of what exactly freedom is. To them, freedom would be to avoid an unwanted marriage and to be able to leave the house. It would be to have some control over one's own body and to have a choice of when and how to become pregnant. Or to study and have a profession. That's how they would define freedom.

As we arrive at Nader's house on another day, three of her sisters are visiting. Under each of their burkas are Indian-style saris with gold embroidery. A red, a yellow, and a purple sister gather on the floor around us, with their eleven children scattering between the kitchen and the reception room. The toddlers cannot make more than a determined crawl back and forth across the floor where we sit barefoot, our sandals piled up in a corner by the door.

"I would not be able to stand it," Nader says, with the abundance of nephews and nieces around her. "I am lucky not to have to be pregnant all the time and to have one after the other. If I were a woman here, that would be my entire life."

Nader's sisters have carefully made-up faces framed by long curly black hair. One sister leans forward as she attempts to explain Nader to me: "Do you understand that it is the wish of every Afghan woman to have been born a man? To be free?"

The other two agree. If they had had their choice, they would have been born as men. Nader is living that fantasy, and that is why other women turn on her sometimes. She does not play by the rules to which they are all subjected. "Nader wants to be her own government," one of the sisters explains. "Not like us, with our husbands as the government always."

To make me understand why some *bacha posh* continue to live as men in Afghanistan when they reach adulthood, another sister asks a rhetorical question that is excruciatingly simple to answer: "If you could walk out the door right now as a man or stay in here forever as a woman, which would you choose?"

She is right. Who would not walk out the door in disguise—if the alternative was to live as a prisoner or slave? Who would really care about long hair or short, pants or skirt, feminine or masculine, if renouncing one's gender gave one access to the world? So much for the mysteries of gender, or the right to a specific one, with this realization. A great many people in this world would be willing to throw out their gender in a second if it could be traded for freedom.

The real story of Nader, Shahed, and other women who live as men in Afghanistan is not so much about how they break gender norms or what they have become by doing that. Rather, it is about this: Between gender and freedom, *freedom* is the bigger and more important idea. In Afghanistan as well as globally. Defining one's gender becomes a concern only *after* freedom is achieved. Then a person can begin to fill the word with new meaning.

<hr />

FREEDOM IS ALSO what the sisters want to question *me* on.

What does a Western woman do with all that supposed freedom they hear about? After they whisper for a bit, one of them turns to me: "You can do anything you want, and you come to *Afghanistan?*"

"Is it the dust?" she jokes. "Or the war? We always have war."

It's more of a statement than a question, and the other sisters are with her; it is very strange for a woman to come to Afghanistan, presuming she could choose to be anywhere else in the world. It is also very strange of my father to allow it, they believe.

Not sure where to begin, I say nothing.

"This is what you do with your life," the sister continues, incredulously, at my silence. "Don't you want a family? To have children?"

She looks a little concerned.

"You should not wait too long to get married. You will be too old to have children!"

Yes. I may be too old already, I say.

Setareh stares at the floor, mortified. All three sisters look around, before one speaks again, with the question they want an answer to.

"Then what is the purpose of your life as a woman? What is the meaning?"

"You might as well have been born a man," another fills in. "What is there now to make you a woman?"

"You have your freedom," the first sister says again. "You can walk out when you want. But we also feel sad for you."

She glances at Nader.

"We know our sister is sad sometimes, too. It is the sad issue of being a man."

Nader looks embarrassed, and perhaps a little irritated. A toddler with three piercings in one ear and a polka-dot jumpsuit has wobbled up to her and maneuvered herself into her lap.

Nader's face changes, and she adjusts her position on the floor to hold her niece with both hands. She leans her head down to inhale the scent of the girl's wispy black hair. She closes her eyes for a moment.

"I have told them to save one for me," she says to me, tilting her head at the sisters. "They have so many. We can pretend one of them is mine."

Her sisters nod. They can all agree on that.

WHEN WE MANEUVER through Kabul's outer neighborhoods on our way home with Nader at the wheel—she insists she is a better and safer driver than any man we might employ for the task—she suddenly has an announcement: "I will take you to my *bachas*."

I press Setareh's hand so she will just say yes and not inquire further. Of course we want to meet Nader's boys.

Setareh catches Nader's phone, tossed from the front seat. We stick our heads together to see what she wants to show us. There, in the middle of a tiny cell phone shot, is Nader, her arms around the shoulders of two teenagers. Both are dressed in suits, with slicked-back gamine hair. They have young, glowing faces with soft features and those confident, defiant eyes. They are not trying to be cute, nor do they look down. They are all grinning, exposing their teeth.

Nader turns around to see our reactions. I know better than to ask her to look at the road when she's driving.

She tells us they are her protégés. Nader has no children, but she has already begun to build her legacy. They are her *bachas*, in training to become the next generation of refusers.

CHAPTER SEVENTEEN

THE REFUSERS

Nader's Boys

ONLOOKERS ARE HUSHED. The coach shouts Korean fighting terms with an Afghan accent. Her arms shoot out, the hands chop down, and fingers point to the floor.

Begin!

The fighters are said to be a girl and a boy. They are in identical white tunics and loose pants, with helmets covering much of their faces, making it impossible to see who is what. All eyes are on the two fighters as they begin their dance in perfect rhythm: *Hop, hop,* apart. *Hop, hop,* together. *Hop, hop, kick.* A leg shoots up, a torso blocks; a head swirls around and dips to the floor. Hit by a surge of adrenaline, they clash for a moment, clinging to each other with guttural sounds coming out. They tear themselves apart again.

The head-scarved coach interrupts: "No, no, no. Fight with your feet. Not with your hands!"

Her hand goes down.

Break.

A quick, respectful bow, and the two panting fighters tear off their tight-fitting helmets. Under the blue helmet is a fighter with slightly fuller lips. She is taller and maybe a year or two older than red helmet, a lanky teenage boy. Both have short black hair glued to their heads and their foreheads glisten with sweat. Two other young students in pants and tunics quietly stand up from the bench. It's their turn now. They are eager to take over the helmets and chest pads—the eighteen students share just one set.

Another girl on the bench has been holding a can of Mountain Dew to her left eye, where she was kicked before. She puts it down and says she is ready for round two. She scored more points than her male opponent in round one, in a system no one here seems to really understand. She was a little faster; her ducking a little smoother.

Sahel leans against one of the mirrors, cracked by a flying body weeks ago. Hands on thighs, she bends her head down and breathes hard. The Korean martial art, named after "the art of hand and foot," is her only physical exercise of the week other than the three flights of stairs she runs up and down daily to and from school. It is far more than most Afghan girls get. Nader walks up to her, patting her on the back. Sahel's mouth curls in a smile. She is Pashtun from Kandahar with three younger sisters. She counts Nader as her mentor and honorary big brother. In her actual family, Sahel is the older brother. At seventeen, she is older than any of her *bacha posh* friends, some of whom have vanished into marriage by now. But Sahel does not intend to go quietly. She has told Nader several times by now: "I am never going to be anyone's servant. Never."

A crumpled bandana comes out of Sahel's pocket; she ties it around her short hair with a knot in the back, biker style. The American eagle rests on her head as she shakes it to emphasize her refusal. She will fight for her freedom, and Nader has promised her support. Unlike Zahra, Sahel is not alone, and unlike Shukur in her time, Sahel is not the only *bacha posh* in a tribe of teenagers approaching adulthood.

A basement in the Khair Khana neighborhood of Kabul is hosting Nader's protégés, who meet here once a week to practice tae kwon do. When Afghanistan had a medalist at the 2008 Beijing Olympic Games, it made this a sport of national pride, on par with football and cricket. Five overgrown *bacha posh* immerse themselves in ritualistic, intense, and explosive close-contact fighting—not at all as a hobby, but because they all aspire to become champions. And in this small underground space, Nader coaches both tae kwon do and her own brand of organized resistance.

Every situation is addressed during downtime on the bench.

How to make yourself useful at home. How to argue for an education and a future income for the family rather than marriage. How to make contingency plans for the day your older brothers decide to put a stop to it all. How to ignore what they say about you in school.

It's better to live outside of society than to be enslaved, Nader preaches to her apprentices. And if *she* could do it, if she could resist becoming a woman for this long, it will be possible for them, too. They have cleared the biggest hurdles already and are almost grownups. Soon, if they have any luck, no one will want to marry them anyway, Nader tells them. In the meantime, if they can just finish their educations and find a profession, they will be of far more value to their parents than they would be as brides for other families.

To Nader, her coaching is not political, or part of any philosophy she has studied. She keeps it practical to her *bachas*: If they resist becoming girls for long enough, both their minds and bodies will grow invincible. They will reach a point of no return, when the male traits take hold. The physical training helps build mental resolve, too, along the lines of what Nader's warrior friend Shahed has prescribed.

"Why do you think the conservatives do not allow women to play sports?" Nader asks, by way of explanation.

"Because you touch each other?" I suggest.

Yes, that's part of it, Nader agrees. This type of coed practice would be highly controversial above ground.

"But it is also because when we use our bodies, we do not feel weak anymore. When a girl feels the strength of her body, she knows she can do other things, too."

Nader is not the first to make the connection between mind and body here. To the intense irritation of many Afghan conservatives, a discreet cadre of sports coaches have spent the last post-Taliban decade working with female teams. I tagged along once with Afghanistan's only girls' cycling team, where athletic women in head scarves and bulky tracksuits navigated muddy backstreets on practice runs, inviting the jeers of men and burka-clad women alike. Young women on bikes are an open provocation and an obscenity on Kabul's streets and they usually avoid inner-city practice. Instead, the coach drives them to a mountain where they can ride in peace. Several boxing clubs also allow young women to practice, sometimes in the company of young men.

Nader coaches soccer, too. Most players are regular girls in head scarves, but several Kabul teams have one or two *bacha posh* in various stages of puberty, too, as evidenced by the Facebook and cell phone photos she directs me to. The team's *bacha posh* usually wears a bandana, or nothing at all on her head, looking defiantly into the camera as she poses lined up next to the others.

WOMEN AND SPORTS are a classic conflict in a culture of honor, similar to that of war. The point of athletic events was to have women admiring male competitors from the sidelines, and later presenting the winner with his reward. The more segregated and conservative the society, the harsher the restrictions on women's sports.

More than a hundred years after the Olympics were revived, Saudi Arabia dispatched its first two female athletes to the 2012 Games in London. Afghanistan sent one—a female runner. In a measured concession, Brunei and Qatar also allowed a few women to participate for the first time. In those countries, women in sports are still a sensitive cultural issue, with a lot of detractors. The same tired historical arguments are still made, often with references to religion or invalid science: Too much physical exercise could be dangerous for women. Men who watch them could get too excited by catching glimpses of female bodies in motion. And the (more important) male athletes may become too distracted to engage in competitive sports at all if women were on the field. And what might be the point of winning, or even playing honorably, if women are not cooing on the sidelines?

The real reasons for those governments' reluctance to have women practicing sports are, of course, exactly what Nader has figured out: A woman who feels her own physical strength may be inspired to think she is capable of other things. And when an entire society is built on gender segregation, such ideas could cause problems for those who would like to hold on to wealth and power.

HANGAM, AN EIGHTEEN-YEAR-OLD Tajik *bacha posh*, joins us. Like Sahel, she has a bandana tied around her head. Hers is in a paisley pattern, and she is panting after having just left the floor. It was not her best game, she tells Nader, admitting to being distraught. She had backed into another car as she was trying to park outside. One of the taillights broke, and she worries that her father will be upset. The car is precious to him. Nader tries to calm her. Her father will be forgiving. With all the gossip the family has had to endure about Hangam's lingering male appearance, her father has still not succumbed to public pressure. He tells neighbors and others to "mind their own business" when they question how he runs his family. There have been many *bacha posh* in Hangam's family, going back generations. Most have eventually moved abroad, as those with money can do.

Her younger sister has a ponytail that sits high on her head. She does not wear a head scarf unless she goes outside. She chimes in about their father. "He offered me to become a *bacha posh,* too, but I said no."

When I met Hangam's father a few days earlier, he told me marriage has not entirely been ruled out for his daughter, if she is willing and remains in Afghanistan. He described her potential husband as "someone educated or liberal; enlightened." The husband must allow Hangam to wear men's clothing if she prefers it, and let her work outside the house, should she want to use the education her father has given her. For he would never allow his daughter to marry "a useless man," he told me.

Such a man might be hard to find in Kabul, but, he believes, not impossible. When he was young, the Russians taught him women should be part of society and not stashed behind closed doors. When he took his family to live in Iran during the Taliban years, he saw *bacha posh* of all ages in their neighborhood in Tehran. His interpretation was that Iranians are clever enough to realize that religious and cultural impositions can be ignored when a country is run by backward-striving people. And that a little resistance is sometimes a good thing. If Afghanistan deteriorates after foreign troops pull out and there is another civil war, he will attempt to return to Tehran. Worst case scenario, he will send Hangam abroad to live on her own. He has the means: He works at a prison, and influences who stays behind bars and who doesn't. And there are always those who pay good money to have their cases "revisited."

AFTER TAE KWON do practice ends, the girls plead for a group shot, lining up against the mirrored wall. They bicker about who gets to be next to Nader. The group of young men finally arrange themselves in a formation fanning out from Nader, who stands broad-legged with one hand in her jean pocket as the ringleader. They all angle their hips forward and pose with their chins down and lips pressed together. Puberty has so far not caused them much trouble—they followed Nader's instructions on how to pray for their chests not to develop. She has helped them stabilize deeper voices, too.

"Show me your best move," I ask of Sahel in the parking lot as we break for the night and are about to part ways.

Before I understand where she is going, she spins backward twice and gently kicks me in the lower back. The other girls whistle in appreciation and offer high fives all around.

"Be careful. She's just a girl," Hangam shouts.

THE SIX GIRLS—including Nader—do not know that their basement in Kabul is just one microcosm in something much bigger, that goes beyond the capital, and beyond Afghanistan.

In immigrant communities all over Europe and the United States, there are women from many other conservative cultures who have their own stories of growing up as boys, for reasons of survival or a desire for freedom. With time, and through dispatches from friends from India, Iran, and elsewhere around the Middle East, I slowly begin to realize that Nader's attempt at resistance can be found in many places where segregation exists and boys are preferred. And that it is a global phenomenon which remains mostly underground. That women in some places take the radical action of refusing their own gender, or change that of their daughters, is not very flattering to societies considering themselves to be somewhat evolved. Nor is it kindly viewed by male religious and political leaders.

But evidence of *bacha posh* variants in other countries is not hard to come by once the right questions are asked. Just across the border in Pakistan, Setareh can present one distant cousin after the other who live as young men, working or going to college. They, too, are *bacha posh,* or *alakaana* in Pashto, often designated as such from birth.

In Urdu-speaking areas of Pakistan and India, they are called *mahi munda,* or "boy-girl." In India, there is a longstanding Hindu tradition of *sadhin,* whereby girls take on the role of honorary men through renouncing their sexuality. Author Anees Jung observed many girls in short hair masquerading as boys detailed in her 2003 book *Beyond the Courtyard.* "It's normal around here," one of the women interviewed in the book explains.

In Egypt, famous deep-voiced balladeer Umm Kulthum began performing dressed as a boy at her father's insistence, to avoid the shame of having a daughter on stage. Middle East scholar and development expert Andrea B. Rugh observed multiple cases of women dressing as men for purposes of work and practicality in the country during her fieldwork in the 1980s.

In parts of Iraq, Kurdish girls have been described by locals just like Zahra: as something in between women and men.

In Cambodia and Myanmar, where sons are also preferred over daughters, who are sometimes sold into the global sex trade, aid organizations confirm that young girls have been known to take on male identities to avoid being drawn into criminal enterprise.

Certain countries even view the practice as so problematic, and apparently so widespread, that it requires intervention by law enforcement: In Iran, with its state-instituted religion, young women who are *pesar posh*—the equivalent to *bacha posh* in Farsi—have been arrested for posing as men in order to work, escape marriage, or just to attend football matches.

And in 2008, religious authorities in Malaysia issued a fatwa against girls with too-short hair who dress and act like boys, with the justification that they are violating Islam and potentially even encouraging same-sex relations.

The Gulf states have the most direct and intriguing parallel to the girls in Kabul: On the streets of Riyadh, in the shopping malls of Mecca, and throughout Kuwait, Bahrain, Oman, and the United Arab Emirates, where some of the world's strictest dress codes for women are enforced, teenage marriage refusers from traditional families call themselves *boyah,* wearing pants and shirts, refusing a head scarf and full-body coverage. They clandestinely drive cars and gather online to exchange images of androgynous fashion and short hairstyles, as well as tips for avoiding authorities. Across the Arabian Peninsula, the perceived threat of *boyah* and of young girls avoiding marriage is taken so seriously that doctors and psychologists blame the phenomenon on unfortunate influences from the West, sometimes dismissing it as a passing phase or a trend.

As in every event where women deviate from traditional gender roles, the economics of strict patriarchy are at stake, always of great concern to male authorities. In places where women are mostly barred from ownership, inheritance, and working outside the house, allowing women to resemble men is regarded as a great risk, since they may eventually begin to claim some of men's rights.

In Qatar, where there is little data on domestic violence, simply because no such crime officially exists according to authorities, and where women have few ways to divorce and keep custody of their children, the government encourages parents to send *boyat* daughters to a state-run "rehabilitation center" offering a program called "My Femininity Is a Gift from My Lord." There, psychologists are employed to diagnose and cure cases of teenage *boyat* girls. Their condition not only defies Islam, the government has proclaimed, but also poses a grave threat to the state itself, since birthrates may be undermined if girls delay or refuse marriage and becoming mothers. The refusal to marry also carries the suspicion of homosexuality, and the spread of that dangerous disease must be stemmed, since it is suspected of being highly contagious. That plague, of course, is said to stem from a degenerate, non-Muslim outside world. The re-education center advises mothers of *boyat* daughters not to complain about their own domestic duties or limited rights, and not to influence daughters to denounce the naturally female way of life and refuse their "biological constitution." Through the center's program, the girls' unwillingness to conform to the ideal of womanhood is promised to be remedied. Once isolated at the center, a girl will be taught to wear a hijab and trained in feminine tasks such as housework and caring for her husband.

THE *BACHA POSH* parallels throughout countries where women lack rights are neither Western nor Eastern, neither Islamic nor un-Islamic. It is a human phenomenon, and it exists throughout our history, in vastly different places, with different religions and in many languages. Posing as someone, or something, else is the story of many women and men who have experienced repression and made a bid for freedom.

It is the story of a gay U.S. Marine who had to pretend he was straight. It is the story of a Jewish family in Nazi Germany posing as Protestants. It is the story of a black South African who tried to make his skin lighter under apartheid. Disguising oneself as a member of the recognized and approved group is at the same time a subversive act of infiltration and a concession to an impossible racist, sexist, or otherwise segregating system.

This type of resistance, discreetly executed by girls and women and parents where gender segregation exists, often in isolation and sometimes in groups, is not only global; it may reach back to the formation of the patriarchal system itself. When the submission of women was codified through law and religion, when the only way to elevate a woman's existence came through marriage, and when the need for sons became absolute in every family, the first *bacha posh* likely soon began to infiltrate male territory.

Just as Zahra's grandmother was told when she was a child: *Bacha posh* existed in Afghanistan "when there were only bows and arrows."

CHAPTER EIGHTEEN
THE GODDESS

REMNANTS OF ONE particular old faith lie just under the surface of the Islamic Republic of Afghanistan.

In the 1970s, Louis Duprée wrote: "The Islam practiced in Afghan villages, nomad camps and most urban areas would be almost unrecognizable to a sophisticated Muslim scholar. Aside from faith in Allah and in Muhammad as the messenger of Allah, most beliefs relate to localized, pre-Muslim customs. Some of the ideals of Afghan tribal society run counter to literate Islamic principles."

That still holds true.

A teacher of religious law at Kabul University has reluctantly offered the first clue. The practice of *bacha posh* can be traced, he believes, at least to "the Sassanid time" in Afghanistan, and with that the belief that such a child will spur actual sons through "magic." It is common knowledge, according to the teacher. But he offers no books to prove it, nor further reference. While most countries have their share of folklore tales and myth, it would be both dangerous and potentially criminal to discuss the existence of influences other than Islam here.

During the Sassanid period, spanning the third to seventh centuries, Persians ruled Afghanistan under an empire stretching all the way to the Balkans. The dominant religion was Zoroastrianism.

Around 1,400 years before Jesus was born, and 2,000 years

before Muhammad, a man named Zoroaster is believed to have lived in Afghanistan. He was the founder and prophet of the faith, where water, fire, earth, and wind are holy elements and the universe is the subject of a constant struggle between good and evil. In Zoroastrianism, humans have the power to choose, and thereby side with either evil or good, through "good deeds, good thoughts, good actions." Zoroaster preached that every person should take responsibility for his or her own actions and not blindly follow the rules of society—a belief system that later came to inspire Friedrich Nietzsche and other philosophers. Zoroastrians were also astronomers and early to astrology, using it to predict cyclical events.

Once you know what to look for, remnants of Zoroastrian practices and beliefs are easily spotted in Afghan society today. A frequent sighting is the young boys (or girls made to look like them) on Kabul streets who offer protection from the evil eye. For a few coins, they rock a canister of burned seeds before passersby, in a ritual mimicking one performed by Zoroastrian temple attendants. Several elements of the traditional Afghan wedding ceremony follow Zoroastrian ritual, in particular the *khastegari* courting process of the bride's parents by the groom's family.

And each spring, Afghans throw a big party to welcome the season. The calendar's most exuberant holiday is the very un-Islamic but entirely Zoroastrian *Nowruz,* meaning "new day." It usually falls on March 21, the first day of spring and the first day of the Persian calendar's new year, when the cycle of life begins anew. The house is cleaned and the best food is brought out. Children receive new clothes. Flower-festooned flagpoles are raised, and bonfires are lit. Young men jump over smaller fires to purify body and mind. Conservative Islamic men in Afghanistan use harsh words for the festival, denouncing it as unacceptable and pagan.

In Zoroastrianism, marriage was an obligation, its main purpose being to produce sons to carry the family name or enter the priesthood, where only men were allowed. In a direct parallel to modern-day Afghan attempts to produce sons, "magic" was employed in various ways to make it happen. The very word that translates as "magic" can be traced to Zoroastrianism, where its priesthood, called *magi,* led rituals, coordinated the worship of fire, and handled all things magical.

In the Sassanid era, it was believed that during pregnancy, a woman could affect the sex of the fetus in her womb by performing certain rituals and relying on magic occurring through prayer, animal sacrifices, and visits to shrines. Appeals in shrines could for instance be directed to the Persian goddess Anahita; still a very popular name for girls in Afghanistan. She was seen as in charge of fertility and the protector of life-giving water, who can heal the wounded and seed women's wombs. By appealing to her, a woman could nudge conception in the right direction.

Today, Afghans pray for sons in mosques, but as Louis Duprée found already in his time, "almost any stone thrown in Afghanistan" will hit a shrine, or a *pir,* which is the Zoroastrian name for a place of worship. In the valley of Paiminar, just north of Kabul, he located at least forty shrines dedicated to fertility, where women come to pray and buy magical amulets guaranteeing sons, often constructing little symbolic beds of straw to remind the saint to help out in the marital bed.

To Sunni Muslims, saints are decidedly un-Islamic, since the prophet Muhammad explicitly forbade revering the tombs of humans. But shrines are still visited by current-day Afghans who come to pray there. Some shrines have been converted into mosques; others are places where followers of the Shia denomination of Islam—which took hold in Iran and later incorporated many Zoroastrian traditions—believe an important holy man is buried. At more modest shrines, the tale of who the buried saint may be—or if one existed at all—may be muddled. But all are still thought to fulfill wishes delivered in prayer, which are often said to revolve around having sons.

In Jalalabad, a shrine dedicated to fertility is well-known and recommended for sons. Many women also take the journey to the Blue Mosque in Mazar-i-Sharif to pray for sons. When a territory is conquered, whatever came before is often erased from history books, and its places of worship eradicated or repurposed. Officially, the Blue Mosque is said to hold the remains of one of the prophet Muhammad's relatives, but it also stands in the middle of what used to be the center for Zoroastrianism: Afghanistan's Balkh province, where Zoroaster is believed to have lived and died.

In Kabul, women can often name at least one or two shrines specializing in boosting fertility. They will offer informed reviews on which shrine produces the best results, based on the successes of sisters, daughters, and friends. The shrines can be ornate or dusty holes-in-the-wall, with male shrine keepers.

These places of worship usually charge a small fee, and some offer tips on specific prayers that may make a son arrive sooner. Fluttering green flags sprinkled across Kabul announce their shrines' locations: There is one on the road to the airport; another next to the Ministry of Communication and Information Technology. At the one by Kabul River, mostly poor women gather to pray and bring sacrifices in the form of sweet desserts for their wishes to be fulfilled. The Shrine of Hazrat Ali, a short drive from Kabul by Kharga Lake, is a popular excursion for newlyweds.

At the Pir Beland Shahib, near a hotel where mostly foreigners stay, seventy-eight irregular steps lead up to an open-air shrine surrounded by brick walls. There, young women and men respectfully enter after removing their shoes, first kissing the flagpole three times, then kissing several of the strips of fabric and scarves tied as wish ribbons throughout the shrines—all typical for a Zoroastrian place of worship. A silent prayer is said, eyes closed facing the sun, followed by the lighting of candles or making a small offering of money or foods.

Forty-year-old Fatima, who is pregnant with a child she has confirmed is a son, is triumphant as she leaves: For some things, shrines just work better than mosques, she explains to Setareh after she and I have raced each other up the steps one day.

Fatima is a Muslim; a devout one at that, she confirms. But she was taking no chances in her desperate need for a son. That could always use a little extra help from the gods.

ANOTHER ZOROASTRIAN TRADITION is to divide foods by the hot or cold effect they have on the body, and the belief that certain foods can heal disease if used and combined correctly. These classifications do not correlate to food that may be heated or spicy, but rather to the effect they are believed to have on a person's blood. It was also thought that the sex of an unborn child could be determined by eating certain types of food, to make a woman's blood more "hot" or "cold." Anthropologist Charles Lindholm recorded these same beliefs and food classification system in his research into Pashtun culture in the 1980s.

According to Professor Nahid Pirnazar, a lecturer of Iranian studies at the University of California in Los Angeles, chapter 16 of the *Avesta,* the Zoroastrian collection of sacred scripture, is a primer for how boys and girls are conceived, respectively.

It reads like a tutorial with Dr. Fareiba, detailing how elements of hot and cold in the body affect conception of either a male or a female child:

> The female seed is cold and moist, and its flow is from the loins, and the color is white, red, and yellow; and the male seed is hot and dry, its flow is from the brain of the head, and the color is white and mud-colored. All the seed of the females which issues beforehand, takes a place within the womb, and the seed of the males will remain above it, and will fill the space of the womb; whatever refrains therefrom becomes blood again, enters into the veins of the females, and at the time any one is born it becomes milk and nourishes him, as all milk arises from the seed of the males, and the blood is that of the females. These four things, they say, are male, and these female: the sky, metal, wind, and fire are male, and are never otherwise; the water, earth, plants, and fish are female, and are never otherwise; the remaining creation consists of male and female.

The belief in magic trickery for conceiving sons is also illustrated by the legend of the rainbow in Afghanistan. The rainbow, a favorite element in every mythology from the Norse to the Navajo people, often symbolizes wish fulfillment. In Afghanistan, finding a rainbow promises a very special reward: It holds magical powers to turn an unborn child into a boy when a pregnant woman walks under it. Afghan girls are also told that they can become boys by walking under a rainbow, and many little girls have tried. As a child, Setareh did it too, she confesses when I probe her on it. All her girlfriends tried to find the rainbow so they could become boys.

The name for the rainbow, *Kaman-e-Rostam,* is a reference to the mythical hero Rostam from the Persian epic *Shahnameh,* which tells the history of greater Persia from that time when Zoroastrianism was the dominant religion and Afghanistan was part of the empire. The Persian epic even has its own *bacha posh*: the warrior woman Gordafarid, an Amazon who disguises herself as a man to intervene in battle and defend her land. Interestingly, the same rainbow myth of gender-changing is told in parts of Eastern Europe, including Albania and Montenegro.

WITH EVERY NEW conqueror—Alexander, the Parthians, and the Sassanids—the Zoroastrian faith was tweaked and expanded upon in Afghanistan. At the height of its reach, the faith had around fifty million followers across the empires. Zoroastrianism and its practices took hold in many places beyond Afghanistan, including Pakistan, India, Iran, parts of Iraq and Turkey, Syria, Lebanon, Israel and Palestine, Jordan, Chechnya, Kuwait, Egypt, parts of Libya and Sudan, and the current-day -stans of the former Soviet Union. Parts of the Balkans—where the "sworn virgins" are found—were also influenced by the Sassanid Empire, with Zoroastrianism as its dominant religion.

As Arabs, Mongols, and Turks arrived and introduced Islam, Zoroastrians were tolerated at first, but eventually temples were burned, priests were killed, and the defeated were forced to convert to Islam. Today, Zoroastrianism officially only has a few thousand followers in the United States, Canada, England, and the Gulf nations. The official number of Zoroastrians in Afghanistan today is zero.

But it is more than coincidental that old myths and remnants of another religion appear in several different places on earth with both a history and some present-day occurrences of girls living as boys. Louis Duprée named the architectural site Surkh Kotal, where a gigantic Zoroastrian fire temple has been excavated in the Afghan province of Balkh, a meeting point between East and West. Greek script has been found on limestone blocks there, indicating Zoroastrian rituals may have spread in both directions from Afghanistan. It also shows how Zoroastrianism has parallels to other prehistoric faiths and cultures, including Norse mythology from the Middle Ages, which also happens to be riddled with women taking the roles of men.

Sweden's Viktor Rydberg, a scholar of comparative mythology, suggested that Zoroastrianism and Old Norse beliefs might have a common Indo-European origin. Zoroastrian scholar Mary Boyce also noted that the earliest recorded prayers of Zoroaster's match Norse religious practices, pointing to an ancient connection between the two worlds.

To those who want to exert absolute control through religion, remnants of other faiths were always a problem, and shreds of Zoroastrianism are a provocation. Religious leaders in Iran, for instance, attempted to abolish Nowruz, but reconsidered when Iranians mounted too much of a protest.

More than just dress codes were enforced by the Taliban's Ministry for the Promotion of Virtue and the Prevention of Vice; they worked hard to destroy ancient Zoroastrian and other archaeological sites in Afghanistan during their rule and banned "sorcery," to make sure no "magic" was employed. Visiting shrines was not permitted, and the Nowruz holiday was abolished. As soon as the Taliban was driven from power, Nowruz was celebrated again.

A certain yearly gathering at the UN General Assembly in New

York also provides a snapshot of how difficult it is to kill an ancient faith and its traditional practices. Particularly, perhaps, when they contain creative elements for how to cope in hardline patriarchal societies.

At the United Nations, ambassadors of countries divided by languages, cultures, wars, religions, and even nuclear threats, stand side by side, taking part in the Nowruz celebration stemming from when they were all part of a Persian Empire. At the event, the UN ambassadors of Afghanistan, Azerbaijan, India, Iran, Iraq, Kazakhstan, Kyrgyzstan, Pakistan, Tajikistan, Turkey, Turkmenistan, and Uzbekistan line up on stage at the headquarters in New York. All wear their best spring outfits, recognizing for a brief moment that they at one time had something in common.

And still do, since girls continue to be born in many places where they are not always welcomed.

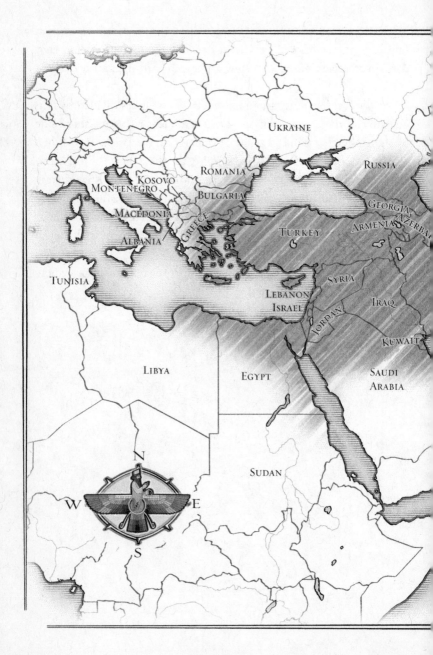

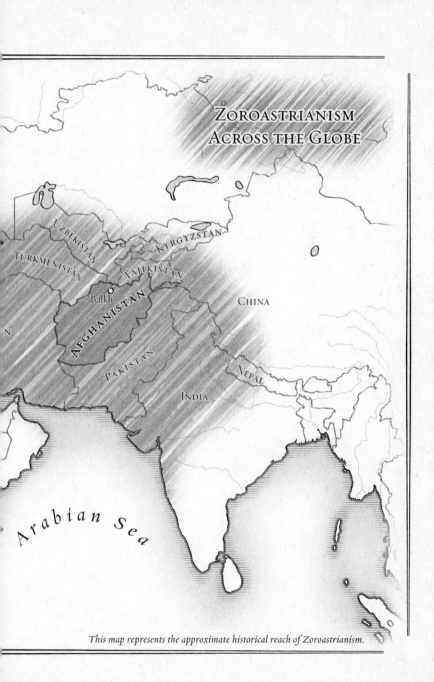

ZOROASTRIANISM ACROSS THE GLOBE

UZBEKISTAN

TURKMENISTAN

KYRGYZSTAN

TAJIKISTAN

Balkh

AFGHANISTAN

CHINA

N

PAKISTAN

NEPAL

INDIA

Arabian Sea

This map represents the approximate historical reach of Zoroastrianism.

PART FOUR
FATHERS

You can if you want to.

—A FATHER TO HIS DAUGHTER
ON A SKI SLOPE IN 1980S SWEDEN

Adam Ferguson

MEHRAN IN BADGHIS

CHAPTER NINETEEN
THE DEFEATED

Azita

*S*he eats.

When she is told a number of ballot boxes from her province are invalid, she eats. When the landlord of the family's apartment gives her a week's notice to move out and find somewhere else to live, she eats. When her husband announces that his first wife and daughter are to come and live with them again in Kabul—and that his decision is final—she eats.

Azita rips through the soft naan bread, she reaches for the rest of Mehran's cookies, she scrapes spoonfuls of rice from pots before doing the dishes.

It's embarrassing, and she cannot stop.

For a woman to become fat, in Afghanistan too, is seen as a sign of weak character; of someone who is no longer in control. But there is no other drug available, and it's not like she can choose to fall apart now. She tries to quell the anxiety as best she can and she overdoses on what is closest and most accessible to her. She eats furiously and she eats mindlessly; she stops only when she is full to the point of feeling ill, allowing nausea to trump worry for a few moments, when blood has left the brain and heads for the stomach, when the sugar spews into every vein and dims the mind.

Azita is no longer the lawmaker for whom people rise to their feet when she walks into a room. In the spring of 2011, almost a year after her failed reelection bid, she is without a salary, invitations from foreign dignitaries, or invitations to attend events abroad. There is not even a gun allowance. She never found the gun they gave her, but it does not matter now. Most of the diplomats and the international organizations have forgotten she even existed.

To them, Azita is not even marginally important anymore.

AT FIRST SHE won. Or at least she thought she had won.

The campaign had sucked the marrow right out of her, with the relentless Ramadan campaigning through desert lands of Badghis wearing a full-length chador and having an empty stomach between dawn and dusk, distributing her tapes and making speeches. Just as in other provinces, Taliban-affiliated groups had managed to retake some districts, which then became off-limits to her. Still, she spent three months knocking on doors, making her pitch to villagers, and feeding hundreds of prospective voters who showed up at her house in Badghis every day for a meal and to get a look at her.

Some of the competition had offered gifts, too, for supporters to show up at rallies, such as clothing, gas for motorbikes, or cash labeled "travel support." Azita wished she could have afforded to give more, but she had only the tapes and her stern-looking posters.

After election day, in one of the primary election counts, she collected the most votes to again secure a seat in the "people's house." The count seemed certain, so victory was declared. She felt excitement paired with relief at the notion of returning to Kabul for a second term. She threw a large party in Badghis, basking in the glow from her proud parents and relatives. But a week later, in a very Afghan twist of politics, at a secondary election count declared even more valid than the first, Azita had suddenly and mysteriously fallen behind. As it turned out, the elections were riddled with fraud, and around the country nearly a fourth of the ballots cast were eventually declared invalid without much examination.

The victory declared then retracted left Azita feeling embarrassed at first. Then she felt numb. She had given the campaign her all; she had no plan B. Her job and her position were her identity, her self-respect, her emotional stability, and her income. It had made possible a somewhat functioning relationship with her husband. And it had promised her daughters a future. She did not know under what guise to step out next. Or if she could reinvent herself. The small expressions of respect her position had afforded her, being greeted by men and sometimes called by her name; these were privileges that would be no more.

Ashamed, she stayed inside the house in Badghis.

When she reluctantly turned her cell phone back on, messages had piled up from supporters, urging her not to throw in the towel. "Everyone" knew there had been foul play, they said. And they knew her not as a quitter who would buckle under corrupt Afghan politics but as a leader who stood for something—was that not exactly what she had told her constituents so many times over? They had gone to the polls for her and would not accept her just folding in the face of some blanket wipeout of votes due to the alleged fraud of others. Of course she had been cheated of her seat; more of the clean votes belonged to her. Unlike many of the others, she had not even been accused of fraud herself. Or did she in fact mean to tell her supporters that their votes were now suddenly worth nothing?

Slowly, Azita came around.

"It's the right of the people who voted for me to see me fight for this. It's a competition, and I won fairly," she told herself.

The image of her daughters back in a Badghis mud house also filled her with determination. They were Kabul girls now, who could make something of their lives. She would not do to them what was once done to her: Invite them to a better life and then exile them back to a province with little prospect of a decent education or a chance to escape an early marriage to a villager. Besides, Azita thought, she had run a clean campaign, so how hard could it be to prove that those additional votes were rightfully hers?

Together with hundreds of other candidates who disputed the election results, she decided to go into battle.

In all, a third of the country's original candidates became embroiled in a heated national conflict, either as contested winners or as runners-up, claiming more votes should be counted toward their own results, or fewer to that of others' results. In the meantime, Afghanistan was left with a frozen, inactive parliament and a crisis for the fragile, untested democracy.

At first, through chaotic official hearings and in the backroom negotiations Azita attended, she was told her chances of a favorable recount were good. They would increase, however, if she paid a fee of $60,000 to certain officials who handled the process. That could even reinstate her without any further queries, she learned. Several colleagues confirmed to her it was indeed the going rate; some even advised her to consider it. It was a small fee to pay to get her job back, suggested one of the officials when she argued that her higher vote count was indeed valid to begin with. She would soon make that kind of money—and more—in her salaried position of power, and by charging those who wanted to pay for the right decisions a little on the side.

"If I even had that money I would give it to the widows," Azita shot back at him before storming out of his office.

At another visit with an official, he suggested she could sign a debt letter toward future income or assets. Several others had done just that, she was told. Surely she, or perhaps her father, had some land that she could put up as collateral? When Azita declined, she was called "a very silly woman." After that, several officials advised her to "just forget about it." Without an "investment" and some good faith money, she was informed it would be difficult to enter parliament again.

Spurred on by the resistance from officials searching to enrich themselves in the political turmoil, Azita put even more energy into tracing her votes and trying to prove their legitimacy. That promise of a new country that had appeared on the horizon when the Taliban first left still resonated deeply with her a decade later. She had not already spent five years in parliament just to sidestep the courts and the official justice system. And regardless of any respect for democracy, she simply did not have the money either.

But now, she was without an income and an office. With little savings, keeping the family afloat in Kabul was becoming harder by the week. Eventually her husband weighed in: This struggle to get back into parliament did not seem to be very fruitful, and it was taking too long. It was time to let go, he argued. They should move back to Badghis, or at least to Herat, where they could live like a normal family again.

It was unthinkable for Azita, who despite her setbacks had grown absolutely certain she should be reinstated as a Badghis representative to Kabul.

Again, she turned to her father and asked him to broker an agreement with her husband; she needed another few months to battle the election commission. Her husband agreed to extend their stay in Kabul, to await the final decision from officials on the makeup of parliament. In return, Azita said she would get a temporary job to support the family while she saw the legal process through.

She would continue, however, to spend almost every day immersed in meetings with election officials, carrying her ragged paper dossier between the ministries, courts, and informal gatherings with colleagues, while telling her family and friends "I am my own lawyer. But I have my supporters. The first is Allah. The second is my people."

FINDING A JOB also proved harder than she had thought. It had become an issue of appearance. A public, high-paying job would potentially make people think she had given up on reentering parliament. A low-paying job would make her seem like a definite loser, which would not work to her advantage in her legal skirmishes either. Regardless, most of her energy went into the legal struggle, and it was not as though anyone were clamoring for her to work for them, either.

As the first months of 2011 went by, her savings ran out. She began to take small loans where she could—from her father, her brother, and from a few friends in politics. She made them promise not to talk about it with others.

The last of her saved money had gone to resettling the family in Golden City, a Pashtun-dominated development at the outskirts of Kabul. The Dubai-inspired houses rose up during Kabul's development mania that followed a massive influx of money in the past decade. At first the buildings had been painted a luxuriously golden yellow that blazed toward the main road leading into the neighborhood. But a few years of desert winds soon sandpapered them into a more matte exterior and now paint was chipping away from the hallways inside.

Golden City has no playground and no football field. There are no trees, or even a patch of green anywhere to be seen. Not that there is a need, either: Children of the mostly conservative Pashtun families who live here are not allowed outside to play much. Azita's husband has decided that their children—including Mehran—must stay inside after school. It's not safe to go out anymore, even for an hour here and there. The children do not have many friends in the new place either, and they left their old ones behind in Macroyan.

Now, every day except Friday consists of the same routine for them: School starts at 7 a.m.; return by midday to do homework, napping, dinner, and then bed. Any play takes place on the apartment's small balcony, but mostly, the children just watch cable television or pirated DVDs, from which the twins can quote most lines by now. Fights flare up more often during the hot summer months, when they circle one another like caged animals in and out of the apartment's small rooms.

But Azita tries to be upbeat and is eager to show off everything that is new when I meet her in the new apartment for the first time, after she has spent months in Badghis and I have been out of the country.

There are wall-to-wall Oriental carpets and thick yellow curtains in every room. There's a dishwasher, an electric oven, and a microwave in the kitchen. A pink porcelain bathroom. Not one but two television sets in the living room. The two wives each have a bedroom. As before, the children share a bedroom. Azita has installed a modern weight-training machine in the children's room. She is planning to lose the weight soon.

A few more of her French-manicured fingers now glimmer with Saudi gold. Her wrists are wrapped in twisted yellow bands, and heavy pearl earrings weigh down her earlobes. That, too, is from the borrowed money. The added bling and the apartment are a careful investment effort, she explains. Around Kabul, appearance is everything, and no one will trust someone who looks like she is on the way out. Visitors still come to their home, and they need to be assured she is still a player. She needs to come off as worldly and sophisticated and confident; as someone who has a rightful place in the national parliament. And, in truth, buying things helps stave off anxiety, she has discovered.

She shrugs when I ask how it can be sustainable without a salary. It's not. Money will need to come from somewhere. Soon.

Ironically, among those who seem not to have fully noticed her setbacks are the threat mongers. They want to make sure she does *not* return to politics. The anonymous calls keep coming, with the message that she needs to stop insisting she should be in parliament. She should behave like a normal woman before God, the callers propose, by staying home. That is, however, not Azita's idea of what God wants for women, and it's not what she wants for herself, either. But the confidence she built while she was in power is harder to challenge now, and only moderately helped by her gold-plated appearance: "Now I take taxis and people do not even greet me anymore," she admits as we sit on pillows, having tea on her bedroom floor. "I feel worthless. I moralize myself up, and then I get down. I get negative ideas in my head that I can't get rid of. I can't focus."

She begins to rise from the floor, to go and change into the all-black clothing for a meeting at the Ministry of Defense. But the four cell phones on the floor between us come alive at the same time. My text message is in all caps:

"ALERT: 1215H EXPLOSION NEAR MOD. AVOID THE AREA."

As soon as a major blast goes off anywhere in Kabul, text messages ripple through the cellular networks, as anyone with a phone tries to ensure the safety of their friends, relatives, and colleagues. With one phone in each hand, Azita and I both perform the same routine, confirming back to each sender that we are nowhere near the Ministry of Defense, which is now under attack. More detailed messages filter in and we take turns filling each other in: A suicide bomber entered the ministry by disguising himself as an Afghan army officer in uniform. Once inside, he shot his way up toward his third-floor target—the minister's office. He then blew himself up in such a way as to maim and kill as many as possible around him. The minister himself appears to have survived, but the total number of fatalities is yet unknown.

After a few minutes of texting, we put our phones down. Azita's second meeting of the day is canceled. She does not mention her close call. It is one of many that have come before. We both know it means neither of us will be going anywhere before roadblocks are cleared. It also means we have more time for tea.

Azita looks down, quietly picking at a piece of cake. It is the bloodiest year yet of the war: American troop losses will reach new highs, and the war will claim the most civilians since counting of them began. In the capital, suicide blasts, kidnappings for ransom, and targeted killings are a regular occurrence.

"This is Kabul now," she says.

AROUND THIS TIME, the military and diplomatic corps in Kabul still officially upheld a rather optimistic view of developments in Afghanistan. But in private, by 2011, many had already lost much of their initial enthusiasm for whether the war could be "won," or how Afghanistan would reach some semblance of peace.

President Obama's two-year "surge" of thirty thousand additional troops meant to quash the insurgency, quickly followed by the announcement of a withdrawal by 2014, had ultimately not prevented various Islamic militants, warlords, criminal networks, and Taliban-affiliated groups from boldly expanding in several provinces. Expensive American efforts to train and equip Afghan government troops to defend their own country still did not prevent the Taliban from successfully widening their territory by aligning with locals and criminal networks, fueled by the ever-expanding opium trade.

And inside the armor-clad and tank-protected enclave of the capital, suicide bombers found new ways to infiltrate and induce terror, at times blasting themselves in pairs, followed by fighters who could hold out for hours, occupying buildings and shutting down entire areas of the city. Rockets were regularly launched at government buildings and even reached as far as the well-protected U.S. Embassy.

Those who could afford protection responded by erecting ever higher walls around themselves.

The pace at which the remaining low-key, elegant 1950s Kabul villas were turning into indistinguishable cement-gray fortresses seemed to increase exponentially for every month with the waning interest of the Western world. One row of sandbags for blast protection became two; those who once employed two guards hired four; and a thick steel door was the new standard. More small huts with security guards for body searches popped up outside houses and hotels, and every tree seemed to be ensnarled in razor wire, preventing both humans and stray cats from getting onto the high walls.

But officially ending America's longest war, with a price tag of upward of $700 billion and counting to American taxpayers, and with its many changing narratives—from "rooting out" terrorism to just fighting the Taliban in general—had become a political necessity back in the United States.

Fear of what would come next was all over Kabul. Those speaking for the foreign military dropped the word "victory" in favor of the more ambiguous "exit," with the silent understanding that battles would most likely continue to rage in some form, ranging from a complete descent into civil war or a full-fledged, lawless narco state, to warlords dividing up provinces through regional battles. The

United States and its allies, however, could no longer afford to be much involved.

What Sherard Cowper-Coles, British ambassador to Afghanistan from 2007 to 2009, writes in his memoir echoes Russian accounts of their journey into the harsh and mountainous country that refused to be conquered or controlled:

> This time it was the United States leading the war in Afghanistan without a clear idea either of what it was getting into or of how it was getting out. Without realizing it, we have become involved in a multi-player, multi-dimensional, multi-decade civil conflict, the origins of which go back many years. It is an unresolved struggle over the nature of Afghan policy, between Islam and secularism, tradition and modernism, town and country, Sunni and Shia, farmer and nomad, Pashtun and Tajik, Uzbek and Hazara.

With the war's downward spiral on everyone's mind in Kabul, finding a viable "exit strategy" was no longer only on the minds of military and foreign policy scholars. Afghans had heard this story before, when six million of them fled the Afghan-Soviet war in the 1980s. After the fall of the Taliban in 2001, many returned from Pakistan and Iran only to find themselves plotting yet another departure a decade later, with those with means hiring smugglers to take them to Europe or Canada.

However, for the foreigners "to leave with some sense of honor intact" and a semblance of at least a "dirty peace," in the words of a European diplomat, some kind of agreement would ideally be brokered with the militant opposition; a stark change of tune from refusing to speak to the Taliban a decade earlier. Paving the way for "peace talks" with the Taliban became a favorite new diplomatic term in Kabul, and already in 2011, "soft" issues, such as the rights of women, had been taken off any high-level agenda, according to several diplomats. That any political deal with extremists would sacrifice every shred of women's rights achieved in the past decade was largely ignored by all but human rights organizations.

As Setareh reached a spokesperson for the Taliban in Kunar province with a burner phone procured especially for the occasion, he confirmed that once—as he fully expects to happen—the Taliban regains more power in Afghanistan when most American and allied forces withdraw, *bacha posh* will immediately be banned, as those who attempt to change their gender wrongly "touch on God's creation." The spokesperson also informed Setareh that women will be removed from all universities, courts, the parliament, and provincial councils, because "God does not want women in any of those places."

ON MOST SPRING Fridays, Babur Gardens in Kabul, which overlook the dust cloud that hovers over the city's downtown, is a picnic destination for families who decide to risk bringing their children outside for a few hours. Teenage boys balance on the stone terracing and climb onto clusters of low trees in high midday sun. Women stay strictly covered and close to their husbands. Teenage girls are rarely seen. Not much actual picnicking takes place on the brown lawns, but a lone ice cream man does good business by offering cones from a battered box held by a strap around his neck. In the afternoons, the park becomes almost pretty as the low sun begins to set. A man on the grass plays a flute and the dust whirls have stilled.

But Azita both looks and feels a bit out of place in her gold-adorned sunglasses and swaths of black fabric, with the pointy heels just visible underneath. She never went to public places like these as a parliamentarian; now, as a regular person and one among many, she is uneasy. She fears someone will recognize her and think she doesn't belong there—that she should confine her children to the family's own private garden, as a richer, more proper woman might do. It's not entirely appropriate for her to be in a crowd like this, within sight of so many other men, though she is in the company of her own husband. More than anything, Azita is hoping she will not run into a friend or a colleague from parliament. It would be best if no one recognized her at all. They may start to ask questions about her family and want an introduction to her husband and his first wife. It would embarrass her, that she—the former parliamentarian—has a polygynous family where she is the second wife.

Azita sits down in a stone alcove while her four girls make a bid for the nearest tree. Mehran, in pants and a shirt, yells in triumph as she hangs upside down from a branch. Twins Beheshta and Benafsha smirk and turn to each other, saying something to the effect of "Enjoy it while you can" to their youngest sister. No one cares that Mehran's untucked shirt falls over her head, exposing her belly as she waves to onlookers.

Now seven, she is still served first in the family, and she still demands to be listened to at all times. Those who surround her encourage her to be smart and strong and loud. The twins don't even attempt to climb the tree; they wouldn't want to get dirty. Middle sister Mehrangis announces that she would actually like to try it, only to be rebuffed by her older sisters. She is too clumsy and chubby, they tell her. She would likely fall and injure herself.

Between the money troubles and the political struggle, Mehran's gender is the least of Azita's concerns right now.

But how does Mehran make a difference as a boy anymore, when Azita is no longer a parliamentarian and the children rarely go out anyway? "Why would I make my daughter into a son if this society was working?" she snaps back at my question. "Nothing has changed, and nothing will change. It's only going in the wrong direction here."

I still don't understand. There used to be a specific purpose to Mehran being a boy?

Azita closes her eyes briefly, in a rare plea for questions to stop. The family's life has changed in many ways since the year before, but now is not a good time to talk about it.

A fifth girl, her dark hair in a ponytail, cautiously watches Mehran in the tree, placing herself a few steps behind the twins. She is their half sister, who moved into their new apartment in Kabul along with her mother a few months ago. At thirteen, she is the oldest child in the family, but next to the twins, who always present as a team and always seem to have something to say, she can rarely find the words. She has been taught not to be loud or move about very much—it's not what girls do.

Her mother carefully sits down on the stone alcove next to Azita. In a white cotton head scarf, she is absolutely still, looking down at her hands. Her bulky jacket and full-length pale blue skirt are typical of how village women dress, and offer a stark contrast to Azita's all-black and gold-ornamented sunglasses.

"Would you like us to pose for a picture together?" Azita asks me.

She moves closer and puts her arm around the other woman, who immediately turns her head away. Where she is from, women are not supposed to have their picture taken. It's awkward, but Azita insists: They are in the capital now—it's different here and they must all adjust. Azita flashes her professional smile, while the woman next to her reluctantly lifts her head just enough to show her eyes under the head scarf.

Their mutual husband is in a good mood, sending Mehran off with ice cream money after only a minimum of begging. He says he feels good. He is a normal husband now, out with his two wives and their children. Actually, it's both a relief and a disappointment that Azita no longer has her seat in parliament. But mostly a relief: It was a long and excruciating campaign, and he was always ambivalent about the prospect of living another five years as the husband of a politician. It also embarrassed him a great deal that they first announced victory and then had to pull back. He certainly doesn't mind the new, bigger apartment, and he knows Azita wants to get back into parliament, but in his view, life is still better this way. He has fewer responsibilities now than when she was in power. Back then, he had to work with her and greet guests or escort constituents who had come traveling. It was exhausting, and sometimes he had to lie down in the afternoons. Most important, for the five years Azita was in parliament, he could not shake the guilt of living in Kabul while his first wife was still in the village.

That situation has been rectified now, to everyone's benefit, he says. He is pleased with his decision: Before, he was too busy, shuttling between them in different provinces. Now the women can share responsibility for the household, making it easier on everyone. And with an uncertain outlook for the country beyond 2014, it is probably for the best that Azita is not in parliament anymore. Her being a politician always posed additional risks for the children. For now, he has agreed to stay in Kabul for a few more months, but he is looking forward to a quieter life in Badghis soon. It will be better for the children, too, not having a mother who is constantly questioned and recognized. As a stay-at-home wife and mother, Azita will be more of a role model to them as they look forward to their own future marriages.

AFGHAN FRIED CHICKEN has only one Kabul branch, and the chipped sign advertises its menu as "Clean, Healthy and Tasty." Azita's daughters have all been there before, on a few special occasions. The four of them almost fall over one another as they jubilantly skip-step into the restaurant, followed by their older half sister, who walks behind them.

The older girls are too tall and too big to fit comfortably inside the main attraction—a plastic play area with a yellow slide and a house to hide in—but they all squeeze in there anyway. Mehran goes on the mechanical rodeo horse three times in a row, with coins from her father's pocket. For her sisters, straddling the toy animal is not an option. Two other families are in the restaurant this evening. They might disapprove, or be offended.

Azita quickly orders for the table. She gets the fried chicken for herself, and the chicken burger special with fries for the children, her husband, and his first wife. This is an expensive restaurant for Kabul—fast food is a Western-style luxury. But Azita has decided to splurge, since the children so rarely leave the house these days. She first took them here to celebrate their move to Kabul and her new position. Her husband sits at one end of the long table, and the wives on the other, with the children's empty seats between them. There is no conversation.

When a burger on a paper plate lands in front of her, the village wife silently looks at it for several seconds, hands still in her lap. Then she removes the bun on top and looks at the piece of fried meat inside. She puts the bun back. As the children are called back to the table, she does not move again until Beheshta has poured ketchup all over her burger. Only after Beheshta's first bite into her burger does her stepmother pick up hers and mimic the move. She chews a small bite carefully and puts the burger down again.

Azita's husband exclaims his confusion out loud. Why is there no bread on the side? There should be bread with every meal, regardless of any burger buns. The restaurant must have made a mistake. He calls on the waiter and complains.

Azita looks down. "It's not easy for him," she mumbles. His daughters can all read and write now, on different levels. Their father has made clear his intention not to learn. Why should he, when Azita makes all the decisions anyway, he has joked.

His first wife hushes the children. She never asked to be brought from the village to the capital, nor does she feel particularly at ease here. After living together and then splitting up the household due to too many conflicts, the two wives had developed a courteous but distant relationship. It worked when they occasionally saw each other in Badghis, when Azita was there campaigning or visiting her parents.

Now it's different.

The first wife never commented much on Azita's children before, but here in Kabul, she has begun to voice her concerns about how frivolous the family has become, adopting strange customs and behaviors. In her view—and she has let it be known—Azita's daughters have become spoiled and inappropriately spirited. They speak back to their parents, are reluctant to help out at home, and in general seem to take too much for granted, she has explained.

The first wife, who is also illiterate, has made it clear to Azita that she will not allow her daughter to be influenced by any such Kabul behavior, which in addition to fantasies of higher studies includes dancing in the living room and watching American movies. She has also noted that Mehran seemed to have her father's ear, more so than the other girls. It has come to bother her quite a bit. There is no reason to extend extra privileges to his youngest, she has told her husband. After all, she is only a girl. But he brushed off her concerns about Mehran's behavior. After that lack of response, the first wife told Mehran to wear a head scarf to school—a demand Mehran completely ignored. The blatant disobedience triggered her stepmother even more. She began to taunt Mehran, to imprint the truth in her: "You are not a real boy—you know that, right? You will never be a real boy."

It works well, as it takes Azita almost a half hour to talk Mehran out of each meltdown that follows.

Just a week earlier, the first wife lectured Mehran about how she should never think she is any closer to her father than the other children, nor that there was a special bond between them. Mehran responded by throwing another fit and yelling at her stepmother. When Azita came in, intending to plead with her husband's first wife to stop, she instead lost her patience with Mehran, who furiously screamed back. Azita slapped her across the face to make her stop.

It was the first time she had hit her daughter.

"You must never speak to your other mother like that again!" she yelled at her daughter. Mehran went silent immediately. Azita froze as she watched the surprised look on her daughter's face and the tears that ensued. The red marks on Mehran's cheek faded, but she did not speak much until the next day.

Azita pleaded with her husband's first wife to recognize that the *bacha posh* arrangement is to their joint advantage. It helps control the pressure to bring another child into the family. Or a third wife. But that argument gains no traction with the first wife, who has firmly argued that Mehran must look, behave, and be treated like the girl she is. Until Azita understands this, it is necessary to remind Mehran that she is indeed a girl—and an ugly one at that—if she misbehaves.

Underneath these forced but polite conversations between the two wives, they both know exactly what is at stake: If Mehran is stripped of her role as a son, it will also remove Azita's fragile status as a somewhat more important wife. There is a traditional ranking order between multiple wives married to one husband, where the first-married holds a higher status and more clout in the family. But that is, in turn, calibrated by who produces the most sons. Mehran is all that stands between Azita as she lives now and potentially reverting to the traditionally lower status of second wife. Making an already complicated childhood even more difficult, Mehran thus holds some of the power balance between her mother and her stepmother.

The first wife has also taken to reminding her husband that his youngest daughter needs to be cultivated into decent marriage material. If nothing else, her current loud and talkative manner will grow into a problem later on. She is already hard to control. He should not let it escalate, she keeps reminding him. "She's a girl, and you have to treat her as one."

Azita's husband has not taken kindly to the brewing conflict centered around his oldest wife and his youngest child, demanding of both wives that they get along and make the children behave. He has even snapped at Mehran a few times himself—something he did not use to do. It should be a happy time for all of them, he insists, now that they are all together again.

After the meal is finished at Afghan Fried Chicken, Azita pays the bill. She wants to leave in order to catch her Turkish television series: In the previous episode, a young woman was being threatened with an arranged marriage, and Azita is curious to see how the drama will evolve. She hurries her husband and the children out through a side door where the four-wheel drive is parked. They had to get a new car to fit the family of eight.

Tonight, Mehran still rides in the front seat.

CHAPTER TWENTY

THE CASTOFF

Shukria

ALL SHE HAD done to become a woman was rendered meaningless in less than thirty seconds. Her sister had been blunt on the phone, repeating what she had just been told by Shukria's husband: "I have another wife, and a baby." Reluctant to break the news directly, he then asked Shukria's sister to pass the message along.

Shukria, who had just come home from a shift at the hospital, was exhausted, and at first thought that she wasn't thinking clearly when she got her sister on the line. But after they hung up, Shukria asked herself how long she had *really* known. A feeling that something was off had certainly been there for a while. And now she looked the fool, for not admitting it to herself and for denying it to others.

She stares into the air at the expensive Lebanese restaurant I have chosen. Or so it looks. Her small, gray-tinted eyeglasses effectively hide her eyes.

Almost two years have passed since we first met at the hospital. She has arrived an hour late today, giving Setareh and me plenty of time to order half the menu, trying to envision what may appeal to Shukria. We had imagined it would be a small celebration—mostly just for being somewhere other than at our usual dark and suffocating meeting place. Now we sit with an ill-suited buffet of grilled chicken, hummus, chopped salads, and melting ice cream on the table between us. Shukria will not eat, and Setareh politely does not touch the food, either.

Of all the intimate details Shukria has shared in the time we have known each other, she has avoided speaking much about her husband. Almost always in passing, she has only mentioned him in a neutral, respectful tone, unwilling to offer up much about their marriage.

Until now.

The first visit her husband took to Tajikistan a few years ago had been a short trip. He had asked Shukria for her saved money to invest in a new business there. There were no opportunities for him in Kabul anymore. The investment optimism of the war's early years had vanished. The construction business was no good anymore; one new development after the other was scrapped or abandoned only half-finished. It seemed foreigners with money wanted out, and most Afghans with money preferred to invest abroad. But Tajikistan next door was ripe for investment, he had heard. It could make them rich, he told Shukria.

She was not convinced but did not want to seem too negative. So she gave him the money. For his second trip, he asked for more, and that time, he was gone longer.

In the next six months, he came home only twice. He had developed a fruit-and-vegetable business in Tajikistan and said that it needed his constant attention. He had a car with a "road pass" allowing him to cross the border, buying his produce on the Afghan side and then selling it in a Tajik border town. He seemed cheerful; things were going well. Shukria need not worry, he assured her. He had taken some other loans, too, in Kabul. It would be up to Shukria to pay the debtors when they came knocking. But surely she understood that they were in this together, and that she needed to contribute her share for his hard work abroad? Shukria swallowed any protest, wanting his good mood to remain. How she would find the money to pay off his debts was a problem for later.

At another homecoming, he mentioned a woman during dinner.

Relating a string of casual anecdotes about his travels, he told her about a particularly silly woman he had run into in Tajikistan. She had fallen in love with him, and said she wanted to marry him. Shukria had not been entertained: "If you want to marry someone else and forget about your wife and three young children, I think you should go ahead," she told her husband.

He laughed at her—she could never take a joke, it seemed. He was not that kind of man. It was just another story. Women so easily got hung up on crazy ideas; that was all. Shukria remembers shooting her husband a weak smile: Yes, how silly women can be, she agreed.

He did not come to her bed that night. Instead, he abruptly said he needed to go visit some relatives. He would stay with them overnight. When he returned the next day, as she was cleaning up after breakfast, he just said it.

"*Talaq. Talaq. Talaq.*"

Then he said it three times again, and left without another word. Shukria heard him perfectly the first time, but she did not understand exactly what it meant until later, when she looked it up. By uttering *talaq*—literally meaning the untying of a knot—her husband was divorcing her. Saying it three times made it final.

Still, she did not understand. It made little sense. *Why* would he want to divorce her? It was impossible to take in. Instead, Shukria went about her day, first going to the bazaar for the shopping she had already planned. She cooked dinner and helped the children with their homework. She told no one about her husband's strange behavior earlier in the day. If she stayed silent, it might never have happened.

Shukria worked her way through the next ten months in that same state of denial. Occasionally, her husband showed up on a visit from Tajikistan, but they did not discuss the divorce. And she tried not to think about it. Until her sister called the other night.

"You must listen now," she demanded of Shukria during the call, speaking each word in an exaggeratedly slow fashion. "I will not allow you to suffer anymore. You have to think of your life and your children."

Besides, the entire family already knew, so she could stop pretending, the sister said. They even knew of the new baby. "You need to live in reality," the sister said.

Shukria's husband had left her, and it was time to accept it. And it struck her for the first time then: She had not only failed as a wife. She had failed at being a woman.

IF AN AFGHAN woman wants to divorce her husband, she needs his explicit agreement. She may also need to produce witnesses to testify that a divorce from her husband is warranted.

A man can divorce for any reason, or for no reason at all. Uttering the same word three times undoes a marriage for a man. It is often left at that.

But in those cases, the woman left behind has hardly been liberated. Unless a marriage is dissolved by a court or a gathering of elders, in the eyes of society a dismissed woman is still married, only with an absent husband. This is the Kafkaesque situation of Shukria: All power over her life still belongs to an absent person, under the law. If she were to attempt to move, travel, or sign anything on behalf of herself or her children, anyone could request the additional and explicit approval of her husband, as he remains the head of her household and her affairs.

Like most women, Shukria wed her husband at home, surrounded by family, in a ceremony conducted by a local mullah. Their marriage, as most Afghan marriages, was not registered anywhere.

Shukria has the option of taking her action for divorce into Afghanistan's official justice system, where civil law, Sharia, and local custom each play a role. It is at best an improvised and unpredictable procedure. She will likely be heard only through a male intermediary. Without her husband present to testify that he has indeed left her, she will need to call her own witnesses, and even so, she risks leaving court without being granted a divorce. Shukria's husband was very clear to her sister: He would never stand in front of his relatives, no less in a court, and declare that he had divorced his wife. It would be embarrassing to him.

A woman seeking a formal divorce also risks frustration and humiliation. It sends a damning message, regardless of the outcome: Such a woman must not have been a good one, as she obviously failed to take care of her husband and her family. Otherwise, why would she have been cast aside?

Shukria would face one or several judges, who may or may not have legal educations but who will each have his own interpretation of the various laws, and who may operate in a confusing maze of rumors and "tradition." The court is formally required to attempt to contact the absent husband, to secure his approval of the divorce. Failing that, her relatives would be called in to verify that the husband is absent. Only then would Shukria have a chance of dissolving her marriage and being awarded the divorce she never asked for.

With very little rule of law in place, most people also bypass the official Afghan justice system altogether in favor of an informal justice system to resolve conflicts, where local laws and judgments vary even more, and rarely to a woman's favor.

Shukria shivers at the notion of being a working divorcée: "If I were a housewife, it would be okay, but now I work on the outside. Everybody will know I am divorced. I could even run into those same judges at the hospital!"

She would be looked upon with suspicion and possibly contempt by both men and women as a failed wife and, by extension, a failed woman. But humiliation would be far from the worst thing. Nor would the fact that she may be forced to move into her parents' house again, where she would formally live under the guardianship of her ailing father. An adult woman cannot live on her own in Afghanistan without a blood relative or a *mahram*. As a divorced woman who still has children living with her, Shukria could not remarry, either, other than to a relative of her husband's. The grave inequality of divorce in Afghanistan is often explained here with the idea that women have less brainpower and may haphazardly ask for a divorce for no good or valid reason.

Now, Shukria's children stand to eventually be taken away from her. According to Afghan civil code, based on Sharia, children belong to the father, since "every child is created by the father." Sharia is considered to be the word of God, and to question it equals blasphemy. Legal arguments challenging the civil code could be interpreted as insults against God, producing a whole new, more serious crime. To question a Sharia argument in a court can be dangerous, since the justice system in Afghanistan is often staffed with ill-educated but self-described pious lawyers and judges.

An Afghan woman who wants to leave her husband will be obliged to also leave her children behind. Making divorce nearly impossible for most women is exactly the point—otherwise, the thinking goes, women could just divorce men left and right, taking the children with them. Women are too emotional, rash, and impulsive—particularly when they are menstruating. They cannot be trusted to make rational decisions. So for their own well-being, the logic goes, children should always remain with the father to avoid being carted off to a series of new husbands whom their whorish mothers may decide to marry at a whim.

Shukria's husband has not yet claimed his children, but she expects it is only a matter of time: "He has no money right now. He wants me to support them a little longer. He will let me raise them and pay for them, and then he could claim them later."

If the father agrees, a son can stay with the mother until he is seven, and a daughter until she is nine. After that, all children become his property. When children reach the age of eighteen they can, in theory, decide with whom they want to live. But in practice, a girl is often married off before then.

SHUKRIA BEGINS TO pick at a chicken kebab. Then she grabs a plate with sautéed mushrooms. "I've never had one of these before. I will try it. I am trying new things."

While chewing, she apologizes for not bringing up the state of her marriage before: "I thought maybe you would become emotional. I did not want to upset you."

"How are you?" I ask, touching her arm carefully.

Looking back at me, she smiles wistfully and tilts her head a little. The announcement of a new baby has made the nightmare she held at bay for ten months excruciatingly real. "I have no feeling right now. There is nothing in my heart. I am like a stone inside. My head is still trying to understand it.

"This is my third destiny," she continues. "First I was a man and then a woman, and now I will be a divorced woman."

The way she sees it, marriage did not quite succeed in fully making her a woman, although childbirth eventually gave her confirmation. But a divorced woman in Afghanistan is something else—without a husband, a woman is lowered to a caste where she is neither man nor woman, nor a respectable citizen. With a divorce often comes the suspicions of a woman being un-Islamic, referencing the prophet Muhammad, who was believed to have expressed that, except for anything that is outright illegal, divorce is what God hates the most. A woman here can be either a daughter or a wife—or a widow—but there is not much in between. When a woman does not belong to her father, with her virginity as capital, or a husband, with her status attached to him, there is no role for her in the patriarchal culture. A divorcée is a fallen woman, who loses all the privileges attached to marriage and her elevated status through her husband. And it is other women who will come down on her the hardest.

If Shukria's husband eventually comes to collect the children there is little she will be able to do. When they are taken away from her, she is reduced to a figure she does not yet know how to name or to describe.

"That will be my fourth destiny. A divorced woman without her children."

She thinks out loud: Perhaps this happened because their marriage was never proper to begin with? She was never a real bride, anyway. She was just Shukur; miserable, in that stupid wedding dress. The marriage probably failed because she could never quite force that man out from inside of her. As her body was put into a dress, she tried to make her mind follow. Nor did she ever get a *mahr*—that sum that should but rarely is paid to the bride to secure her.

"Right now I am nothing. I was nothing and I am nothing. I was never a man and never a woman. I was a wife and now I will not be a wife anymore. When he takes my children away from me, I will not be a mother. To whom do I have value? Can you tell me—to whom?"

She wags her head from side to side, her voice bristling.

"To your children, your parents, and to your patients," I say. "To us. You have value to us."

But Shukria still shakes her head.

"How many lives should I have? How many people must I be?"

CHAPTER TWENTY-ONE

THE WIFE

Azita

T HE PRODUCER ASKED for color, so she added the turquoise scarf to break up her all-black. He is happy with the small concession, nodding in approval as Azita walks back onto the television set. Then he turns to the production assistant right behind him. Something is still not quite right: Azita needs more *eyes*. The assistant springs into action, and Azita patiently allows her eyes to be lined with even thicker strokes of black kohl while the female sound operator attaches a small microphone at the neckline of her black coat. Azita remains still. She knows it will be faster if a professional does it. They are all waiting for her now.

"Ready?"

Azita nods to the producer. Ready. And the tape rolls again.

Heat is rising quickly on the hillside terrace, but little can dampen her energy today, where she is placed on a small stage in front of three cameras and a local production crew. Her delivery is flawless and moving; she tells the story of how she came from a dirt-floor house in the provinces and took the seat for Badghis in parliament. It's her success narrative and she doesn't miss a beat when she ties it to the future of Afghanistan: "Our nation is in trouble, but it will never go anywhere by itself," she exclaims to the future viewers. "The responsibility for your future lies with you. No one will take care of it for you."

Azita is still waiting, hoping to be reinstated in parliament. But this is a good diversion, allowing her to play the role of a politician again for few hours.

She is one of three judges on a television program meant to get young Afghans—a majority of the population is under 25—interested in politics. In this *American Idol*–format, each young contestant will make a speech in front of the panel of experienced politicians, who will offer on-air coaching and finally cast votes on his performance. No young women have signed up, but dozens of young men have gathered for this production funded by one of the American nonprofits aimed at "democracy promotion" abroad. Each participant wears his Friday best, ranging from a traditional *shalwar* to a camouflage jacket and cowboy boots.

The strong lighting on the set makes Azita's eyes glimmer and gives her the familiar rush. She has a momentary flashback to the introduction she used to read to her sisters back in Badghis when they played television: *"Welcome, ladies and gentlemen. This is the news hour."* Today, being a female television anchor would be a far from respectable job. For a woman to expose herself on television is to be seen by many men at once. Azita could not work in television; it would kill her political aspirations for good. Even appearing on this show could seem a little low-class for a woman. She knows it. But it offers her a chance to get out of the house. And for as long as the camera is on, she is on. To her delight, the production crew had even sent a car and a driver to pick her up that morning, as though she was someone important.

The past few weeks have not offered much reprieve from her confinement in Golden City. Her husband is the only one who can drive her now, and he will do so only when he is willing and in a good mood. He no longer allows her to take taxis, and every meeting outside the house needs to be negotiated with him in advance. With Kabul deteriorating, it is for her own safety, he has stated. Because he cares about her. On some days, he decides they will not leave the house at all.

One at a time, the show's contestants walk out before the judges. Each participant will touch his chest with the right hand and exclaim a respectful *"Salam aleikum"* greeting before making his political speech about Afghanistan's future. Most presentations are far from Azita's upbeat tone: A dominant theme is that foreign troops should leave sooner rather than later. Such statements are usually met with cheering approval by other contestants awaiting their turns, even though they have been asked to be silent.

Azita takes the role of a coach, altering between gentle criticism—"I don't understand if you even have a political idea"—to praise, suddenly exclaiming *"afaim"* or *"bravo"* when she hears something good. When one young man is struck dumb as he faces the judges, Azita slowly talks him out of paralysis: "Breathe. Feel yourself. We are your friends."

He delivers his three allotted minutes in a rambling stream of words. If he were in power, his first and most urgent priority would be to put an end to the stealing of aid money by officials and make sure it was used better. He gets the highest score from the judges. He has hit on a topic that enrages many Afghans, and he is still in the running to become Afghanistan's "Hope for the Future."

FOREIGN AID WORKERS, who can be the most cynical of all about their own difficult field, will sometimes mutter a one-sentence response to why, after a decade of aid to Afghanistan, it still ranks close to the bottom of the Human Development Index: "Too much money." And too many cooks.

Afghanistan has historically been called "the Graveyard of Empires" in war memoirs. In our time, it may also be called "the Playground of Foreign Aid Experimentation."

The ambitious project, much like what the Russians set out to do, of turning around a country where many still perform daily tasks according to hundred-year-old traditions and where infrastructure is virtually nonexistent has prompted disillusioned aid workers to routinely trade stories of engendering epic chaos: when dozens of "projects" and millions of dollars converge on a single province, as each nationality and each organization attempts to execute its own version of democracy and development—usually without ever speaking to one another. Add to that confused and increasingly frustrated Afghans caught in the middle.

Countries wanting to remain in good diplomatic standing with Washington, D.C., after 2001 contributed not only troops but also generous offerings of foreign aid. Between 2006 and 2011, a total of more than $30 billion was spent on development aid to Afghanistan by about thirty countries and a few large multilateral organizations such as the European Union, the United Nations, and the World Bank. The single biggest contribution came from the United States, which also had the biggest staff and the most fanciful projects. Plus the more than one thousand nongovernmental organizations registered to operate in Afghanistan—all with different agendas and ideas of what works best.

A fundamental quandary for all those entities is that they need to demonstrate some progress for the money to keep flowing from donors. Just not too much, as abundant optimism could risk that same flow of money. Delivering foreign aid to a weak, war-torn country with few functioning institutions, where war still rages in many places, raises the bar even higher. In that state, Afghanistan was simply unable to absorb much of the money that was pushed into the country. Instead, the massive, well-meaning funds fueled mismanagement and corruption.

Norwegian political scientist Astri Suhrke offers a scathing review in her 2011 book *When More Is Less: The International Project in Afghanistan*. With twenty-five years of experience in Afghanistan, she describes the "very modest results" of foreign aid there as a direct consequence of overly confident organizations setting out to entirely rebuild Afghanistan, aided by a very powerful foreign aid lobby that reacts to every visible failure by appealing for more funds to rectify them. Together, these entities have not only largely failed to help

Afghanistan, but also caused irrevocable harm by creating "a rentier state unparalleled in Afghan history and nearly unique in the world of international assistance," she writes, with a complete dependency on foreign aid and little accountability toward its own citizens.

Afghanistan holds a spot at the very bottom of Transparency International's corruption index, and as the war is drawing to a close, Afghan officials are openly trying to cash in as much as possible before most troops—and money—leave for good. Of the aid contributed by U.S. taxpayers, for instance, as little as ten cents on the dollar may at times have reached its intended recipients, according to an auditor at the Office of the Special Inspector General for Afghanistan Reconstruction. Much of the rest has fueled a fragile and corrupt economy where a select few—both Afghans and foreigners—have been made extraordinarily wealthy.

The strong urge by Western donors to help, in particular, Afghan women has also proved fraught with failures and strange priorities.

One of the most heralded achievements—education, and especially of girls—touts impressive official numbers: close to ten million students registered, compared with around fifty thousand under the Taliban. But half of Afghanistan's newly created schools have no actual buildings, many lack teachers, most students never graduate, and one-fifth of the registered students are permanently absent.

Many students also find that the foreigners' interest in schooling does not extend to higher studies. Mostly located in urban areas, universities have limited slots available and charge fees too high for most. As 40 percent of Afghan girls will marry before the age of eighteen, when childbearing and managing a household will take precedence over education, it is hard to understand why more slots and scholarships have not been offered to those young women who have the ability and permission to get higher educations.

In a single year, more than seven hundred "projects" related to gender and improving the lives of women and girls in Afghanistan were also sponsored by foreign donors. A report by Norwegian political scientist Torunn Wimpelmann explains that despite some progress, especially in the urban centers, "gains are on the whole modest and reversible." But more notably, "the emergence of a jet-setting strata of English-speaking women activists" in Kabul, focusing mainly on an international audience, has managed to create an even larger gap between urban and rural women and those separated by class, wealth, and education. One consequence of this, Wimpelmann writes, is that women's rights have increasingly become viewed as an elite and Western-backed issue by many in Afghanistan. Now, taking a conservative stand on women's rights has therefore become the necessary norm for many politicians or influential power brokers who want to demonstrate their nationalist and Islamic credentials. That will be the unfortunate legacy of "women's issues" in Afghanistan for some time to come, similar to the Russian experience. A long-term investment in a strengthened justice system and a functioning parliament would have benefited women and girls more, Wimpelmann contends, echoing the words of Azita.

NOT UNTIL ELECTRICITY on the television set goes out for the third time does Azita relinquish her chair on the set and walk back to the shade inside, as taping for the show breaks by midday. The producer has arranged for a lunch of meat stew and Mountain Dew. Azita declines the bread. She explains to the two fellow male judges that she is trying to lose weight.

They are also politicians, about twice her age. She wants to use the opportunity to secure their support for her reinstatement in parliament, and the men politely ask after the health of her father, who they know from his "political days." How is he?

Azita is equally polite in her response: He is doing well. Not so political these days. His old age and all.

But they persist. He must have inspired her to take up a career in politics?

Azita smiles. It was all so long ago. She really doesn't want to talk about her father. He is retired now.

A better topic, she suggests, is how they can support her in the struggle to claim her rightful seat. "Being at home is not restful. It's depressing. It's not who I am. I feel useless there. It's when I am outside the house that I feel valuable," she tells them.

They seem to understand. They know she is more than a housewife—that she is her father's daughter. She beams at their affirmation.

But when Azita returns home this afternoon, she will find Mehran in tears again, refusing to speak or eat. Her stepmother has invented her most efficient line so far, and she has been hammering it all day, while Azita has been out of the house: "You are not Mehran. You are Mahnoush. You are *Mahnoush-Mahnoush-Mahnoush*."

IN THE HOUR after dinner, Azita will pay even more dearly for her outing, when her husband prompts her on when his regular monthly allowance will be reinstated. It is a conversation they have had several times now, and at first, Azita just listens to him.

In his opinion, the fact that Azita no longer receives a salary from parliament is no excuse. Their agreement from years ago stills stands: He allows her to work on the condition of a marital kickback. She cannot change those terms now, just because she is temporarily unemployed. Her husband makes his case again: He agreed to move to Kabul and live there once she got into parliament. He agreed to stay for these additional months as she continues to try to get her seat back—and he should be compensated accordingly. He has stood by her side and acted as her "house husband," as his only job. And it has not been without effort. So she cannot just stop paying him. Their deal was always the same—part of what she brings in is handed over to him, in cash. What she keeps is for food, school fees, and rent.

Even so, he argues, the money he got was rarely enough for the sacrifice he has made: suffering questions and humiliation from others over how he could allow his wife such freedom—to work outside the house and to mingle with other men.

Most of his money is invested now, in a relative's nut business, and that money is his alone and she is never to question him about it. Over the years, his compensation has gradually increased, and rightfully so. What's more, the relocation of the family to Kabul is saving Azita money, he points out. His bimonthly trips to the province to see his first wife and eldest girl were costly. But now, for her to just end those payments? It's unacceptable, he tells her, and he will have none of her excuses.

Perhaps she is lying about the lack of money? She is hiding it, right? At first, it's a question, but he soon says that he is actually sure of it: She has money saved somewhere. All parliamentarians do—he has seen how they live. Azita's new washing machine shrinks next to their cars, villas, and vacations abroad. It must be that she prefers to keep the extra profits to herself instead of making good on their agreement. She can keep denying it, but he won't be fooled. He may lack an education, but he knows *her.*

Azita finally protests, offended at the suggestion of deception. If she had the money, she truly would hand it over, she tells him. What he accuses her of—having money stashed away somewhere—is particularly insulting. She is not one of those corrupt politicians who takes kickbacks and bribes for passing on suggestions of who should get contracts, or what minister to support with a vote of confidence. Were she that person, Azita retorts, surely they, too, could have owned a house in Dubai by now, or even in a European capital? At least they could have owned something in Kabul. But they are renters. She worked for one of the poorest provinces in the country, so how dare he compare her to those who pillage and steal?

But the more Azita speaks, the more she infuriates her husband.

"Shut your mouth or I will make it silent," he warns her. He will not hear of any more. He reminds her of how simple it would be for him to shame her, ending any of her political ambitions for good: "I will go to people and say you are not a good wife and that you have relations with other men."

Azita has received variations on that threat before.

In the past, the solution was always straightforward: more money.

She would give him an even larger chunk of her salary. If she was planning a trip abroad, she would also give him an extra wad of cash to compensate for the time she would be gone.

Those trips always caused arguments—like the time her flight from Dubai was delayed and she was forced to spend a night at the airport. He had gone on for weeks about it. Sometimes accusations were combined: She is having an affair and she is hiding money from him. Or she is giving the money to the man she is having an affair with. With a mix of apologies, flattery, and, in the end, more money, Azita has usually managed to appease him. But now, when she has no money to offer, their argument cannot be easily resolved. What little she kept for herself she has already spent. There is no money, she tells him again.

Being accused of having an affair also disturbs her more than usual. After thirteen years, he should know better than that. When would she even have time for an affair? When she is not arguing with election officials, she is trying to find a job. Or cooking. Or taking care of the children.

How about if he offered some support, instead of repeating these same insulting accusations, she tosses back at her husband. As the mother of his children, she should at least be treated with some respect. Using veiled ways of saying she is a prostitute should be beneath him.

It's not like he is perfect, either, Azita blurts out, suddenly losing her forced cool: "According to the Koran, a wife can leave her husband if he does not support her. I am still supporting you."

She looks at him before she goes for what is meant to be the final line of their argument: "There is no husband here."

He seems surprised when she says it. It is a graver insult than most things she has launched at him before: to call him something other than a man and a husband. When he responds, he parses each word: "You are nothing. I *made* you an MP."

"So do it," she tells him, still defiant. "I do not care. Destroy me if you want. Because it was never you. It was all me."

That is when her face hits the wall.

Her eyes close as her knees fold. Covering her head with her arms and hands, she crouches on the floor below him, turning toward the wall, with only her neck exposed. It is where the blows fall next.

Now she has a choice: Beg him to stop. Or just stay silent until he tires. She tries to calculate where the children might be, and how much they can hear. They will see her later; there is nothing she can do about that. But it is better that they do not see or hear them in this exact moment.

Her husband's voice from above is almost soothing. "I will support my family. In the village. In Badghis. When we go back there I will support you all. We will not have to worry about money."

She knows what he means. He has mentioned it before: the bride price for their daughters. It will secure the family for years. If war returns, the girls will need to be married off sooner anyway. It's not good for a family to have five daughters in the house. And, as he is fond of saying, she keeps forgetting that he is a simple man—all the luxuries of this Kabul existence are not for him anyway. They would all be better off in the province where a man can provide for his family. And get some respect at home.

"MAYBE I SHOULD just end this stupid life."

It is a strange thing for Azita to say, even after spending another night with the wet towel on her forehead.

Her style has always been different from both Afghan men and women in this regard—she does not tell her stories with exaggerated dramatic flair, involving elements of potential death at each turn.

We are at a small Kabul café. With the turmoil at the house, I am no longer invited to visit, but we have carved out some time after another meeting for which she gained permission from her husband to attend. We are the only guests outside, in a dusty garden full of plastic chairs. Wearing "big makeup"—her code for covering bruises—has become a regular occurrence now.

Over the past two years, despite both her own and the country's setbacks, Azita has been the constant optimist. But today she cries, slowly, without much sound. Embarrassed, she turns her head away each time her eyes fill up with tears and she quickly wipes them away.

As always, when I don't know what else to do, I try to sound matter-of-fact: "It is only a turn of phrase for you, right? 'This stupid life'?"

She says nothing, which usually indicates there's something she's not saying—something contrary to the confident image she wants to project. It is hard enough to admit that domestic violence has returned to her family.

"Have you ever tried to kill yourself?" I ask.

Her eyes flicker and turn down to the table.

It was early in her marriage, in Badghis. She had panic attacks that developed into seizures, when she would go catatonic. They usually lasted only minutes, but sometimes longer. The first such episode came right after the wedding. It began with sharp chest pain, followed by shortness of breath. After that, her hands and feet would go cold, and she could not move them. Nor could she speak or move her head. With time, she found the attacks would subside when her feet and hands were rubbed. A doctor also gave her phenobarbital, an antiseizure medicine. She was newly pregnant with the twins, and, following instructions, she took two a day.

One day, she took twelve.

It was a watermelon that pushed her over the edge, or more accurately, the fantasy of one. She was locked inside the house, thinking of the watermelons in the field outside in the family's plot. She could not stand most foods, but she craved that cool, crisp melon. But they were outside the locked door where she could not go. And none were for her, anyway; they were to be sold at the market.

The twelve tablets put her in a deep sleep for two hours.

When she woke up again she immediately apologized to everyone for mistakenly taking too much medicine. How stupid of her. She is still not sure why she took them; maybe it was indeed a mistake. But she never wants to revisit that low again. It was the weakest her spirit had ever been. That she was so close to abandoning her daughters before they had even been born is her greatest shame.

She looks up at me and apologizes for her initial remark—of course she does not want to end her life. She really does not. But it does feel as though there is something wrong with her mind these days. Where she used to be able to think of solutions, she now feels blocked. With the increased insecurity in Kabul, with the foreigners leaving, the parliament still in chaos: She always saw a way before, but it feels harder now. Or maybe she is getting older? The thought of Afghanistan descending into chaos after foreign troops leave is something she cannot even contemplate.

"I think maybe I should have left," she suddenly says.

She has never said that before. Hardly even thought it, in a real way. Divorce was just never an option. Just like Shukria, Azita knows seeking a divorce would not be in her favor—especially not with the accusations of infidelity, which could land her in prison. And she would most likely lose her children.

But the "leaving" Azita refers to is of a different kind. Unlike for many of her colleagues in politics, the thought of living life abroad after the foreign troop withdrawal has never held much allure for her. The concept was almost unspeakable for an idealist who always swore she would stick by her country and its future.

"When I was an MP I had lots of friends and contacts. Visas were never a problem. I could have gone anywhere. The children could travel on my passport, even. Now I just have a tourist passport. I was so busy with my work. I feel so guilty for them now. I was so selfish. I was thinking of my country and its future. And my work. I should have only taken care of my family."

In wanting to create a better future for her daughters she had always imagined it would be in an Afghanistan she had helped reform. Trying to teach her daughters resilience, strength, and pride for their country, she also wanted them to be proud of *her* for the effort. To then plan for a comfortable exit abroad like several of her colleagues seemed so . . . hypocritical.

Before leaving for campaign training in the United States a few years ago, she had joked with the twins about seeking asylum there. It was already a popular topic among her colleagues, back then. Several of the other MPs had sent their children to study, or to apply for asylum in Europe, so they could eventually travel back and forth and get better educations. But Azita assured her daughters that she would, of course, always return to them, to Kabul and to their family. Besides, she had no dreams of America. Her dreams included only Afghanistan. She had felt pleased with herself after giving her daughters that speech, thinking she had taught them a little something about character and national pride.

But on one recent evening, Benafsha, the quieter of the twins, had suddenly spoken up after another suicide bombing not far from their house. She reminded Azita of the conversation about foreign countries and how she had said they would always stay in Afghanistan. "You made your choice, Mother," Benafsha said. Now, none of them would ever leave.

It was in that moment when Azita's image of herself as a selfless patriot began to shift, replacing it with that of a selfish careerist. A sense of shame came over her. She was someone who would choose her country over her daughters, and they had always known it. She had not seen it herself until it was too late. She had taken a chance on Afghanistan with the new foreigners and had believed that it could get better. She had reached for something impossible, and she had been a fool to do it. Maybe it had always been unrealistic that Afghanistan would change much in her lifetime, and she had gambled away the lives of her daughters on it.

"Are you still thinking of leaving?"

"No. Never. I could never leave them," Azita says. "But maybe I was very stupid before."

She must carry on for the sake of her parents, too. Her father's decision to marry her off will stand in war or peace, whether she is in parliament or not, and regardless of her relationship with her husband.

"I would like to meet him," I say. "The man who holds all this power, always and from the beginning. Do you think he would speak to me?"

"Probably no."

CHAPTER TWENTY-TWO

THE FATHER

Azita

N O REGULAR AIRLINE flies to Azita's home province, and the roads snaking up to the northwestern corner of Afghanistan are known to be riddled with homemade explosives and criminal gangs.

Foreigners, on the other hand, can travel anywhere for free on UN flights that run on an ad hoc timetable based on when any of their more prominent officials need to take off. A ticket, or "travel authorization," for Setareh, who holds an Afghan passport, comes at the price of my attending a half-day lecture at an air-conditioned UN office on the suffering of Afghan women. After that, we will spend the next day hanging around the United Nations' private terminal at Kabul airport, a hangar filled with aid workers and diplomats where planes randomly take off outside.

The women waiting to fly somewhere all look foreign-born, and all are in the very distinctive ethnic war-chic resort style rarely seen outside fortified expatriate compounds and never on regular Afghan women. Long, flowing silk tunics in light colors are paired with delicate, embroidered head scarves, slightly slipped back, Benazir Bhutto–style, allowing strands of expertly blow-dried and high-lighted hair to escape. Exquisite antique Kuchi-nomad silver jewelry once made by hand for tribal weddings in the provinces clatters on wrists and necks. The standard male diplomat wardrobe is made up of different gradations of khaki. Some are are sockless in loafers and pair the pants with navy, gold-buttoned blazers. Most of the elegant foreigners carry small point-and-shoot cameras to document their work in the field. Their accompanying "body men" are about double the size of any diplomat, and carry German automatic weapons strapped onto their backs.

A mid-level foreign aid worker can take in a salary of $15,000 per month, tax free. Plus various bonuses for "hardship," which a posting like Afghanistan is considered to be. But the enthusiastic caravan that has rolled into Afghanistan in the past decade is not all about money, although that has certainly drawn more than a few. Many are young idealists looking for adventure. Others are seasoned bureaucrats who have seen every war of the past three decades and signed up for yet another tour.

There is the Balkan gang and those who used to dine together in Baghdad. They demonstrate their status by sharing stories of wars past with the brand-new Afghanistan experts from elite universities on the American East Coast. Just as the European colonialists before them, these current-day explorers live well before they return home with exotic tales of foreign lands.

Decor inside the embassy compounds, air-conditioned by powerful military-grade generators, aims to showcase the best of each country's culture and design. A Dane will recline on exquisite Scandinavian midcentury classics that were bubble-wrapped and shipped in secure containers from Copenhagen. The British offer the best-stocked bar in town at the queen's outpost in Kabul, named "The Inn Fidel." They are also known for some of the most elaborate costume parties, where in a favorite tradition of both historical and current-day European aristocracy, guests are thrilled to pose as someone else for an evening. American embassy workers can swim in a beautiful lap pool with a barbecue hut close by, where a trusted Afghan in a white chef's hat will cook anything to country club perfection.

Americans there will sometimes proudly proclaim that they haven't set foot outside the compound since they were picked up at Kabul airport and won't again until it's time to return home. No need for that. The U.S. Embassy seems to be constantly expanding, and the grass truly is greener in the green zone, where water is never scarce. The dust inside the perimeter is swept away so diligently that the air feels easier to breathe than in the rest of Kabul, where thousands of children die each year from respiratory ailments caused by garbage bonfires, cars burning cheap gasoline, and the microbes spewing from open sewers.

The benefits of being a foreigner in Afghanistan are well-known to those who get drunk together on Thursday nights around Kabul. No matter who they were in the outside world, or what social class they belonged to, in Kabul a foreigner instantly becomes a member of an upper, ruling class. Like any war zone, this is a place for personal reinvention, where a new, improved persona can be crafted, the past temporarily erased, as demands and social codes of the outside world are put on hold. Joining the expatriate set in Afghanistan is an effective disguise, and one that brings power and access.

AFTER A DAY and a half spent waiting at this *karavan serai,* as an irritated Setareh dubs the hangar scene, I have tried everything from the kiosk of foreign and Afghan delicacies, and she has refused most of it. We conclude that we are not on anyone's preferred passenger list, and that if we are to ever meet Azita's father, we must concede defeat and make our own way to Badghis.

So we fly to Herat on one of Afghanistan's own local airlines and eventually, with some help by both Azita's and Setareh's relatives, we find an Afghan army helicopter crew willing to take us further into the land. As we arrive at the base in a faux-fur-lined taxi, we are met with a breakfast that appeals more to Setareh: sweet tea, chewy flatbread, and mulberry jam. The local commander cautions us that while he can take us into Badghis, we may not get out, since he is not planning on sending anyone back there for a while. But Setareh has already plotted our exit by road: She has gone out and bought two light blue burkas and tucked them into her black wheeled carry-on, smirking at my backpack once again. For our planned stay in Badghis, which is close to Iran, we have also gone shopping for some more black; Setareh is in what we come to translate as "Herati dress," a very large sheet of dark fabric swept around her head that reaches all the way down to her shoes, making her look like a little friendly ghost with a serious face. I have opted for the full hijab, "Iranian style." In the black head-to-toe cloak and tightly pinned black head scarf, plus sunglasses, I am all mind and no body. If even that.

IN THE HELICOPTER we are seated on the floor in the glass bulb next to the pilots, with the earth moving underneath us.

First pilot Azizi trained under the Russians. The Cyrillic letters inside the cockpit are an issue for the constant rotations of young Americans who arrive on the base to advance Azizi's skills. After too many jumbled conversations over the radio, the Americans now allow him to be mostly silent on the radio once he is up in the air. They have provided him with a brand-new portable GPS to navigate; he proudly wears it strapped to his leg. As we hover over burned-yellow wheat fields and clusters of pistachio forests, he makes a point of not looking at it. He knows where he is going.

Like Zahra's pilot father, he is also a fan of the Americans. They are decent people. Their names are simple to pronounce, too: Bill. Joe. Hank. They trade stories about their kids and their families. Most are younger than Azizi, but he has made a few new friends. He is useful to them: He translates the Cyrillic letters on the dashboards inside the sturdy and reasonably reliable helicopters his division flies. He has tried to teach them the Russian technical terms he knows. They, in turn, try to teach him some in English. But many times, they have found that sounds and letters have no equivalent in the other language, so Afghan-American military partnership gets by using mostly "Ringlish" (Russian via Persian English) and "Pinglish" (the closest possible English versions of Persian words in Azizi's Dari dialect).

Americans have a different way of expressing themselves beyond words, too, Azizi has found. They are direct, detailed, and insistent with their ideas. Afghans prefer to be indirect. Bad news or an opinion that differs is seldom presented without some tiptoeing first—or is just left unspoken for each person to figure out on their own. By now, Azizi has learned how to behave when the Americans ask for something impossible. He does not want to seem uncollaborative, and he gathers Americans eventually find out what is possible or not anyway. So he always says yes. And "no problem."

As long as they let him get up in the air, he doesn't really care who they are. He got along fine with the Russians; it just annoyed him slightly that they were always trying to push their political beliefs on him. You needed to be a party member to get ahead. Like most Afghans I have asked, he declines to say whether he actually joined the Communist party back then; it was a long time ago. He thinks he likes the Americans better though; they don't try to talk politics with him. "They are just soldiers, like me."

When the Americans leave, he will fly for whoever comes next. The electrical sockets were changed in the hangar from two-pronged to three-pronged when the Americans came. If they are changed again, it doesn't matter much to him. He can adapt.

If not for the landscape moving below, he would seem to be making conversation at afternoon tea. As we slowly make our weightless way across the dried-out land that resembles the cracked heel of a foot, he steers straight toward every steep mountainside that rises up before us until the rotor blades are almost close enough to touch it. Only then, with just a minimal flick of the wrist, will he force his machine to rise up horizontally along the mountainside. Each time, he rewards himself with a wide grin as we reach an open sky.

BIENVENIDO A QALA-E-NAW. The greeting is spray-painted across the sandbags, where we slowly descend into a swirl of dust.

This is northwest Afghanistan, bordering on Iran, with its own elected Afghan governor. But it was the Spanish military who fixed up the modest airfield when they were assigned the Badghis province. They installed their "reconstruction team" in the small capital and unfurled the dark blue NATO flags alongside Spain's yellow and red. No pole was left for the black, red, and green flag of the Islamic Republic of Afghanistan.

The helicopter finally lands about as elegantly as an overweight water bug. Our fellow passengers, all Afghan military officers in desert camouflage, with well-tended black mustaches, climb out. This is the desert land, complete with sand dunes and a few pine trees surrounding the mud houses leading into the city, with a cupcake-like turquoise mosque at its center.

Before 2001, this could not even be called a city, says the governor's aide who greets us carrying under his arm a pink notebook with pigtail cartoon characters. You take what you can get in terms of office supplies here.

There are no hotels, but he has agreed to host us in the governor's guesthouse on the condition that we do not move around too much or let anyone know that women are staying there. As we drive into Qala-e-Naw, it still looks like more of a village, with scattered mud houses surrounded by low walls. Everything is small and brown, tone on tone with the desert itself. The main street counts six shops on each side, in one- or two-story buildings. There is a women's market, where fully veiled or burka-clad women can shop in the company of other women only, while the men wait on the other side.

On the men's side, such items as spare car parts, used cell phones, and carpets are for sale. The women's area mostly consists of vendors selling dry goods, children's clothing, and wedding supplies. Brightly hued garlands of paper and nylon fabric hang outside in the sweeping dust-wind. Even though Iran is closer, almost everything is imported from Pakistan. The foreign American-led troops are stingy about letting Iranian imports through wherever they control the border. Here, the language I have come to know as Dari is called "Kabuli," and a different, more Iranian-sounding Persian dialect, closer to Farsi, is spoken.

Several UN agencies and the U.S. Agency for International Development have helped build what the governor calls a "very modern" place compared to how it looked ten years ago. Most people still get their drinking water from wells, but at least the wells are no longer contaminated. And most women still give birth at home, but at least the city has one midwife-in-training available for those who would welcome her. Tuberculosis, malaria, and diphtheria are still rampant in the province despite major improvements by the Spanish on garbage disposal and sanitation. Now, there are some small schools, a few clinics, and even a sewage system created by the Spanish equivalent of the army corps of engineers, who dug canals underground.

THE GOVERNOR'S GUESTHOUSE is pink, and with its peach-colored curtains and soft carpets, it's the most luxurious accommodation in town. Spotty electricity arrives for a few hours every day, and there are indoor bathrooms, albeit without running water. We are given a small room, littered with the belongings of two male guests who, by gender discrimination in our favor, are told to get out and sleep on the roof instead. On top of the makeshift beds are mattresses with the manufacturer's plastic wrapping still intact. Setareh fishes out her shiny blue burka and spreads it out over the bed before she lies down, bouncing right back up again after inhaling the odor left by previous guests who have slept in the 100-degree summer.

We will spend days waiting in this little room with pink walls and a peach glow through the curtains.

Everybody seems to know of Azita's father, as he is still one of the very few residents of this province with a university degree. But we are informed that he is old and tired, and has no interest in discussing times past.

In the meantime, our efforts to lie low and dress appropriately—Setareh in her sheet and I in my black cloak, hair completely covered and my eyes darkened with kohl that no amount of baby wipes will re-move at night—render some unexpected praise from our housemates. After a few days, Setareh overhears the men staying in the room next to us. Forgoing all courtesy phrases and looking down as we pass them, at all times entirely mute and with most of our faces covered, we seem to have met their approval. "The Iranian and the Hazara," they conclude, "are very good girls. Very covered, and very shy."

Our modesty has appealed so much to one man that he decides he likes us both "very much." For a moment, he ponders whether to ask each of us to pose for a cell phone picture with him. But it would probably be too forward, he tells his friend, and not something the good and proper girls would ever agree to.

After translating the mumblings next door, Setareh and I declare success for my efforts to become a woman. After removing my body, my voice, and most of my face, I have finally arrived.

THE VILLAGE WHERE Azita's mother-in-law still lives is about ten minutes by car from the city center, on a small road where a group of Kuchi nomads—a mostly Pashtun minority—have settled, their red and green fabric tents shaking in the wind, and small children herding bony goats. A narrow bridge sprouts from a hillside, which Azita is credited with convincing the Spanish military to help rein-force. The village is said to have a thousand houses, but we do not count more than a few dozen on the small hill. There are a few small fields of green where farmer families live in tents or under tarps with UNICEF logos and where, when we pass, the women turn away and hide their faces with their large *chadori* sheets. Those tarps are for sale at the market, just like the seeds handed out to women by an-other NGO. Eggplants are budding in one field, where Afghan pop music unexpectedly streams out from a transistor radio. Two boys play naked in a small water stream.

Our driver, who has on enough cologne to kill the entire popula-tion of the backseat, takes us to a metal gate. The scent wafting from the car competes with the stench from an open sewer that hits as soon as we enter the small compound.

This is what poverty looks like.

Small barefoot girls in synthetic dresses flock around us. Two teenage girls are holding babies whose faces are spotted with lazy flies. They are the grown-ups. One girl looks at me from under a mass of tousled dirty hair and remains silent. She may be around six, but she acts like an older sister to the others. For the next two hours, she will just keep looking at us, the whites of her eyes contrasting with her darkly tanned skin.

The mother-in-law's one-story house is the color of dried mud without a single tree to protect it from the blinding sunlight. Mud and straw, the least expensive building materials, provide natural insulation through all seasons; they are organic and practical compared to the cinder block houses that the military is fond of putting up as aid projects. Afghans often reject those; they feel like freezers in the winter and bake ovens in summer.

An exhausted-looking goat is tied to a pin in the stone wall inside a fenced area just outside. Another small patch of land is dedicated to the cultivation of kitchen vegetables. It is surrounded by barbed wire to prevent animals and children from raiding the tomatoes, potatoes, and onions. From above, it all looks dead. Food is cooked outside, over an open fire. A small naan oven is built into a corner. There is no electric heat. In the winter, firewood is used to heat the house. The wood is collected in the summer from the bottom of the hill, about a twenty-minute walk away.

A small, hunched-over woman steps out. The girls instantly part to let her through. She is dressed all in white, with a thin, white head scarf wrapped like a turban around her head to protect her from the sun. Her face looks much like how the desert appeared from our helicopter—a burnt shade of brown, cut by the ancient marks of riverbeds.

She embraces me and kisses me on both cheeks with a stream of respectful greetings. Setareh and I greet her in return. On her left shoulder, a set of tiny keys is attached with a safety pin. They make a small rattling sound as she moves. "I found them on the road. I like to wear them for decoration. Like jewelry," she explains when I ask what they are for.

Her other son, Azita's brother-in-law, has two wives. His first, who lacks most of her teeth, is the mother of seven daughters. His second wife is fourteen and has just given birth to a son, the mother-in-law's first grandson.

This recent marriage happened according to the tribal exchange tradition, so the family did not have to pay for her. In order to secure a new wife who might bear a son, the family made a trade with the neighbor, where a thirteen-year-old daughter was offered to the neighbor's family. She is now married and pregnant by the neighbor's fifteen-year-old son, who is proudly referred to as a Koran student. Like other Koran students here, he is instructed by an illiterate mullah on what the religious texts say, since he himself is not able to read or write.

Inside, all the cupboards in the kitchen have padlocks. A few large storage containers and a glass cabinet with dishes are also locked. We are shown into the main salon, a small room painted in a shiny turquoise color. A photo of Azita hangs on the wall, surrounded by a fuchsia paper garland from when she first celebrated her election to parliament. This is the room Azita's children would live in with their mother were they to return to their father's house. We sit on the dirt floor and exchange more greetings. The low, bulky door is pushed almost shut so the family's women and children cannot enter. We are in what currently serves as a guest receiving room, and only the mother-in-law and her son are allowed here.

The women remain outside the door, eagerly trying to get a peek at the visitors. The children pile on top of one another to make the most of the thin strip of visibility through the door opening. Every now and then, a small child tries to force the door open, only to be pushed away by her grandmother. Azita's brother-in-law brings in a special treat: a square box with liquid in it and a large table fan. He places the acid battery in the window and hooks up the fan. Moments later, Setareh and I are ensconced in a thick stream of warm air blowing straight into our eyes, and we must raise our voices to be heard over the noise of the engine.

Through vivid gestures and rapid speech, showing her few remaining front teeth, Azita's mother-in-law describes how she runs the house: "It would be impossible for everyone if I were not here. Yes, I can't leave the house. I need to stay here and take care of my son and my grandson. And my son needs to work on the plantation outside."

Being the oldest surviving member of the family, she gets to advise everyone on how to do things. How old exactly?

"I'm seventy or eighty. I don't really know." Her son offers another estimate: "She's eighty-five or ninety." In any case, she is by far the longest-living woman in her village, they believe. Since men work with the animals, the women run the household, under her direction. Some of her granddaughters go to school for a few hours each day, but other than that, none of them are allowed to leave the house.

She *loves* Azita.

She says it over and over, with great emphasis. Her oldest son reaffirms it: Azita is the family's great pride. They are now known in the village as "the husband family" of the powerful politician in Kabul. People treat them with more respect and admiration now. The family is of course sad Azita does not live with them anymore, but they are well aware she has more important things to do. They always knew she was destined for greater things. Hopefully, she will return to them one day, with her daughters. It is a burden to her husband, though, to lead the stressful life of Kabul, but they understand it is a sacrifice he is making. Those same statements come back in response to almost every question we ask, before we are ushered out for a tour of the humble premises by Azita's brother-in-law, who feels his elderly mother should no longer be bothered: They both agree that Azita's success is thanks to her husband.

Later, we make our way on the narrow road back to town, and we pass a little girl who is wandering alone on the road. She is barefoot and seems unable to walk straight, her small frame moving unsteadily back and forth along the roadside. The shoulder straps on her dress are untied, hanging down from her naked torso. The driver circles his finger in the air: She is sick in the head. Nobody cares how she dresses or that she is out walking alone. She will never marry anyone.

"DID YOU SEE the keys?" Azita's brother asks when we meet him in the trailer where he works on a USAID-funded project to convert Taliban sympathizers in the province by offering them cash payments.

He emits a hollow laugh.

Those keys were the very thing his sister's life revolved around for many years. She could not even drink a glass of water, no less eat, without access to those keys, which came only with her mother-in-law's permission. It makes him angry to talk about them. He was the one who went to check on Azita each Friday. The trip took one hour by foot, and forty-five minutes by donkey. And at the age of ten, he was the one who tried to challenge his brother-in-law by refusing to leave so his sister would not be harmed again. When he was twelve, he started spending the night in the village, so he could visit her on two consecutive days.

"And you think they are poor?"

He smacks his tongue after hearing my account of the village. "That family has both money and land! But it is how villagers live."

When he smiles, showing all his teeth, he looks just like Azita. His eyes glimmer just like hers, and his speech is only an octave or two deeper. And just like his sister's, his fluent English is self-taught. He is twenty-four and the only son of his parents. But he is not on speaking terms with them; he married a Pashtun woman they did not approve of. He does not want children, either. Why would he want that, in this society, with its impossible rules to live by for both men and women, he asks me.

As a son, he has not been able to please his parents more than his sisters; quite the opposite. Before his marriage, he had refused his father's dictated career path of becoming a mullah. During the Taliban period, young boys were obliged to study under religious leaders, and to Azita's brother, those years felt completely wasted. His father was still disappointed; the path to a future with some recognition would come only through studying religion, he told his son. It would help not just him, but the entire family, he had argued. It was the beginning of a rift between them that only widened in the years after the Taliban left.

He expected more from an educated man like his father. But maybe the wars got to him in a way that changed him for good. When their father was young, he was an idealist who wanted to take on and change the world, but he was struck down. He was said to be "the most liberal of everyone" back then. Azita's brother does not hesitate to say out loud what I have suspected for a while now: "Everybody here knows he was a Communist. It's not a secret. Today, he just says it was something in his youth."

Azita's father's joining the party at that time explains how he came by the university job, and how his daughter attended elite schools. And later, why his library was burned and the family had to flee from Kabul. It is also the reason why Azita does not want to involve her father too much in her politics—he was aligned with other foreigners, who are not appreciated by the new ones she is currently aligned with. Nor by her Afghan constituents.

It makes their journeys eerily similar, and perhaps typical for many Afghans of these two war generations.

Azita is the "collaborator," as her father was in his time. "Communists" were viewed as those who sold their country to the Russians, similar to how Azita has been part of a foreign-backed government. Her father placed his trust and loyalty in those who promised to reform the country; he bet everything on it. When those ideas were shut down and the foreigners left, after his family's life fell apart, he was filled with regret and distrust.

"She is just like him," Azita's brother says, as if to confirm my train of thought. "She is her father's daughter. Anything she could do to make him proud she has always done."

And just like her father was, she will be disappointed, her brother predicts. When he travels to the capital, he wears jeans and a leather jacket. That would raise too many eyebrows and might even be dangerous in Badghis, where he sticks to the flowing white *peran tonban* he detests. In his view, Afghanistan has dark days ahead.

"I used to cry when the Afghan flag was raised. But just look at my sister's situation—that political game. The internationals have been playing a game with us, too. When they leave, there will be a civil war, after just this short time of peace that we have had now."

Azita's brother predicts she, too, has too much faith in the political process, just as their father once did. Kabul's elite has always aligned itself with whichever foreigners pull into town, and, eventually, Afghans who stay pay a price when those foreigners leave. Those who can will leave the country, and will again be replaced by those with more conservative values. And there will be consequences for Azita, too—the threat against her will only increase once the foreigners leave. She will likely never try to separate from her husband; her brother is sure of it. She would not do it to her parents, nor to her children.

But, he says, "Every human has her limits."

ONE OF THE most prominent families in town is about to marry off another daughter.

The price for Azita was $1,000 and some land. The price for her three-years-younger sister was set to $4,000.

Now, thanks to Azita's status, the family's stock has risen, and a daughter of the house fetches one of the highest prices of any bride of Badghis. The asking price for Azita's third sister, Anita, has been met at $14,000.

Preparations at Azita's parents' house have been going on for months now, with cars shuttling between Herat and Qala-e-Naw. An entire room of the house is dedicated to the bride's loot: Brand-new pots, pans, and plastic containers are hidden under a large blanket. Decorations have been brought from Herat, and pastel-colored garlands and paper napkins are stored in a large box. In the garden sit five large shipping containers from Pakistan, now emptied of their contents. Few expenses are spared in the wedding preparations, and the future husband is paying for everything. Azita's father has also contributed several gifts: A double bed. A washing machine. A dishwasher. An electric heater. Cooking gas.

At twenty-six, Anita is not a young bride, but she has some education and works as a teacher. She lives here with her parents in one of Qala-e-Naw's best houses on an avenue-like street, where high iron doors with ornaments open onto a garden of well-tended red and white roses. A small, simpler house sits to the right, next to the larger, white-painted main house with stately entrance pillars. High palm trees shade the big house entirely. Its greatest luxury, an indoor bathroom, is said to be the envy of the neighborhood. Not even the governor's mansion has that. The toilet is still outside, but there is running water in the house, in a white and yellow porcelain washbasin. Thick wall-to-wall carpets in soft pastel colors soak up any noise, and heavy brocade curtains seem to keep the desert sand out, making the indoor air easier to breathe. Azita has mentioned, not without bitterness, that her parents collect a healthy income from their old apartment in Kabul's Macroyan neighborhood. Her mother also runs a kindergarten school.

The lady of the house is Azita's mother, Siddiqua.

She strides toward us at the entrance, in a sheer white head scarf and a long brown cotton jacket and skirt. The whole family is busy with the wedding preparations, she tells us. Very busy indeed. But they can see us for a brief moment, since we have traveled far. Azita's mother is striking, with a sharp nose and high cheekbones. She has a few gray strands blending into her dark hair, the same color as her thick eyebrows. As we sit down for cardamom tea and imported chocolates in shiny wrappers, Siddiqua remarks on how she, of course, finds it an honor, but a bit curious, that someone would travel all this way to speak about her oldest daughter.

Is there any chance we might see Azita's father as well? I wonder.

She shakes her head. He is a man of his own mind, and he is not always in the mood for visitors.

How long might we be in Badghis? In polite code, Setareh explains that we are in no hurry and will remain for as long as we need to. In even more polite code, Siddiqua in return assures us that she will welcome us every day, without guarantees of a meeting with the patriarch himself.

Her daughter Anita joins us. She is young and a little shy, but proud to be at the center of her parents' attention as a bride to be. Her bushy eyebrows, which have grown together in the middle, will soon be plucked to thin strands for her wedding. Anita has been engaged for six months now. So far, there has been no direct conversation with her husband-to-be, nor has she spent any time alone with him.

"Afghan girls go blind into their marriage," she jokes.

Her mother does not laugh. "He is educated, from a good family, just like you," she says, addressing her daughter. "He has a good personality, and everybody was happy with him. So I think we did a good job for you."

Anita looks down. It's true. "Nobody forced me. And I have refused others."

Siddiqua turns to me: "Lots of suitors came, several in one week even, from difference provinces. We are a well-known family here, and everybody knows about our daughters. All the others cried when we announced that she was engaged. And Anita said nothing when we asked if she would agree to this one."

When asked about a husband, silence means consent. It would be impolite of a daughter to address her parents directly with any objection.

"What made you say yes?" I ask Anita.

"We were both teachers in a college center. We got familiar with each other. I knew his family's status is high."

"So you have actually spoken, then?" Setareh and I glance at each other. This sounds interesting.

"We have greeted each other. But he seems like a good man."

He never told her he would propose, either. That would have made him a dishonorable man who "plays with girls." Such matters are discussed with parents only. He is Tajik, so Anita is considered to be "marrying up" from her mixed lineage, as opposed to Azita, who married into one of Afghanistan's smaller minorities.

"Do you feel happy?"

Embarrassed smile. "Yes."

"Do you think he will allow you to keep working?"

Anita looks at her hands. "I don't know. It will be the decision of my husband, and I will respect it."

Siddiqua has been fanning herself with a piece of plastic while listening to Anita. Now she breaks in: "They are a very good match."

She has been married for thirty-seven years herself.

"Tell me," I ask Siddiqua, "what is the secret to being married for so long?"

She looks at me like I am clueless. "It's very hard to get divorced here," she says, throwing her hands up in a gesture of "What else did you imagine?"

But what is important is loyalty, she adds after a pause, in an attempt to smooth over her statement. Mourtaza was chosen for her, and of course parents try hard to select the best husband for a daughter. Just like she is trying to do for her own. From that point, you work with what you have, she explains.

I nod, to indicate that I understand. The conversation is going exactly where I want it to go.

Siddiqua understands that too, and quickly volunteers her take on Azita's marriage: "I did not agree. I had a very bad reaction to it. I was thinking she would become a doctor. I was shocked when my husband brought it up. It was very hard for me. In the end, I felt that I had to give up. I was unhappy, but I accepted it."

HIS SNOW-WHITE BEARD enters first. It is almost an entity of its own, floating freely around his face, reaching up to his white hair, water-combed flat just moments ago.

Azita's father places himself so he is looking directly at me, towering above all of us on the floor. It is as though he has been listening and just waiting for his moment to enter the conversation. He sits down before we have a chance to rise, and spits out his *naswar,* a strong green chewing tobacco, on a teacup saucer.

Setareh, ever the professional, attempts to make an introduction, but he cuts her off. "I know who she is. And I know what she wants to talk about."

With his eyes still fixed on me, he begins to speak.

"I am not a dark or close-minded man who will lock my girls in the house. I was a professor before. I like my children to be educated and go to school. I worked with Russian advisers during the Russian times."

It is not exactly a reference to Communism, but meant to underscore that he was at the pinnacle of society.

"I am so proud of Azita," he continues. "There are so few of her kind. The other woman politicians are with different groups and have their powerful backers. My girl is independent. She is very bright, a hard worker, and she knows what she is doing. She has come so far."

He looks pleased.

"But this almost did not happen," I say. "When you decided she should get married, how could she know she was even going to be able to work?"

"I was forced to do so. There was civil war in Afghanistan. There were rebels here in Badghis. No rules. There was war. Everybody wanted to take your girls. It was a terrible time in my life. I was so worried all the time. 'How can I protect my family?' I thought. In Kabul, my girls were potential victims. I considered Pakistan and Tajikistan. Finally I settled on my ancestral place—Badghis. I came here for my family to live. Society was very unsafe for girls, and law and order had broken down completely. If anybody realized you had a beautiful girl or an educated girl in your house, they would just come and take her, to 'have relations' with her. And that would have ruined my family. I am not happy about it, but I was forced to give my daughter to my brother's son. It was that or have my daughters end up in the mountains as brides of warlords. This is how it happened that I gave my daughter to an uneducated man. He was the best solution at a time of war."

Siddiqua objects: "But this was during the Taliban. There was no war."

Mourtaza flinches, a little startled by being cut off by his wife. "This was when the Taliban were forming. Some very powerful people came to me and asked for my girl. They would have taken her without hesitation. Marrying her off would close their eyes on her."

"What about the fact that he already had a wife? Was that a problem?" I ask.

Siddiqua hisses, and her voice turns sharp. "Of course it was a problem that he had a wife already. I mean, how would you like it? Just imagine."

"Do you ever think you made a mistake, or did you make the right decision?"

Mourtaza sighs.

"It was not my desire or ambition to marry my girl to an uneducated person. But if you had been here then, you would have said I made the right decision. This was a question of life and death. I wanted her to survive. Not to die in some cave in a mountain with rebels. I wanted my daughters to go to the best schools and universities, and to marry educated men. That was my hope for all of them. But today I have all my girls. Alive. If I had had my desire, it would have been different. Completely different. My heart did not want to do it."

Azita had to be married not only for her own protection, but also for the sake of the entire family and its reputation, he explains again. In the society Mourtaza and everyone else here must live in, individual needs and achievement are secondary to those of the family, because they must be. One member cannot go off and plan his or her life alone, without regard for anyone else. It does not work that way—the entire family and its reputation always need to be taken into account.

Mourtaza says he always had Azita's best in mind, but he had to take into account his own interests, as well as those of his other children, and his family's legacy. Perhaps someday, after years of peace and prosperity, social rules will loosen up and allow cultivation of individual choice and happiness. But for now, one's family and its standing are the only possible constants between wars, and that needs to be carefully preserved. Mourtaza has even cut off his son for disobeying him on the question of marriage.

As Azita's father explains this, I recall Azita's brother's words: "What's the difference between the mountain and the village he sent her to? We are a large tribe. We would have been protected. He could have picked someone educated."

But an educated man may not necessarily have been better, in Mourtaza's view: "Azita is not in a bad situation today. Her husband will do what I advise. Yes, I forced her to marry him. Yes, he was a poor and uneducated man. But he didn't stop her from working. At the time, there was no one else I could trust. What if she had married someone rich and educated, who did not allow her to go out of the house? At least he didn't prevent her progress."

The way Azita's father sees it, his daughter's achievements are thanks to him. Surely she will have her seat in parliament back soon, and if she does not, she has still reached higher than anyone in their family ever has, by his doing. To her family, and to their province, she is considered a success. Yes, the union with her husband could have been better. But it could also have been a lot worse, in her father's view. Azita has some freedoms that most women in Afghanistan do not have, as her husband allows her to work. Even though she and her husband are going through a hard time right now—and both parents are convinced it will pass—her life is still better than that of other Afghan women.

MOURTAZA WINCES AGAIN when I bring up the abuse.

It was the abuse of his daughter that made him cry on her door-step as he was leaving many years ago. He remembers it today; he felt like he had beaten his own daughter by putting her inside the home of a man who did not even recognize it as a crime.

Whatever the exact circumstances and motivations of Mourtaza's decision to marry off Azita to her older cousin may have been, this visibly moves him. He takes a deep breath and bursts into a speech that may hint of the political convictions of his youth:

"Afghanistan is not a developed country. It's not an educated country. Even in educated families, people are immature. There are no rights for women here and most men feel like women should just obey them. This makes our society miserable. The violence . . . it's so common here and it's not even a matter of my daughter's life. It happens to the wives of ministers. In Azita's family, her mother-in-law and her sister-in-law . . . their level of understanding is low. They think they must discipline girls. This is not good. They give no rights to women. Violence against women is everywhere. Men want to talk, and for their wives to be quiet. Of course, I felt horrible when it happened. I talked to my son-in-law. But it's not easy."

He shakes his head.

Both he and his daughter are part of a system that he alone cannot change or even revolt against. Time has taught him that. But it's still unbearable for him to think that anyone has laid a hand on his daughter. He has been tempted to strike back, to literally punch out his son-in-law to extract a promise that the abuse will stop. But once a daughter has been given away for marriage, her husband must be respected. Even by the father-in-law. Mourtaza knows this.

"Afghan men are immature," he repeats. "I am a man myself, but this is true. I can only advise my son-in-law. I cannot change society. We can't hide anywhere. Our society is sick."

Throwing his hand out toward Siddiqua, who still wears her head scarf inside the house, he says: "I was always against girls wearing scarves and being kept inside. I don't care if she wears a miniskirt."

Siddiqua looks a little taken aback. It was a long time ago that she wore a miniskirt. When they were both young and lived in Kabul.

"I advocate freedom and awareness," Mourtaza says. "That's how I grew up. But my children have been brought up with these stupid, *stupid* rules imposed on them by society."

Siddiqua nods. Society. The greater evil.

It takes the blame, and the responsibility, away from the individual. But realistically, how far can personal responsibility go in a time of war, when entire families are just trying to survive?

Siddiqua appears upset, not so much from my questions, but from speaking about the abuse of her daughter. "This is what we have today, so we have to accept it," she says, turning toward me.

"I know my son-in-law now, and I know he is not a bad man. Even though my girl takes care of the family. This is common here—you have to fit yourself into the situation. She is doing well. We were so happy when she was born. It took four years for us to have a child. My husband never had any sisters. She got a lot of attention for three years, before my second child arrived. I loved to dress her up, in every color and every style. She was wild. Just like a boy. Very fast. Quick in the head. And she grew up in the best of situations, in the best of times. There was peace, she went to the best schools with the best facilities. They even had laboratories. She was singing. . . ."

Siddiqua interrupts herself. "If there had not been war, everything would have been different for her. But Azita is the daughter of her father. She is strong. We are who we must be."

That their youngest granddaughter is growing up as a boy is just another concession to their own society. Over the years, they have made many.

WE ARE STUCK. I have promised Setareh's family to take her back to Kabul soon, and my own visa is about to expire. But after saying good-bye to Azita's family, we soon realize we may actually not get very far.

Our Afghan military friends are busy elsewhere, and the United Nations is not flying into the remote province at all, due to the current "security situation," the details of which are not shared. It's either the road or we stay put, hoping the United Nations will change its policy. When I tell Setareh this, she looks about as crestfallen as I feel, faced with the prospect of several more weeks in the now 104-degree heat of Badghis.

As we stare at each other, I realize that of course there is one, and only one, air service that runs reliably in Afghanistan. The American one.

We do not have enough clout to work our way into the U.S. military's infrastructure, nor do we really want to, having successfully avoided any entanglement with them so far. But the U.S. Agency for International Development routinely charters small private planes manned by tan Western pilots in white, short-sleeved epaulet shirts for every impossible-to-get-to corner of this country. However I am well aware, as I am often told by Americans, that "Sweden doesn't matter." In this particular situation, my humble and presumed neutral Swedish passport will not necessarily get us anywhere at all.

Time has come to fully shape-shift into my studied American immigrant persona again, honed for a decade among impossibly assertive New Yorkers. I finagle the number for the lone USAID officer, who controls both agricultural policy and flight manifests for the entire province.

And whether it is my best attempt to sound confident with a thick American accent, or a dose of Afghan magic, the generous State Department employee on the phone offers us two leather-clad seats on one of their scheduled flights out of Badghis, courtesy of American taxpayers—one for me, and one for my "Afghan partner," as I have just dubbed Setareh in a poor attempt at official-speak. There is no request for any kind of security vetting or discussion about her ethnicity or her father's clan: a small miracle of its own. I exclaim a mimed "God Bless America" to Setareh, who offers a silent high five in return.

LATER, WITH OUR departure sorted, on our final night in Badghis, Setareh has a request. "Do you know how to *couple dance?*"

It's when a man and a woman dance together, she clarifies when I look puzzled. She has seen pictures of it online—two people hold on to each other while moving across the floor. Setareh has only ever danced by herself, or with other women, corralled in the bride's area at weddings. So could I teach her this other way of dancing, please?

After checking to make sure the staircase is empty and that no one seems to be coming, I place my arm around her waist and her hand on my shoulder.

Our soundtrack is a Viennese waltz, hummed by me, as we go over the steps. *One-two-three, one-two-three.* Anything more modern than a waltz would require more brainpower on my part, and the waltz seems fitting—it is how I was taught to dance for my first formal dinner party in Stockholm when I was sixteen.

As I lead Setareh out in a barefoot swirl on the carpets of the governor's guesthouse in northern Afghanistan, we tell each other about our big gowns with flowing trains. Or maybe I am in tails, with slicked-back hair and shiny patent leather shoes.

After a few staggering rounds, we move smoothly through the thick dark air streaming through tattered mosquito nets. Setareh bends her back outward against my hand, letting her uncovered waist-length black hair fall toward the floor.

She has been my bodyguard and my negotiator and my researcher and my buddy, whom I in return have taught things no proper woman should speak of. She is all woman, all the time, of a certain, very confident kind. But just like several of the *bacha posh,* she has a trusting and progressive father, who has allowed her to work and travel with me, into the unknown. She has risked her life for me, and I will always guard her secrets.

If Afghanistan again takes a more fundamentalist turn, all the Setarehs, all the Mehrans, all the Azitas, and all the refuser girls will go first. Whatever they wear and regardless of the gender they display, they will once again risk being locked behind closed doors, in darkness; their education, wisdom, and spunk wasted. These women who have sprouted up in the past decade will disappear from a magical place full of secrets, bristling with power and promise, that they could have helped run.

As we waltz in our sweat-drenched pants and tunics with a touch of Swedish bug repellent, most certainly ridiculed by Afghan mosquitoes, I think about how I should dance more when I return to my world.

ONE OF THE BOYS

THE WAY I have come to see it now is that *bacha posh* is a missing piece in the history of women.

We have an idea of how patriarchy was formed. But back then, a resistance was also born. *Bacha posh* is both historical and present-day rejection of patriarchy by those who refuse to accept the ruling order for themselves and their daughters. Most *bacha posh,* including Zahra, Shukria, Shahed, Nader, and Mehran, have paid dearly for living as boys, and their circumstances were rarely chosen. But once they found themselves on the other side, they fought back. And it was noted. So can a story of concession and resistance, of tragedy and hope, exist at the same time?

For women, it always has.

Despite Afghans' awareness of the practice, individual *bacha posh* are often isolated, and left alone to ponder their notions of gender. But each older *bacha posh* I have come to know has at one point turned to me and asked if there are others like her. Some have been stunned to learn that there are—not only in Afghanistan, but also in other countries. How can we speak to them? they have asked. How can we meet? Or, as Shahed once asked me, how could they build a village where they would all live together?

Nader is trying to do just that, in her own small way, by building resistance among her group of tae kwon do students.

It is a beginning, and we should do a lot more to help her expand that circle. Because throughout history, when European and American women disguised themselves as men to fight wars, pursue higher educations, and, for instance, become doctors—all of which were initially off-limits to women—it was eventually followed by a larger shift, where more areas slowly and painfully were pried open to women. Single acts of dressing like men did not cause that shift, but they were part of something bigger—an underground of women slowly coming to disregard what they had been told about their weaker gender by learning to imitate and disguise themselves as the other.

Some may call that tragic—that women "are not allowed to be women," to wear billowy skirts and flowers in their hair, and instead adopt the exterior and mien of men. But that is what *most* women, in *most* countries, have had to forgo in order to infiltrate male territory. Ask female executives, lawyers, and those who work on Wall Street how much femininity they can allow themselves to display on a daily basis. And who is to say that those embellishments are what make a woman?

Afghanistan is a story of patriarchy, in a raw form. In that, it is also a story of Western history, with elements of the lives our foremothers and forefathers led. By learning about an ill-functioning system in Afghanistan, we can also begin to see how most of us—men and women, regardless of nationality and ethnicity—at times perpetuate a problematic culture of honor, where women and men are both trapped by traditional gender roles. Because we all prefer those roles—or maybe because it is how we were brought up and we know of nothing else.

BACHA POSH ALSO provides clues for the larger question of when and how the strict patriarchal and patrilineal system can begin to disintegrate in Afghanistan. Westerners have sometimes attempted to teach Afghan women about gender, freedom, human rights, and how they might conjure up the confidence to speak for themselves.

But dressing your daughter as a son, or walking out the door as a man, are only two of the creative ways Afghan women buck an impossible system. It tells us this: Being born with power, as a boy, doesn't necessarily spur innovation. But being born entirely without it forces innovation in women, who must learn to survive almost from the moment they are born. Afghan women do not need much well-intentioned training on that.

But as Azita says, the burkas, and any other ways of hiding, will disappear only once there is safety and rule of law in Afghanistan. Until then, nothing much will happen in terms of easing harsh social codes or opening up opportunities for women. Because most of all, and first of all, there needs to be peace.

In times of war, the argument for pulling a teenage daughter out of school is simple to make—just as it's easy to argue for marrying her off at a young age, or to use her to pay off a debt. In war, there are few dreams; the future may not exist and the prospect of reaching old age is abstract. War does away with ambition for change and even faith. The fear that the extreme insecurity of war creates fuels conservatism and closes minds, making families turn inward and trust no one. Alliances through marriage, in which women are used as trading chips, become even more important. To effect change on a larger, political scale—to defy society or one's own family in a time of war—may be too much to ask of most.

AFTER THAT, it is about following the money.

The value of women in society can be fully realized and accepted—by men, women, and governments—only when they begin to achieve some economic parity. Increasing financial power makes possible political power—and political power is necessary to advocate for real change in family law, in banishing polygyny, in allowing women to get a divorce and sharing custody of children, and in prosecuting domestic abuse and sexualized violence. And only educated women, who can gain economic power, will be able to challenge flawed interpretations of religion and culture that prescribe segregation and certain behavior of one gender. It is not just a human rights argument, it is the Warren Buffett argument and the Christine Lagarde argument: Countries that want to develop their economies and standards of living cannot afford to shut out one-half of their population. And it is the Virginia Woolf argument: In order to create, a woman needs money and a room of her own.

Conservatives and extremists in any society are extremely aware of this fact. Those who control life, and the bodies of women, control the money and hold the power. Women who are kept indoors, whether because of references to religion, culture, or honor, cannot make money and will not hold any power. Women who are married off and locked up, and raped by older husbands in order to produce male heirs, will never rule a country or explore its natural resources. Or go to war, for that matter. Women who never receive an education are not likely to demand their rightful inheritance. Women who do not have a say over their own bodies' reproduction will never be able to challenge men on economic power. Those who hold the power to create life control the universe.

MEN ARE THE key to infiltrating and subverting patriarchy.

As the U.S.-led war ends, many will still say that Afghanistan's treatment of women is due to its culture and religion. That the case for women's rights in Afghanistan is a hopeless one. That Afghans are simply too conservative and too set in their thousand-year-old ways. But that is not true. I believe most Afghan men, on an individual level, are far from extremist or fundamentalist.

Hope rests with those men, who control what happens to their daughters. Behind every discreetly ambitious young Afghan woman with budding plans to take on the world, there is an interesting father. And in every successful grown woman who has managed to break new ground and do something women usually do not, there is a determined father, who is redefining honor and society by promoting his daughter. There will always be a small group of elite women with wealthy parents who can choose to go abroad or to take high positions in politics. They will certainly inspire others, but in order for significant numbers of women to take advantage of higher education and participate in the economy on a larger scale, it will take powerful men educating many other men.

Those hundreds of "gender projects" funded by aid money might have been more effective if they had also included *men*. The fact that Westerners often came in intending to promote only women in a country where the majority are unemployed also contributed to the perception that the entire idea of human rights and gender equity was a stand *against men*.

This is why visible young girls and women, supported by fathers, need to be cultivated and stand as indigenous examples of how promoting daughters leads to better economic prosperity. For all. Because she brings in much more as an educated young woman than as a bride, while not making her father any less of a man, but rather one with a bigger house. Through that, the idea of honor can be redefined by men to other men. What is honorable is not to beat a woman, to sell her, or to take another wife; it is to have an educated daughter. Men, too, suffer under the current system of honor, where they alone bear the burden of supporting and protecting their families.

Just as the civil rights moment expanded to include those of any color, and as straight people joined the fight for gay people to marry, it is harder for conservatives to resist when a new economy takes hold and social norms around gender are moved by both women and men.

We should strongly desire such a development in Afghanistan, not just out of the goodness of our hearts or any idealist notions, but because research overwhelmingly shows that countries with increased equality are much less violent and more economically stable. In terms of "national security" and foreign affairs, Afghan women, as well as women globally, should be everyone's concern, up to and including the military.

In *Sex and World Peace*, a study on the relationship between gender and violence, political science scholars conclude that violence on a micro level—for instance between a husband and wife—is directly reflected in how violent a *society* is. Both within its borders and against outsiders. Countries that suppress its women are more likely to threaten their neighbors as well as other countries farther away. So the more progress for women Afghanistan sees, the less of a threat the country is to the rest of the world.

Why, then, are women so often relegated to an "issue" and not standing at the top of every agenda on foreign policy?

Women were never an "issue." Afghanistan's history in the last decades is one example of how women—and control over them—were always at the very core of conflict. The authors of the study, which, together with the work of Gerda Lerner, should be required reading for students everywhere, go as far as to suggest that the "clash of civilizations" of the future will be based not on ethnopolitical differences but on gender beliefs. From that perspective, what is mistakenly referred to as "women's rights" is not even just about human rights. It's about evolution and building peaceful civilizations.

Gerda Lerner, after she had researched the origins of patriarchy, predicted that the construct would one day come to an end, since it is a human-made idea. There will perhaps always be sexism, just as there is racism today. But slavery is officially abolished in most places on earth. The journey toward freedom for Afghan women will continue for a long time yet. But it does not have to be endless.

SOMEDAY IN OUR FUTURE it may be possible for women everywhere not to be restricted to those roles society deems natural, God-given, or appropriately feminine. A woman will not need to be disguised as a man to go outside, to climb a tree, or to make money. She will not need to make an effort to resemble a man, or to think like one. Instead, she can speak a language that men will want to understand. She will be free to wear a suit or a skirt or something entirely different. She will not count as three-quarters of a man, and her testimony will not be worth half of a man's. She will be recognized as someone's sister, mother, and daughter. And maybe, someday, her identity will not be confined to how she relates to a brother, a son, or a father. Instead, she will be recognized as an individual, whose life holds value only in itself.

It will not be the end of the world, the nation-state, or sexuality. It will not solve all the world's problems. But it is an exciting promise of how we might continue to evolve, through small bursts of individual greatness alongside a slow overhaul of our civilization.

This possible future could only expand the human experience and be liberating to men and women alike. And it will be interesting to all. Because, maybe what Azita once said about why she was glad to have been born a girl holds some truth:

"We know what it's like to be men. But they know nothing about us."

VIERGE MODERNE

I am no woman. I am a neuter.
I am a child, a page-boy, and a bold decision,
I am a laughing glimpse of a burning sun

I am a net for all voracious fish,
I am a toast to every woman's honor,
I am a step toward chance and disaster,
I am a leap in freedom and the self

I am the blood's whisper in a man's ear,
I am the soul's shiver, the flesh's longing and denial,
I am an entry sign to new paradises

I am a flame, seeking and jolly,
I am a water, deep, but daring up to the knees,
I am fire and water, in sincere context, on free terms

EDITH SÖDERGRAN
Finland, 1916

AUTHOR'S NOTE

AS SHE APPROACHED her tenth birthday, Mehran became a student, along with her older sisters, at an all-girls school in Kabul. She wears the uniform for girls. In the afternoons, she is allowed to switch into boys' clothing at home and when she is out in the neighborhood. She keeps her hair short and is still considered to be the wildest member of the family.

AZITA NEVER REENTERED parliament. In late 2011, along with dozens of other candidates, her victory was acknowledged as valid by a court appointed to resolve the political impasse from the fraught elections of the year before. But Afghanistan's president Hamid Karzai ultimately agreed only to reinstate ten parliamentarians in the lower house, with the blessing of the United Nations. Azita was not among them. Instead, she helped form a new political party in opposition to the government and eventually got a job with a European aid organization. Her modest salary allowed her to keep the family in Kabul and her daughters in school. The family of eight moved to a smaller apartment and now shares three rooms. In the summer of 2013, she sought medical treatment due to blunt strokes to her neck and chest, which were photographed and copies were forwarded to me. In an interview in Kabul, her husband confirmed that their marriage had again come to include violence.

In early 2014 Azita was let go from her job, as the funding for her organization was to expire.

AT SEVENTEEN, ZAHRA adopted a new hairstyle that she says is an attempt to replicate Justin Bieber's. She still wears male clothing. She has dropped out of school; she could no longer bear exhortations by her Pashto teacher to dress like a woman. Her mother still insists she should get married. Her father says he will never force her. Zahra refuses to go to weddings, fearing she may be spotted by a future mother-in-law. She holds on to a dream of immigrating to another country, where there are more of her kind.

SHUKRIA LIVES WITH her three children in Kabul. She continues to work full-time as a nurse and is studying to become a doctor.

NADER STILL DRIVES her car around Kabul and teaches tae kwon do in a basement.

IN A FAILED attempt to flee Afghanistan through Tajikistan, Shahed had all her savings stolen by a smuggler.

FINALLY, A NOTE on Setareh: She is the only character in the book who in reality is a construct of several people. I worked with several translators who, for an extra layer of protection and according to their wishes, I have called by a single name. For each character interviewed, and for different occasions, my translator needed to possess different skills and knowledge of different ethnicities, neighborhoods, and cities. So "Setareh" is Pashtun and she is Tajik and she is Hazara. She speaks several dialects of Dari, as well as Pashto, Urdu, and English. She has a degree in literature, in law, and in political science, and she is a very clever street kid. She is a poet, a teacher, an aspiring lawyer, and a budding businesswoman. She is upper class and middle class and she is a refugee. She is a student. She wears a full hijab and a sloppy head scarf; she prays five times a day and not at all. And within each young woman who took the role of Setareh for me, there are many more who are constantly shape-shifting and adapting to whatever circumstances they are thrown into. The way Afghans always do.

New York, February 2014
@nordbergj
bachaposh.com

NOTES

x   **"But Not an Afghan Woman"**   First published by the U.S. nonprofit Afghan Women's Writing Project (awwproject.org) in 2010. AWWP was founded by American journalist and author Masha Hamilton. The organization serves as a platform for and offers training to young female writers in Afghanistan.

PROLOGUE

1   **announced that U.S. troops would begin to withdraw**   In "Remarks by the President in Address to the Nation on the Way Forward in Afghanistan and Pakistan," December 1, 2009, whitehouse.gov, the president discussed his policy for withdrawing U.S. soldiers from Afghanistan after the surge: "And as Commander-in-Chief, I have determined that it is in our vital national interest to send an additional 30,000 U.S. troops to Afghanistan. After 18 months, our troops will begin to come home."

In 2011, the president reiterated his commitment to troop withdrawal. See "Remarks by the President on the Way Forward in Afghanistan," June 22, 2011, whitehouse.gov, where he says: "By 2014, this process of transition will be complete, and the Afghan people will be responsible for their own security." In 2014, the president announced that U.S. troop withdrawal would be completed by 2016.

CHAPTER 1: THE REBEL MOTHER

9   **Elected to the Wolesi Jirga**   For more background on the Wolesi Jirga, see Martine van Bijlert and Sari Kouvo, eds., *Snapshots of an Intervention, The Unlearned Lessons of Afghanistan's Decade of Assistance (2001–11)* (Kabul: Afghanistan Analysts Network [AAN], 2012).

9   **heavily populated with drug kingpins and warlords**   See Declan Walsh, "Warlords and Women Take Seats in Afghan Parliament," *The Guardian,* December 18, 2005, theguardian.com.

11   **more girls are enrolled in school**   The World Bank's arm for helping the poorest countries, International Development Association, worldbank.org, cites the following figures: "Enrollment in grades 1–12 increased from 3.9 million in 2004 to 6.2 million in 2008. Girls' enrollment skyrocketed from 839,000 to more than 2.2 million, and boys' from 2.6 million to 3.9 million—the highest enrollment in the history of Afghanistan."

11   **The majority of marriages are still forced**   UNIFEM Afghanistan Mission, "UNIFEM Afghanistan Fact Sheet 2007," unifem.org. This states: "70 to 80% of women face forced marriages in Afghanistan."

11   **honor killings are not unusual**   Human Rights, United Nations Assistance Mission in Afghanistan Kabul, Office of the United Nations High Commissioner for Human Rights Geneva, *Harmful Traditional Practices and Implementation of the Law on Elimination of Violence against Women in Afghanistan,* December 9, 2010, unama.unmissions.org. The report cites one of several harmful traditional practices: "So-called 'honour' killings recognize a man's right to kill a woman with impunity because of the damage that her immoral actions have caused to family honour. It is a killing of a family member by one or several relatives who believe the victim has brought shame upon the family."

11   **involvement of the justice system in a rape case**   Human Rights, United Nations Assistance Mission in Afghanistan Kabul, Office of the United Nations High Commissioner for Human Rights Geneva, *Silence Is Violence: End the Abuse of Women in Afghanistan,* Kabul, July 8, 2009. This report discusses the high incidence of rape in Afghanistan, as well as why victims are reluctant to report it or to seek redress. In particular, it notes: "Shame is attached to rape victims rather than to the perpetrator. Victims often find themselves being prosecuted for the offence of *zina* (adultery) and are denied access to justice."

11   **Women burn themselves to death**   Human Rights, United Nations Assistance Mission in Afghanistan Kabul, Office of the United Nations High Commissioner for Human Rights Geneva, *Harmful Tradi-*

tional Practices and Implementation of the Law on Elimination of Violence against Women in Afghanistan, December 9, 2010, unama.unmissions.org. "Among the most tragic consequences of harmful traditional practices is self-immolation—an apparently growing trend in some parts of Afghanistan."

11   **daughters are still a viable, informal currency**   Human Rights, United Nations Assistance Mission in Afghanistan Kabul, Office of the United Nations High Commissioner for Human Rights Geneva, *Silence Is Violence: End the Abuse of Women in Afghanistan,* Kabul, July 8, 2009. It states: "Monetary compensation or *baad* is often also part of what is seen as an acceptable solution to all parties."

13   **literacy rate is no more than 10 percent**   Ibid.: "The adult literacy rate of Afghans over 15 years is 28% including 12.6% for females. In rural areas, where 74% of Afghans reside, it is estimated that 90% of women cannot read or write."

CHAPTER 2: THE FOREIGNER

17   **lives of Afghan women were to be improved**   For information on European Commission aid for Afghanistan and the inclusion of "gender" in its programs, see European Commission, *Country Strategy Paper Islamic Republic of Afghanistan 2007–2013,* eeas.europa.eu.

21   **Celebrated for publishing several travel guides**   See Nancy Hatch Duprée, *An Historical Guide to Afghanistan* (Kabul: Afghan Air Authority, Afghan Tourist Organization, 1977).

22   **the country's last king, who was ousted in 1973**   Afghanistan's last king ruled for forty years before he was removed. See Barry Bearak, "Mohammad Zahir Shah, Last Afghan King, Dies at 92," *New York Times,* July 24, 2007, nytimes.com.

22   **stand guard in Ḥabībullāh Khan's harem**   Ḥabībullāh Khan ruled Afghanistan from 1901 to 1919. See Encyclopaedia Britannica Online, www.britannica.com.

22   **Afghans have been driven out**   Zarif Nazar and Farangis Najibullah, "Kabul Housing Shortage Leaves the Middle Class Behind," Radio Free Europe, January 31, 2011, rferl.org.

23   **figures ranging from twenty-three to twenty-nine million**   Andrew Pinney, *Snapshots of an Intervention, The Unlearned Lessons of Afghanistan's Decade of Assistance (2001–11)* (Kabul: Afghanistan Analysts Network [AAN], 2012).

24   **for an illiterate person to have memorized**   See Louis Duprée, *Afghanistan* (New York: Oxford University Press, 1973, sixth impres-

sion, 2010), pp. 74–75, in which he says Afghanistan "has a literate *culture,* but a non-literate *society.*" Duprée's book, written before the Soviet invasion, is still one of the most comprehensive sourcebooks on Afghanistan, as Louis Duprée was a lifelong researcher of the country. The Louis and Nancy Hatch Duprée Foundation at Kabul University is dedicated to helping to preserve the cultural heritage of the people of Afghanistan and support education about it: dupree foundation.org.

CHAPTER 3: THE CHOSEN ONE

27   **The Taliban no longer rules**   The Revolutionary Association of the Women of Afghanistan, "Some of the Restrictions Imposed by Taliban on Women in Afghanistan," rawa.org/rules.htm (accessed January 31, 2014), notes: "18. Ban on women's wearing brightly colored clothes. In Taliban terms, these are 'sexually attracting colors.'"

29   **Afghan police are among the most popular targets**   See Jon Boone, "Afghan Police Hit by High Death Rate and 'Quick Fix' Training, Says EU," *The Guardian,* October 1, 2009, theguardian.com; and Susan G. Chesser, "Afghanistan Casualties: Military Forces and Civilians," Congressional Research Service, December 6, 2012, fas.org. Statistics in this report state that in 2008, Afghanistan national army casualties were 259 killed, 875 wounded; Afghanistan national, local, and border police casualties in 2008 were 724 killed, 1,209 wounded.

29   **the conviction of martyrdom and the prospect of virgins**   Ibn Warraq, "Virgins? What Virgins?" *The Guardian,* January 11, 2002, theguardian .com.

30   **Afghanistan is the world's largest producer of opium**   Seventy-four percent of global illicit opium production in 2012 came from Afghanistan, and Afghan opium cultivation reached a record high in 2013. See United Nations Office on Drugs and Crime, UNODC, *World Drug Report 2013,* unodc.org; and United Nations Office on Drugs and Crime, Islamic Republic of Afghanistan, Ministry of Counter Narcotics, *Afghanistan Opium Survey 2013 Summary Findings,* November 2013, unodc.org.

31   **Saur Revolution, when the Communist People's Democratic Party**   The Saur Revolution took place on April 27, 1978. See "Afghanistan: 20 Years of Bloodshed," BBC News, April 26, 1998, news.bbc.co.uk/2/ hi/south_asia/83854.stm.

31   **With ideological and financial backing from Moscow**   Orzala Ashraf Nemat, *Afghan Women at the Crossroads: Agents of Peace—Or Its Victims?,*

The Century Foundation, 2011. Nemat writes: "The massive reforms of the PDPA regime were all directly supported by the Soviet Union and facilitated by Soviet advisors—which led the majority of the Afghan population to see the government in Kabul more as an agent of alien outside power rather than as an internal grassroots movement."

31   **setting out to replace religious law with a more secular system**   For background on the People's Democratic Party of Afghanistan (PDPA), its ties to Moscow, its aims of secularization and reforms that came to be considered "un-Islamic" by many, see Asta Olesen, *Islam and Politics in Afghanistan* (Nordic Institute of Asian Studies) (Kindle Locations 8046–49), Taylor and Francis, Kindle Edition.

31   **Amanollah Khan had tried to assert rights for women**   Valentine M. Hoghadam, "Revolution, Religion and Gender Politics: Iran and Afghanistan Compared," *Journal of Women's History* (Johns Hopkins University Press) 10, no. 4 (Winter 1999). Hoghadam states: "The king was forced to abdicate by a tribal rebellion opposed to schooling for girls, restrictions on polygyny and prohibition of the bride price."

31   **Soraya, who famously cast off her veil**   See Sunita Mehta and Homaira Mamoor, ed. Sunita Mehta, *Women for Afghan Women* (New York: Palgrave Macmillan, 2002), where the authors note that "as early as 1921, King Amanollah Shah abolished the mandatory donning of the burqa, and his wife, Queen Soraya, appeared in the public unveiled and wearing skirts that revealed her legs."

32   **equal rights in the Constitution of 1964**   See Arline Lederman, "The *Zan* of Afghanistan—A 35-Year Perspective on Women in Afghanistan," in Mehta and Mamoor, ed. by Sunita Mehta, *Women for Afghan Women*, in which Lederman mentions women's role in drafting Afghanistan's 1964 constitution.

32   **receive mandatory educations**   Dr. Huma Ahmed-Ghosh discusses the many social and economic reform programs under PDPA rule and how tribal chiefs "viewed compulsory education, especially for women, as going against the grain of tradition, anti-religious and a challenge to male authority" in "A History of Women in Afghanistan: Lessons Learnt for the Future or Yesterdays and Tomorrow: Women in Afghanistan," *Journal of International Women's Studies* 4, no. 3 (May 2003).

34   **Rapid attempts at reforming society and culture**   See Hoghadam, "Revolution, Religion and Gender Politics." The author explains one of the most controversial government decrees, Decree No. 7, which "fundamentally would change the institution of marriage

and position of women." In the decree, "the government outlawed traditional cultural practices widely regarded as 'Islamic.' Thus, the PDPA placed a limit on bride price, banned forced marriages and the practice of levirate, and prohibited marriage through subterfuge or coercion. Whereas girls usually were wed immediately upon puberty, the new government set a minimum age of marriage of sixteen years for women and eighteen years for men."

35   **"the greatest threat to peace since the Second World War."**   President Carter's quote is mentioned in Elizabeth Gould and Paul Fitzgerald, "Excerpts from The Apostle's Diary," in Mehta and Mamoor, ed. by Sunita Mehta, *Women for Afghan Women*. The authors offer background on the similar goals that the U.S. administration (fighting "Godless communism") and Islamic fundamentalists in Afghanstan had in the struggle against the Soviet Union, since they shared "a crusader mentality."

36   **In the spring of 1992, Kabul erupted**   President Mohammad Najibullah's regime fell in April 1992 and the mujahideen entered Kabul. See Alfred Aghajanian, ed. by Peter R. Blood, *Afghanistan: Past and Present/ Comprised of Afghanistan, A Country Study and Country Profile: Afghanistan, A Report by the U.S. Government's Federal Research Division,* September 2007.

36   **like most other children in Kabul**   Ahmed Rashid notes the horrors Kabul's children saw at this time in *Taliban: Militant Islam, Oil and Fundamentalism in Central Asia,* 2nd ed. (New Haven: Yale University Press, 2010). The author cites: "A UNICEF survey of Kabul's children conducted by Dr. Leila Gupta found that most children had witnessed extreme violence and did not expect to survive. Two-thirds of children interviewed had seen somebody killed by a rocket and scattered corpses or body parts. More than 70 percent had lost a family member and no longer trusted adults" (p. 109).

CHAPTER 4: THE SON MAKER

40   **the United Nations calls the worst place in the world to be born**   Stephanie Nebehay, "Afghanistan Is World's Worst Place to Be Born: U.N.," Reuters, November 20, 2009, reuters.com. Nebehay reports that "Afghanistan has the highest infant mortality rate in the world—257 deaths per 1,000 live births, and 70 percent of the population lacks access to clean water."

40   **And the most dangerous place in which to be a woman**   See Lisa Anderson, "Afghanistan Is Most Dangerous Country for Women,"

Thomson Reuters Foundation, 2011, trust.org, listing "violence, dis-
mal healthcare and brutal poverty" as the three primary reasons.

42   **eighteen thousand Afghan women dying each year**   Statistics are available at United Nations Population Fund (UNFPA), "The State of
the World's Midwifery 2011," unfpa.org.

42   **on par with the poorest and most war-torn nations**   See UNFPA,
"Trends in Maternal Mortality 1990–2010," unfpa.org.

42   **The life expectancy of a woman here is forty-four**   According to the
World Food Programme Country Overview of Afghanistan, wfp.org
/countries/afghanistan/overview (accessed January 31, 2014): "While
life expectancy has increased slightly to 44.5 years for men and 44
for women, many of the country's health indicators are alarming."
However, the CIA World Factbook estimates for 2014 a life expectancy of 50.49 years for the total population in Afghanistan, of which
male life expectancy is 49.17 years and female life expectancy is 51.88
years.

44   **Gerda Lerner pioneered the study of women's history**   Historian Gerda
Lerner (1920–2013) discovered that the existing historical record was
deeply lacking on half the population—that of women. Instead, history books mostly told the story of men throughout the ages. Lerner
set out to collect and analyze the existing research on ancient civilization, to understand how humankind began to organize societies from
the very beginning. In her book *The Creation of Patriarchy* (New York:
Oxford University Press, 1986), she explains how patriarchy is not
"natural" nor "God-given" but "a historic creation formed by men and
women in a process that took nearly 2,500 years to its completion" (p.
212) and provides context for many things that happen in Afghanistan to this day.

CHAPTER 5: THE POLITICIAN

49   **most rural and undeveloped provinces**   Badghis ranks as the thirty-
first least-developed province out of Afghanistan's thirty-two and is
61 percent worse off than the world's least-developed countries. See
UNICEF, Best Estimates Provincial Fact Sheet, unicef.org (accessed
January 31, 2014).

49   **Badghis is dominated by Tajik tribes and has a Pashtun minority**   The
Naval Postgraduate School's Program for Culture and Conflict Studies fact sheet for Badghis province, nps.edu (accessed January 31,
2014), states: "The province is inhabited by Tajiks who are thought

to make up 62 percent of the population with Pashtuns making up approximately 28 percent."

50   **Ahmed Rashid describes those who fought**   See Ahmed Rashid, "A Vanished Gender," in *Taliban: Militant Islam, Oil and Fundamentalism in Central Asia*, 2nd ed. (New Haven and London: Yale University Press, 2010), pp. 105–116.

54   **upheld by 130,000 troops from forty-eight countries**   Ninety thousand of the 130,930 ISAF troops were American. See International Security Assistance Force (ISAF): "Key Facts and Figures," November 15, 2010, isaf.nato.int.

54   **the standard playbook of "state building"**   In his chapter, "The Failure of Airborne Democracy," in van Bijlert and Kouvo's *Snapshots of an Intervention,* Afghanistan analyst Thomas Ruttig describes how the 2001 Bonn conference "already had substantial democratic deficits" as the Taliban was excluded, in favor of warlords and groups sponsored by Pakistan and Iran. As a result, he writes, "warlords . . . were allowed to take over not only the 'new' democratic institutions but virtually everything else that mattered in the country. Today they constitute the inner circle of advisors for an over-centralised presidential system and, because of their religious self-legitimisation, are difficult to challenge politically. They simply have put themselves above the law."

55   **as one more rationale for the war**   On November 17, 2001, First Lady Laura Bush took over the president's weekly radio address, a transcript of which can be found at presidency.ucsb.edu. She said: "Because of our recent military gains in much of Afghanistan, women are no longer imprisoned in their homes. . . . The fight against terrorism is also a fight for the rights and dignity of women."

55   **After years of being unable to peer out of any window**   The many Taliban restrictions on women, which included the compulsory painting of all windows, are enumerated in "Some of the Restrictions Imposed by Taliban on Women in Afghanistan," Revolutionary Association of the Women of Afghanistan, at rawa.org/rules.htm.

55   **the mandated 25-percent-minimum female share of seats**   Article 83(6) in Afghanistan's constitution from January 2004 states that two female delegates should be elected from each province; see servat.unibe .ch. Afghanistan's electoral law of 2005 further details how the quota should be drawn from the respective province; see ecoi.net/file_upload /1504_1215701180_electoral-law.pdf.

55   **just as the Koran does**   The Koran is believed to contain the words of God, directly spoken to the Prophet Muhammad, and later recorded

by scribes. Translations into other languages from the original can
vary and are sometimes debated. In Iranian-American Muslim translator Laleh Bakhtiar's English version, *The Sublime Quran* (Kazi Publi-
cations, 2007), sublimequran.org, which is supported by the Islamic
Society of North America, several verses affirm the equal standing
of men and women. For example, see verses 3:195 ("each one of you
is from the other") and 33:35 (which lays out how God asks the same
of both men and women). As for 4:34, the original text that is often
quoted in other translations as men being the "protectors" of women
and therefore interpreted as though they should have some decision-
making power over women, Laleh Bakhtiar instead translates as men
being the "supporters" of women.

55   **that men and women are equal**   The Constitution of Afghanistan,
ratified January 26, 2004, "Chapter Two: Fundamental Rights and
Duties of Citizens," Article 22, states: "Any kind of discrimination
and distinction between citizens of Afghanistan shall be forbidden.
The citizens of Afghanistan, man and woman, have equal rights and
duties before the law."

57   **share no common cause**   Orzala Ashraf Nemat, *Afghan Women at the
Crossroads: Agents of Peace—or Its Victims?* The Century Foundation,
2011, discusses the realities of the women members' roles in parliament: "Not all of them were there to carry women's voices, however.
In fact, most of the women in the parliament are linked in different
ways to powerful warlords and other power brokers, and do not have
any agenda to change or improve legislation in favor of women and
human rights. Only few outstanding voices came out of the parliament to champion women's needs, while in general, the record of its
achievements is very weak—almost total failure—in terms of legal reforms in support of women."

57   **laws ratified that actually discriminate**   According to Human Rights
Watch: "The law [passed during Karzai's administration] gives a
husband the right to withdraw basic maintenance from his wife, including food, if she refuses to obey his sexual demands. . . . It also effectively allows a rapist to avoid prosecution by paying 'blood money'
to a girl who was injured when he raped her." See "Afghanistan: Law
Curbing Women's Rights Takes Effect—President Karzai Makes
Shia Women Second-Class Citizens for Electoral Gain," August 14,
2009, hrw.org.

57   **amnesty has been handed out for war crimes**   Nemat's *Afghan Women
at the Crossroads* says this about the amnesty law: "Despite having 27
percent of the parliamentary seats filled by women, the parliament

has approved a controversial amnesty law, calling for immunity for all those involved in war-time violations of human rights and women's rights; approved the Shiite Personal Status Law, subjecting Shiite women to traditional religious controls, which later on was reviewed and amended to some extent; and pointedly did *not* approve presidential nominees for the position of minister of women's affairs."

58   **The largest religious authority in the country**   "The Ulama Council: Paid to Win Public Minds—but Do They?" by Borhan Osman for Afghan Analysts Network, November 5, 2012, afghanistan-analysts. org, explains the complicated role of the Ulama Council in Afghan politics and society.

59   **Louis Duprée described this contradiction**   See Louis Duprée, *Afghanistan* (Princeton: Oxford University Press, 1973, sixth impression, 2010), p. 104.

CHAPTER 6: THE UNDERGROUND GIRLS

65   **Husbands otherwise have an absolute right to the children**   Orzala Ashraf Nemat provides an analysis about divorce in an Islamic context under Afghanistan's civil law in "Roundtable Conference: Comparative Analysis of Family Law in the Context of Islam," Kabul, August 15–17, 2006, af.boell.org. The Afghan Civil Code affords the husband a unilateral right to divorce the wife for any reason, or for no reason, at any time (Article 135). In addition, Afghan Civil Code, Articles 236 through 255, cover custody issues.

71   **Nine out of ten Afghan women will experience**   For information on the statistics of domestic abuse in Afghanistan, see "Living with Violence: A National Report on Domestic Abuse in Afghanistan," Global Rights: Partners for Justice, March 2008, globalrights.org. This report notes "an overwhelming majority of women, 87.2%, experienced at least one form of physical, sexual or psychological violence or forced marriage, and most, 62.0%, experienced multiple forms of violence."

71   **According to Mara Hvistendahl**   Mara Hvistendahl's *Unnatural Selection: Choosing Boys over Girls, and the Consequences of a World Full of Men* (Public Affairs, 2011) reports on the sex-selective abortions of female fetuses throughout Asia.

CHAPTER 7: THE NAUGHTY ONE

76   **but in the 1980s, Dr. Eleanor Galenson**   The research was presented in Eleanor Galenson and Herman Roiphe's *Infantile Origins of Sexual Identity* (New York: International Universities Press, 1981).

80   **Christian countries did not recognize marital rape**   See websites of RAINN—Rape, Abuse and Incest National Network, rainn.org, and Rape Crisis, rapecrisis.org.uk/maritalrape2.php (accessed January 31, 2014).

85   **When the United States, the United Kingdom**   The Sunday, October 7, 2001, online edition of *The Guardian* had a timeline of the attack on Afghanistan; see theguardian.com.

87   **the UN-mandated 2002 emergency *loya jirga***   The structure of the *loya jirga* is described in press briefing notes from the UN, un.org/News/dh/latest/afghan/concept.pdf.

88   **Afghans have been tortured to death by U.S. forces**   See Tim Golden, "In U.S. Report, Brutal Details of 2 Afghan Inmates' Deaths," *New York Times,* May 20, 2005, nytimes.com.

CHAPTER 8: THE TOMBOY

98   **King James I of England denounced**   See Anastasia S. Bierman, *In Counterfeit Passion: Cross-Dressing, Transgression, and Fraud in Shakespeare and Middleton* (University of Nebraska—Lincoln, Department of English thesis, 2013), digitalcommons.unl.edu.

98   **France implemented a law in 1800 that said women**   Lizzy Duffy, "Parisian Women Now (Officially) Allowed to Wear Pants," National Public Radio, February 4, 2013, npr.org.

102   **just as the Bible**   For instance, Timothy 2:9 says: "Likewise, I want women to adorn themselves with proper clothing, modestly and discreetly, not with braided hair and gold or pearls or costly garments, but rather by means of good works, as is proper for women making a claim to godliness."

102   **Veiling predates Islam**   See Leila Ahmed, *Women and Gender in Islam: Historical Roots of a Modern Debate* (New Haven: Yale University Press, 1992), pp. 5, 11, 12, 55. She writes that veiling was apparently introduced in Arabia by Muhammad, but already existed among the upper-class Greeks, Romans, Jews, and Assyrians. Veiling is nowhere explicitly prescribed in the Koran.

107   **According to one Islamic hadith**   Everett K. Rowson, "The Effeminates of Early Medina," *Journal of the American Oriental Society* 111, no. 4

(October–December 1991): 671–93. Rowson notes that the Prophet did not really seem to have a problem with cross-dressers, which were common in his time, but he may have grown to believe it threatened established social norms. The hadith is here translated as: "The Prophet cursed effeminate men and mannish women."

107 **The Koran can be read in many ways**   Sadakat Kadri, *Heaven on Earth: A Journey Through Shari'a Law from the Deserts of Ancient Arabia to the Streets of the Modern Muslim World* (New York: Farrar, Straus and Giroux, 2012), offers a fascinating view into how Islamic law and its many intepretations have developed through the centuries.

108 **title of mullah is open to anyone**   Louis Duprée describes the role of mullahs in his book *Afghanistan*: "Those at the bottom of the hierarchy, the village mullah, often non-literate farmers, often function as part time religious leaders. Technically, Islam has no organized clergy, and every man can be a mullah. Anyone can lead in prayer" (p. 107).

109 **a marketing gimmick invented in the United States in the forties**   Background on the use of color for gender identification was found in Jeanne Maglaty, "When Did Girls Start Wearing Pink?," April 8, 2011, smithsonianmag.com.

114 **famous warrior Malalai of Maiwand**   Abdullah Qazi, "The Plight of the Afghan Woman: Afghan Women's History," January 2, 2009, Afghanistan Online, afghan-web.com.

115 **"Before Islam" would be sometime**   See Library of Congress: Federal Research Division, "Country Profile of Afghanistan, August 2008," loc.gov, which states: "After defeating the Sassanians at the Battle of Qadisiya in 637, Arab Muslims began a 100-year process of conquering the Afghan tribes and introducing Islam."

CHAPTER 9: THE CANDIDATE

116 **Shah Massoud, the "Lion of Panjshir,"**   See Farangis Najibullah, "What If Ahmad Shah Masud, Afghanistan's 'Lion of Panjshir,' Hadn't Been Killed?" Radio Free Europe, September 9, 2011, rferl.org.

121 **from the war that killed one million Afghans**   See Rafael Reuveny and Aseem Prakash, "The Afghanistan War and the Breakdown of the Soviet Union," *Review of International Studies* (1999), faculty.washington.edu.

123 **in Afghanistan, a man is allowed**   The Afghan Civil Code, Article 86, asianlii.org, states:

Polygamy can take place after the following conditions are fulfilled:
1. When there is no fear of injustice between the wives

2. When the person has financial sufficiency to sustain the wives. That is, when he can provide food, clothes, suitable house, and medical treatment.

3. When there is legal expediency, that is when the first wife is childless or when she suffers from diseases which are hard to be treated.

Polygamy, however, means that both parties could be married to several people, so what the law allows in Afghanistan is actually *polygyny*.

CHAPTER 10: THE PASHTUN TEA PARTY

135 **It makes her a very unusual young woman**   According to *Higher Education in Afghanistan—An Emerging Mountainscape,* A World Bank Study, August 2013, www-wds.worldbank.org, which states: "Second, education attainment among women is particularly low in Afghanistan. The three percent enrolled in higher education consists disproportionately of male students. Females comprised only 19% of all students enrolled in public universities and higher education institutions in 2012 [MoHE (2013)]."

137 **Afghanistan Independent Human Rights Commission**   Detailed information about the organization's mission can be found at their website with a profile of Dr. Samar, www.aihrc.org.af.

138 **The word itself is not mentioned once**   See the full text of the Convention on the Rights of the Child at United Nations Office of the High Commissioner for Human Rights, ohchr.org.

CHAPTER 11: THE FUTURE BRIDE

147 **The three pillars of Pashtunwali**   The three pillars are explained further in Charles Lindholm, *Generosity and Jealousy: The Swat Pukhtun of Northern Pakistan* (New York: Columbia University Press, 1982).

147 *gender identity disorder* and *transsexualism*   The International Classification of Diseases's ICD-10 Classification of Mental and Behavioural Disorders, World Health Organization, Geneva, 1993, who.int, lists the detailed criteria for gender identity disorders in section F64.

CHAPTER 12: THE SISTERHOOD

152 **Marriage is a core component**   Gerda Lerner explains how marriage was always a key part of the patriarchal system in *The Creation of Patriarchy* (New York: Oxford University Press, 1986). She writes: "For

women, class is mediated through their sexual ties to a man. It is through the man that women have access to or are denied access to the means of production and to resources. It is through their sexual behavior that they gain access to class. 'Respectable women' gain access to class through their fathers and husbands, but breaking the sexual rules can at once declass them."

158   **Afghan prosecutor Maria Bashir**   See Jeremy Kelly, "Afghan 'Defender of Women's Rights' Maria Bashir Puts 100 in Jail for Adultery," October 22, 2012, thetimes.co.uk.

159   **the rules of succession**   See Max Fisher, "Last Vestiges of the British Empire Complicate Royal Baby's Succession to the Throne," July 22, 2013, washingtonpost.com.

CHAPTER 13: THE BODYGUARD

176   **According to Butler, just as little children**   See Butler in a video explaining her work at http://bigthink.com/videos/your-behavior-creates-your-gender. "Nobody really is a gender from the start," Butler proposes in the video. See also Judith Butler, *Gender Trouble: Feminism and the Subversion of Identity* (New York: Routledge, 1990), p. 191, where the author writes, "In what senses, then, is gender an act? As in other ritual social dramas, the action of gender requires a performance that is *repeated*. This repetition is at once a reenactment and reexperiencing of a set of meanings already socially established; and it is the mundane and ritualized form of their legitimation."

177   **central argument in nineteenth-century Europe**   Barbara Ehrenreich and Deirdre English's book *For Her Own Good—Two Centuries of the Experts' Advice to Women,* first published in 1978 by Anchor Books and later by Random House in 2005, recounts the efforts of medicine and science to shut women out of public life and intellectual thought for much of history.

178   **group individuals by traditional "male" or "female" traits**   Sociomedical scientist Rebecca M. Jordan-Young critiques brain studies in *Brain Storm: The Flaws in the Science of Sex Differences* (Cambridge, Mass.: Harvard University Press, 2011). She spent thirteen years going over brain studies dating back to 1967. Most studies had concluded that the male and female brain were very different from birth, making a strong argument for inherent gender differences. But Jordan-Young found the brain studies to be problematic at the outset, mainly because experiments had often been performed on rats, with the results transferred to assumptions about humans. Studies did show great

differences between the brains of newborns in general, just as their bodies and skin color were also very different. But the differences between the brains of boys and girls did not constitute two distinct and separable categories.

178 *more different* **than a random man put next to a random woman** Janet Shibley Hyde, "The Gender Similarities Hypothesis," *American Psychologist* (2005). In this paper, University of Wisconsin–Madison psychologist Shibley Hyde offers the following conclusion: "The gender similarities hypothesis stands in stark contrast to the differences model, which holds that men and women, and boys and girls, are vastly different psychologically. The gender similarities hypothesis states, instead, that males and females are alike on most—but not all—psychological variables. Extensive evidence from meta-analyses of research on gender differences supports the gender similarities hypothesis."

178 **With time, nurture can *become* nature.** Lise Eliot, a neuroscientist at Chicago Medical School, explains brain-based differences in *Pink Brain, Blue Brain: How Small Differences Grow into Troublesome Gaps—and What We Can Do About It* (New York: First Mariner Books, 2010). According to Eliot, physical differences do exist in the brains of boys and girls, but they are not responsible for gender dissimilarities. Instead, very early on in life, different behaviors and skills are expected from each sex. The language used with each gender is different, and each child, depending on whether it's a boy or a girl, is encouraged to develop what we think of as typical traits and behavior—for instance, that girls are more quiet and that boys are more active. Through that process of learning and forming habits, the brain will physically develop along the same lines. The brain—especially a growing brain—is so malleable that it will grow, form, and adjust according to the repetitive patterns to which it is exposed. Behavior is ingrained in the brain as it develops and comes to feel "natural."

CHAPTER 14: THE ROMANTIC

184 **research by Dr. Alfred Kinsey and others** See Theodore M. Brown and Elizabeth Fee, "Alfred C. Kinsey: A Pioneer of Sex Research," *American Journal of Public Health* (June 2003), ncbi.nlm.nih.gov.

184 **how a woman's uterus could be surgically removed** See Ehrenreich and English's *For Her Own Good.*

186 **only "paltry" references to lesbianism** The quote is from page 97 in chapter 5, "Woman-Woman Love in Islamic Societies," by Stephen O. Murray, in Stephen O. Murray and Will Roscoe, *Islamic*

Homosexualities: Culture, History, and Literature (New York: New York University Press, 1997). Murray also quotes the passage from Muslim geographer and cartographer Sharif al-Idrisi, who lived in the twelfth century, on page 99.

188   **"Very powerful warlords and regional commanders"**   For a fuller context of Coomaraswamy's remark, see "New UN–Afghan Pact Will Help Curb Recruitment, Sexual Abuse of Children," UN News Centre, February 3, 2011. Also see "An Unwanted Truth? Focusing the G8: Shining a Spotlight on Sexual Violence Against Children in Conflict," Warchild UK, April 2013, cdn.warchild.org.uk. In this report, the British NGO Warchild UK, which focuses on providing assistance to children in areas of conflict, said of *bacha bazi*: "The issue remains one of virtual silence and inaction, however, due to the acutely taboo nature of the subject and complicity of senior figures of authority."

188   **the number of boys sexually abused**   John Frederick for UNICEF, "Sexual Abuse and Exploitation of Boys in South Asia and a Review of Research Findings, Legislation, Policy and Programme Responses," April 2010, unicef-irc.org. See also a Save the Children report from 2003: "Mapping of Psychosocial Support for Girls and Boys Affected by Child Sexual Abuse in Four Countries in South and Central Asia," sca.savethechildren.se, which states: "Men are seen as needing 'sexual release,' the lack of which can even result in poor health. On the other hand, the ideal construction of the female is asexual before marriage, and sexually passive after. There are traditional precedents for 'accepted' child abuse. Reports of men using young boys for sexual gratification are well-known and talked about. Traditionally, 'keeping' good-looking boys adds status and prestige to the man, and adds to his image (self or imposed) of virility. Under the Taliban, a strict ban on homosexuality made more overt aspects of practise go underground. However, the practise of boys under 18 being brought to parties for entertainment is reported to still be taking place in some rural areas and in and around Kandahar."

189   **"The first sexual experiences"**   Charles Lindholm, *Generosity and Jealousy: The Swat Pukhtun of Northern Pakistan* (New York: Columbia University Press, 1982), p. 225.

189   **Author Hamid Zaher recounts**   Hamid Zaher, *It Is Your Enemy Who Is Dock-tailed: A Memoir* (iUniverse, 2012), originally written in Farsi in 2009, Kindle Edition.

192   **defined three different forms of love**   Helen Fisher, "The Nature of Romantic Love"—commentary in *Journal of NIH Research,* April 1994, helenfisher.com.

CHAPTER 15: THE DRIVER

197   **Forty-five-year-old Amir Bibi in Khost**   For Bibi's interview, see Terese Christiansson, *De är kvinnorna med makt i Afghanistan,* Expressen, December 4, 2010, expressen.se.

198   **In a study of medieval Europe**   Valerie R. Hotchkiss, *Clothes Make the Man: Female Cross Dressing in Medieval Europe* (New York: Garland Publishing, 1996), p. 13.

198   **Lotte C. van de Pol and Rudolf M. Dekker**   Rudolf M. Dekker and Lotte C. van de Pol, *The Tradition of Female Transvestism in Early Modern Europe* (London: Macmillan Press, 1989).

199   **orphan Ulrika Eleonora Stålhammar**   The information on Stålhammar is at the National Swedish Army museum's website, sfhm.se.

199   **Briton Hannah Snell famously served**   See Julie Wheelwright, *Amazons and Military Maids: Women Who Dressed as Men in Pursuit of Life, Liberty and Happiness* (San Francisco: Pandora/Harper Collins, 1989).

199   **German women were also found**   See Dekker and van de Pol, *The Tradition of Female Transvestism,* p. 96.

199   **among the conquistadors in South America**   Ibid. See also Wheelwright, *Amazons and Military Maids.*

199   **British anthropologist Antonia Young tracked down women**   Antonia Young's *Women Who Become Men: Albanian Sworn Virgins* (Oxford and New York: Berg, 2000) reads in large parts like a book on Afghanistan today, even though the two countries are twenty-six hundred miles and an Arab peninsula apart. Information on Albanian virgins cited in this section is from her book as well as an interview.

    See also Rene Gremaux, "Mannish Women of the Balkan Mountains," theol.eldoc.ub.rug.nl, from 1989.

    Gremaux also contributed the chapter "Woman Becomes Man in the Balkans" to the book *Third Sex, Third Gender: Beyond Sexual Dimorphism in Culture and History,* edited by Gilbert Herdt (Zone Books, 1993). He writes of these women: "Belonging to an intermediate gender category may have caused much inconvenience to the individual's psyche, yet being betwixt and between also opened new perspectives and brought about opportunitites."

    For a recent documentation of Albanian virgins, see Pepa Hristova, *Sworn Virgins* (Heidelberg: Kehrer Verlag, 2013).

201   **Albanian laws stemming from the fifteenth century**   See Young, *Women Who Become Men: Albanian Sworn Virgins.*

CHAPTER 16: THE WARRIOR

205   **children still freeze to death**   See Rod Nordland, "Driven Away by a War, Now Stalked by Winter's Cold," *New York Times,* February 3, 2012, nytimes.com.

209   **his 1990 study Manhood in the Making**   David D. Gilmore, *Manhood in the Making: Cultural Concepts of Masculinity* (New Haven: Yale University Press, 1990).

210   **a "natural" aggression in sons**   Joshua S. Goldstein, *War and Gender: How Gender Shapes the War System and Vice Versa* (New York: Cambridge University Press, 2001).

210   **women today make up 15 percent of troops**   The ACLU press release "ACLU Challenges Ongoing Exclusion of Women from Combat Positions," October 31, 2013, www.aclu.org, reads: "Women make up more than 14 percent of the 1.4 million active military personnel, yet are still excluded from over 200,000 positions despite the repeal of the 1994 combat exclusion policy in January."

CHAPTER 17: THE REFUSERS

221   **a longstanding Hindu tradition of sadhin**   See Serena Nanda, *Gender Diversity* (Long Grove, IL: Waveland Press, 2000), p. 40.

221   **"It's normal around here"**   See Anees Jung, *Beyond the Courtyard* (New York: Viking by Penguin Books India, 2003), p. 125.

221   **women dressing as men for purposes**   See Andrea B. Rugh, *Reveal and Conceal: Dress in Contemporary Egypt, Contemporary Issues in the Middle East* (Syracuse, NY: Syracuse University Press, 1986).

222   **religious authorities in Malaysia**   "Malaysia Bans Tomboys Saying Girls with Short Hair Who Act Like Boys 'Violate Islam,'" *Daily Mail,* October 24, 2008, dailymail.co.uk.

222   **call themselves boyah**   Lorenz Nigst and José Sánchez García, "Boyat in the Gulf: Identity, Contestation and Social Control," Universities of Vienna and Barcelona, Middle East Critique, Spring 2010. See also Shereen El Feki, *Sex and the Citadel: Intimate Life in a Changing Arab World* (New York: Pantheon, 2013). El Feki visits a rehabilitation center, and what she is told by a psychologist at the center echoes the story in Afghanistan, in that most teenage girls she counseled who had been brought up as boys didn't consider themselves troubled or needing a cure. "They feel it's their freedom; they don't feel it's wrong," a psychologist is quoted as saying.

CHAPTER 18: THE GODDESS

224 **In the 1970s, Louis Duprée wrote** See Louis Duprée, *Afghanistan* (Oxford University Press, 1973, sixth impression, 2010) p. 104.

224 **Around 1,400 years before Jesus was born** See Mary Boyce, *Zoroastrians: Their Religious Beliefs and Practices,* first published in 1979 by Routledge; and Jenny Rose, *Zoroastrianism: An Introduction* (London: I. B. Tauris, 2011).

226 **"almost any stone thrown in Afghanistan"** See Louis Duprée's *Afghanistan,* p. 104.

228 **recorded these same beliefs** Lindholm writes, on page 166 of his book *Generosity and Jealousy:* "Swatis share with other Pakistanis and South Asians a firm belief that food, drink and even people are either 'hot' or 'cold.' The logic by which these divisions are made are by no means clear, and sometimes people disagree on whether a particular unusual food is 'hot' or 'cold' but there is widespread agreement about the major parameters of the system."

228 **a primer for how boys and girls** Chapter 16 of the *Avesta,* "The Bundahishn ('Creation'), or Knowledge from the Zand," can be found in English translation at avesta.org.

229 **The Persian epic** See Djalal Khaleghi Motlagh, *Women in the Shāhnāmeh: Their History and Social Status Within the Framework of Ancient and Medieval Sources,* ed. by Nahid Pirnazar, trans. from German by Brigitte Neuenschwander (Santa Ana, Calif.: Mazda Publishers, 2012), p. 42.

229 **the same rainbow myth of gender-changing** See Raymond L. Lee and Alistair B. Fraser, *The Rainbow Bridge: Rainbows in Art, Myth and Science* (Pennsylvania State University Press, 2001).

230 **Norse mythology from the Middle Ages** See Helga Kress, "Taming the Shrew: The Rise of Patriarchy and the Subordination of the Feminine in Old Norse Literature," in *Cold Counsel: Women in Old Norse Literature and Mythology: A Collection of Essays,* ed. by Sarah M. Anderson with Karen Swenson (New York: Routledge, 2002), p. 90.

230 **a common Indo-European origin** Viktor Rydberg wrote about this in "Fädernas Gudasaga" of 1923.

230 **the earliest recorded prayers of Zoroaster's** Mary Boyce, *Zoroastrians: Their Religious Beliefs and Practices* (Routledge, 1979), p 17.

CHAPTER 19: THE DEFEATED

240 **embroiled in a heated national conflict**   Rod Nordland, "Candidates for Parliament Protest Afghan Elections," *New York Times,* November 7, 2010, nytimes.com, tells the story of the fraught election procedure: "Nationwide, the election commission invalidated 1.33 million or nearly a fourth of the 5.74 million votes recorded, according to an official fact sheet."

244 **bloodiest year yet of the war**   Comparative numbers are found in Susan G. Chesser, "Afghanistan Casualties: Military Forces and Civilians," Congressional Research Service, December 6, 2012, www.fas.org. American casualties in 2002: 49, wounded: 74, American casualties in 2011: 404, wounded: 5,204. The report also mentions that "up to 11,864 civilians were killed in Afghanistan from 2007, when the United Nations began reporting statistics, to the end of 2011." In 2011, the civilian casualty toll was 3,021 killed and 4,507 injured—the highest numbers since UN reporting began in 2007.

244 **President Obama's two-year "surge"**   Peter Baker, "How Obama Came to Plan for 'Surge' in Afghanistan," *New York Times,* December 5, 2009, describes the thinking behind Obama's decision to temporarily send more troops into Afghanistan.

245 **$700 billion and counting to American taxpayers**   Anthony H. Cordesman, "The US Cost of the Afghan War: FY2002–FY2013, Cost in Military Operating Expenditures and Aid, and Prospects for 'Transition,'" May 15, 2012, csis.org.

246 **"This time it was the United States"**   The quote comparing the U.S. involvement to the Soviet Union's is on page 290 of Sherard Cowper-Coles, *Cables from Kabul: The Inside Story of the West's Afghanistan Campaign* (Harper Press, 2011).

247 **ignored by all but human rights organizations**   Several groups have warned about the dangers for women of any negotiated political deal with the extremists, including the Afghan-led Afghanistan Human Rights and Democracy Organization, in its 2012 report "Afghan Women After the Taliban: Will History Repeat Itself?," ahrdo.org. They write: "The current US and Afghan government-backed process of negotiating with extremist groups, and especially the Taliban, promises to increase the vulnerability of women in Afghanistan in the medium- to long-term. Any political deal with these forces means the selling out of women's hard-gained achievements in the last ten years while most likely incurring unbearable cost for Afghan women."

CHAPTER 20: THE CASTOFF

257   **If an Afghan woman wants to divorce**   See "I Had to Run Away, The Imprisonment of Women and Girls for 'Moral Crimes' in Afghanistan," A Human Rights Watch Report, 2012, hrw.org, which explains: "Laws governing divorce in Afghanistan are discriminatory against women. The Afghan Civil Code of 1977, the key source of statutory family law in Afghanistan, allows men to divorce women very easily. Article 139 of the Afghan Civil Code states that: (1) A husband can divorce his wife orally or in writing. When a husband lacks these two means, divorce can happen by usual gestures which clearly implies divorce. (2) Divorce happens with clear wordings which, in customs, convey the meaning of divorce without intention. Women, however, face far greater obstacles in obtaining a divorce. Absent consent from their husband, women can only obtain a divorce through a court and must show cause on the grounds of (1) defect, for example because of illness; (2) harm; (3) non-payment of alimony; or (4) absence. Obtaining a 'for cause' divorce for women in Afghanistan is not easy, legally or practically. . . . Compounding these problems, many judges do not even apply the provisions of the Civil Code, but instead invoke their own interpretation of Islamic law, with some judges not even admitting that women are entitled to seek divorce."

CHAPTER 21: THE WIFE

264   **close to the bottom of the Human Development Index**   A yearly report by the United Nations Development Programme, UNDP, measures "development by combining indicators of life expectancy, educational attainment and income into a composite human development index, the HDI" and can be found at undp.org. See also *The Forgotten Front: Water Security and the Crisis in Sanitation,* Afghanistan Human Development Report 2011, Centre for Policy and Human Development, Kabul University, cphd.af. The report analyzes Afghanistan after almost a decade of foreign aid: "[T]here has been progress in recent years, but the progress has been uneven and far too slow. According to the Human Development Index for 2010, Afghanistan is ranked 155th among 169 United Nations member states . . . 84 percent of Afghan households are multi dimensionally poor."

265   **more than $30 billion**   The figures regarding Afghanistan's aid are according to "Investments to End Poverty: Real Money, Real Choices,

Real Lives," a report by British research group Development Initiatives, London 2013, which collects global data on development aid from both donor and recipient countries; see devinit.org.

265 a scathing review Astri Suhrke, *When More Is Less: The International Project in Afghanistan* (New York: Columbia University Press, 2011). Dr. Astri Suhrke is a senior researcher at the Chr. Michelsen Institute in Norway. Her work focuses on "the social, political and humanitarian consequences of violent conflict, and strategies of response." She is a member of a committee of experts serving the Norwegian Nobel Committee; see http://www.cmi.no/staff/?astri-suhrke. What Dr. Suhkre in her book calls "the liberal project" in Afghanistan began already in 2002, with sixty government donors in the country. She describes in detail the aid community's planning and implementation stages, and the mismanagement that ensued. For instance, she writes: "There were parallel structures of administration on virtually all levels of government. International advisers, contractors and NGOs were ubiquitous. About two-thirds of all aid was channelled through an 'external budget' administered directly by foreign donors."

Suhrke's book is just one of several evaluations of how the foreign aid to Afghanistan has not only been questionably effective but may also have brought long-term negative consequences for the country and its economy. See also: "Evaluating U.S. Foreign Assistance to Afghanistan: A majority staff report prepared for the use of the Senate Foreign Relations Committee" of June 8, 2011, U.S. Government Printing Office. The report cautions that Afghanistan may suffer a severe economic depression when foreign troops leave in 2014 due to the almost complete foreign aid dependency: "Foreign aid, when misspent, can fuel corruption, distort labor and goods markets, undermine the host government's ability to exert control over resources, and contribute to insecurity. According to the World Bank, an estimated 97 percent of Afghanistan's gross domestic product (GDP) is derived from spending related to the international military and donor community presence."

266 an auditor at the Office of the Special Inspector General James R. Petersen served as senior auditor for the special inspector general for Afghanistan Reconstruction. In his *Politico* story "Was $73B of Afghan Aid Wasted?" January 11, 2012, politico.com, he offers an idea of how much of the foreign aid funds actually go to helping anyone at all due to high overheads and corruption: "But a mere 30 cents out of every dollar for Afghanistan goes to aid. It gets worse. Of that 30 cents, frequently only half reaches the intended recipient. The remainder is lost, stolen or misappropriated by Afghan workers and officials. Many projects don't even attain their own internal goals, according to reports from inspectors general and the Commission on War-Time Contracting. The June 2011, Senate Foreign Relations Committee report concluded that few, if any, of these aid programs are sustainable in the long term. Add in the cost of the USAID's bureaucratic superstructure—including $500,000 annually for each U.S. employee in Kabul, and the supporting staffs in Washington—and sometimes less than 10 cents of every dollar actually goes to aiding Afghans." For more details, see sigar.mil for quarterly reports on Afghanistan reconstruction.

266 **close to ten million students registered** Rod Nordland, "Despite Education Advances, a Host of Afghan School Woes," *New York Times,* July 20, 2013, nytimes.com, goes behind the numbers to reveal that only about 10 percent of students make it through to graduation and that graduation rates are even worse for girls.

266 **more than seven hundred "projects"** Again, information on 2011 foreign aid projects and numbers relating to "gender" were provided for this book by the British research group Development Initiatives; see devinit.org.

266 **"gains are on the whole modest and reversible"** Torunn Wimpelmann's 2012 report for NOREF, Norwegian Peacebuilding Resource Centre, is called "Promoting Women's Rights in Afghanistan: A Call for Less Aid and More Politics," cmi.no. Norway is a large donor of foreign aid globally, and one of the largest to Afghanistan. Wimpelmann's research, based on extensive fieldwork in the country, explains the discrepancy between the foreign aid bubble of Kabul and the actual needs of Afghan women: "The polarised and politicised situation regarding women's issues in Afghanistan clearly demonstrates that women's rights can never be secured, at least not in a sustainable manner, in isolation from broader political developments. Yet this is exactly what Western governments often have attempted. High-profile-declarations of commitments to and funding for women's rights have been occurring in parallel with other policies that have undermined the very institutions and conditions on which such gains depend, such as a formal justice system, a functioning parliament and a non-militarised political landscape."

EPILOGUE: ONE OF THE BOYS

304   **the relationship between gender and violence**   Valerie M. Hudson, Bonnie Ballif-Spanvill, Mary Caprioli, and Chad F. Emmett, *Sex and World Peace* (New York: Columbia University Press, 2012). These authors' research clearly shows what Afghanistan has seen many times over—that the treatment of women and girls is at the center of war and conflict, and never a side "issue." In fact, they are the very best measure of the level of conflict both internally and externally, as "the treatment of women—what is happening in intimate interpersonal relationships between men and women—creates a context in which violence and exploitation seem natural" (p. 15).

Their book also proposes the involvement of men to a greater degree, in redefining honor and advocating for women, maintaining that "societies that are more gender-equal are less likely to go to war" (p. 3). We would do well to remember this important conclusion: "We have found in conventional aggregate empirical testing that the best predictor of a state's peacefulness is not its level of wealth, or its level of democracy, or whether it is Islamic or not. The very best predictor of a state's peacefulness is its level of violence against women.... And the less willing a country is to enforce laws protecting women within its own borders, the less likely it is to comply with international treaty obligations. These empirical findings, we believe, are only the tip of the iceberg" (p. 205).

ACKNOWLEDGMENTS

To those who have helped me, enlightened me, challenged me,
corrected me, and kept me safe:
Stephen Farran-Lee. Lennie Goodings. Rachel Wareham. Carol le Duc.
Terese Cristiansson. Helena Bengtsson. Ola Henriksson. Lisa Furugård.
Robert Peszkowski. Torbjörn Pettersson. Magnus Forsberg.
Naeemullah Sephahizada. Björn-Åke Törnblom. Afzal Nooristani.
Kim Sundström. Susan Chira. Kirk Kraeutler. Adam Ferguson.
Familjen Nordberg. Nuri Kino. Claire Potter. Vanessa Mobley.
David Halpern. Louise Quayle. Rachelle Bergstein. Laura Minnear.
Dana Roberson. Gennine Kelly. Naheed Bahram. Lee Mitchell. Laurie Gerber.
Ted Achilles. Solmaz Sharif. Ashk Dahlén. Phoebe Eaton. Anders Fänge.
Hanneke Kouwenberg. Doug Frantz. Sari Kuovo. Mujahid Jawad.
Saeedullah Reshteen. Diana Saqeb. Thank you.

To those generous organizations from which I have received
invaluable intelligence and support:
The Swedish Committee for Afghanistan, swedishcommittee.org
Women for Afghan Women, womenforafghanwomen.org
SOLA—School of Leadership Afghanistan, sola-afghanistan.org
Afghanistan Analysts Network, afghanistan-analysts.org
Stiftelsen Natur & Kultur
Publicistklubben
Thank you.

To those brave friends who have asked not to be named. Thank you.

To Nils Horner. Thank you.

#pressfreedom

INDEX

42, 46, 65, 70–71, 90, 112–13, 128,
    184, 199–200, 207, 223, 303
    traditional (Western) values of, 178
    and weddings, 151–54
Fareiba, Dr.:
    on Afghan culture, 45–46, 61, 115
    children of, 43, 44
    hospital work of, 40–43, 69–70
    on hot and cold elements, 228
    on need for sons, 40, 43–44, 45–46,
        70
    on puberty, 96, 147
    and Shukria, 164
    sons created by, 46–48, 69, 72, 159,
        185
Fatima, visitor to shrine, 227
Fisher, Helen, 192
foreign aid:
    anticommunist, 35
    corruption in, 120, 264–67
    houses built with, 283
    ineffectiveness of, 333–35
    for little girls, 138
    and refugee camps, 205
    and wealth gap, 267
    women's rights as focus of, 17, 138,
        266–67
    worker salaries and, 276
France, dress codes in, 98, 323
Freud, Sigmund, 76

Galenson, Eleanor, 76
Garofalo, Robert, 148–49, 184
gay rights movement, 304
gender:
    binary view of, 149
    in childhood, 23–24, 48, 138
    in cultural construct, 176
    equality in, 31, 32

as forbidden topic, 138, 139
intermediate category of, 329
learned behaviors of, 176, 326
and magic, 72, 159, 194, 224, 225–26,
    229
mainstreaming, 17
nature vs. nurture in, 177–78, 327
and power, 98
segregation by, 18, 24, 50–51, 70, 97,
    101, 200, 219, 221, 223
traditional roles of, 34, 43–44, 149,
    301, 326
and violence, 335–36
and war, 209–11
workshops about, 17, 302
gender differences, 104–5, 175, 176–78,
    326–27
blurring lines of, 76
in brains, 177–78, 326
gender experts:
    ignorance of girl/boy system, 17–18
    misplaced focus of, 17, 119, 304, 315
gender identity:
    creating, 176–79
    development of, 76, 148
    and freedom, 212, 306
    as idea vs. reality, 211
    and survival strategy, 208
gender identity disorder, 147–50
gender similarities hypothesis, 326–27
Gilmore, David D., Manhood in the
    Making, 209
girls:
    becoming boys, 14–15, 48, 67, 68, 70,
        113, 114, 220–23, 300; see also bacha
        posh
    boys changing back to, 15, 70, 96–97,
        126–27, 133–34, 137, 139, 176
    career ambitions of, 156

ABOUT THE AUTHOR

JENNY NORDBERG is an award-winning journalist based in New York. A correspondent and columnist
for the Swedish national newspaper *Svenska Dagbladet,* she
has a long record of investigative reports for, among others, the *New York Times,* where she contributed to a series
that won the 2005 Pulitzer Prize for National Reporting. In 2010, she was awarded the Robert F. Kennedy
Award for Excellence in Journalism for a television doc-
umentary on Afghan women. She is a member of the
International Consortium of Investigative Journalists.

THE UNDERGROUND
GIRLS OF KABUL

EXTRA LIBRIS

ESSAYS,
READER'S GUIDES,
AND MORE

A Note from the Author

What happens now?

This book begins and ends in Afghanistan. But when I was editing the final draft, I kept thinking of the millions of Afghan refugees who live as expatriates, forced to leave their own country due to decades of war.

Some grew up as *bacha posh*. I kept wondering what happened to them when they abruptly found themselves in societies where women had more freedom—did they still want to continue living on the other side, wearing their adopted male identity?

I heard about one *bacha posh* who had gone to the United States to study. Arriving in America as Faheem, she had eventually graduated college as *Faheema* and was now living in a small New England town. When we first met, she had already read my book. She told me she liked it and that it had inspired her to to share her own story.

As she prepares to go back to Afghanistan in the spring of 2015, I am hoping that she will be a part of the community that Shahed—the Afghan special forces soldier—once dreamed of: a place where *bacha posh* can find their own voices, share their stories, and connect with others who have had similar experiences.

Women who have lived as men and boys—and still do—exist everywhere. They are both an important part of history and a reflection of the world we currently live in. But what if they could learn from one another and at the same time educate us more about the resilience, resistance, and struggles of women and girls against a global system of oppression? I think it's time for these women to speak for themselves. They have spent far too long in hiding.

For the next chapter of their journey, I have created bachaposh.com.

I also hope that you, as a reader of this book, will join me in contributing your own experiences and thoughts at bachaposh.com.

With gratitude,
Jenny Nordberg

I Was a Bacha Posh:
The Story of Faheema

Liberating. That's how it felt, walking out the door for the first time as a boy. I was twelve. I was no longer Faheema, who needed to be proper and watch her every move, but *Faheem,* who had guts and could go where he wanted. That was now my right as a *bacha posh.* It's what they call girls who are disguised as boys in Afghanistan. And I suppose it's the term for those who eventually become boys on the inside, too.

My family had returned to Kabul in 2002 after the Taliban was toppled; society in Afghanistan was so much more conservative than in Pakistan, where we had lived as refugees. Afghan girls were looked down upon and their lives were much more restricted and difficult. Women were harassed on the street; they had to wear headscarves; they couldn't speak to boys or adult men or even look them in the eyes.

But I was different. I was always brought up as a boy. I just didn't look like one at first.

At home I was the one who got things done. We were carpet weavers and I ran the family business from our house. Seven other, younger children took orders from me. My parents often told me they wished I had been born a boy. They have said it for as long as I can remember—my father in particular. It would have made more sense, he said, since I was a harder worker than any of my brothers.

Most *bacha posh* in Afghanistan are made that way by their parents. But my story is different. I made the decision to switch. I gave them what they asked for, but it was my choice. I wanted to have more freedom.

It worked.

The attitude, the lowered voice, how I moved with more confidence. I did not have to make myself smaller by hunching over. I could disappear in a crowd. And others bought it. I found that the more divided a society is, the easier it is to live in disguise. As a boy I was seen as a complete person. I did everything Afghan culture said I couldn't do as a girl. I became strong. I took responsibility. It was practical, too. I could protect my sisters and escort them to class in winter. And it pleased my parents. At least they did not protest. But I still felt inadequate.

I had always thought being *bacha posh* was my own choice, that I was doing it for myself, of my own free will. But that was not entirely true, I realize now. I felt pressured by my parents' wish for me to be a boy. I took it too literally.

When I was eighteen, I still had no breasts. My periods were irregular and when my mother had sought out a doctor in Kabul, he said that my psyche might be turning into a man's. It had scared her. She wor-

ried I may never be able to return to life as a girl.
That I was permanently changed.

I spent nine years living as a boy. A few years ago,
I came to a small town in America to go to college
and I started thinking about what it means to be a
woman. Why should I need to hide? Could I not have
the same pride, and the same abilities, as a girl? Why
did I think that I could only have those qualities as
a boy? I thought, in my disguise, I had outsmarted
the system. That I had won. But confronted with a
less restrictive culture, I became increasingly angry.
I wondered how long I would have to do this.

Coming back was hard. I began letting my hair
grow out. Now it's almost all the way down to my
waist. I also went to see a psychologist at my university. We talked about what in me is male and what is
female. I still don't know what normal is, but I am not
as angry anymore.

Of course, the differences between men and
women are enforced here, too, but there is no need
for me to pretend to be a man in order to go outside
or to be considered a complete human being. But in
some ways America is also a conservative society, as
there isn't a lot of room for gender ambiguity. It's so
important for many people to be *either* male or female. I have both in me now and that's how I'll always be.

I think often about what it means.

Being a man gives you so many privileges that
you become less observant. You don't see the small
things. You own the world and everything is yours.

As a boy I was obsessed by everything I needed and wanted. That's what you do. You focus on yourself. A lot is expected of you as a man, so you have to think constantly about how to meet those expectations.

As a woman you see more. You notice what's around you. To me that is the essence of it. You relate to others. As a woman I have a soft core that melts with everything. I can feel what others feel. I see what they see. And I cry with them. I think of that as the female in me. I allow that now.

Today I'm in my twenties, but I don't expect to live long. A woman's average lifespan in Afghanistan is forty-four years, so mine is probably halfway over. I would like to stay here, in the United States, and become an anthropologist. But my American visa expires in a few months; then I'll have to return home.

Even now, my father only accepts me as a boy, not as a girl. We talk on Skype: He is a macho colonel in Afghanistan who calls me every day. Like my close friends, he is still allowed to call me by my boys' name. But I know now that both my family and much of my society were wrong when they said that only boys can do certain things. It's they who don't allow girls to do anything.

I have complicated feelings about the freedom I have here in the West. It's borrowed. It's not really mine. Deep down you know it could be taken away at any moment. Just like that of a *bacha posh*.

A Conversation with
Jenny Nordberg

Q. When you first broke the story of *bacha posh*
for the *New York Times* in 2010, it drew millions
of views and a massive response from readers
worldwide. What drew you to this topic and
inspired you to expand the article into a full-
length book?

A. It's the story of a lifetime. How often does a journalist come upon an actual secret that unspools into
a story no one has ever told before? And this secret
cut right to the most difficult questions of human
existence: war, oppression, differences between the
sexes. When I first discovered and started researching the *bacha posh*, I was frustrated to find that none
of the Western experts on Afghanistan I consulted
had any idea this was happening. In time I realized I
had to become the expert.

As a woman, the experience of *bacha posh* opens
a window onto a very raw form of patriarchy, where
people like me are unwanted, despised, and abused.
Writing a full-length book gave me the space to go

much more in-depth on this issue and to try to understand why that is.

But this is also a story that goes beyond the experience of being female in one part of the world; as a reader of my original *Times* piece said: "What woman hasn't wondered how life would have been different if she had been born a boy?" Her comment helped me realize that this is not just a story about Afghanistan—it's a story about all women and the history we share, one that should be read and understood by women (and men) everywhere.

Q. Most *bacha posh* are forced to become girls before they hit puberty, sometimes after living their whole lives as boys. What kind of lasting impact—if any—did this have on the women you interviewed?

A. My research, based on interviews with dozens of *bacha posh*, shows that the impact on adult females depends very much on when their transition back to life as a woman takes place. A few years as a boy when they're still children may be remembered as an empowering experience. But for those who go through puberty and beyond as young men, things quickly become much more complicated. Aside from the psychological conundrum, those who are nurtured as boys and young men through their teens and beyond can see a delay in the development of female identity and even the onset of puberty. It's an example of how the mind affects the body. *Bacha posh* really is a singular, contemporary case study in the nurture versus nature debate.

Q. To research and write this book, you have spent a great deal of time in Afghanistan over the past few years. What was it like?

A. Working in a country at war can be physically and mentally exhausting; you're on high alert most of the time. There's a feeling that there is no time to lose, because who knows for how long you can be lucky and not be in the wrong place when a blast goes off? Imagine how Afghans who have lived with this for more than thirty years feel. Of course, this environment has its advantages. Afghans are extremely polite and hospitable, and there is very little time for indecision or procrastination; interactions are much more immediate. With the constant presence of potential disaster, life takes sharper contours. And you laugh a lot together.

Q. You worked closely with this book's subjects. Did you become friends with the women you interviewed?

A. A classic tenet of journalism dictates that a journalist should not make friends with her subjects. But I believe you can be a professional and a human being at the same time. With all my main characters I have developed an intimate, respectful bond. Over the years I've asked them to tell me things they have never spoken of before, about their bodies, about sex, about religion—all the forbidden topics. In return I have shared some secrets of my own with them.

At the same time, there were no blurred lines about who the journalist was and who the subjects were. Each of these very brave women made a conscious choice to be part of this book, and I have tried to honor that by offering a lot of transparency about my work. For instance, when I had a somewhat finished manuscript in the summer of 2013, I went back to Kabul to see each of them again. We read it together, and for those who could not read, I read it out loud. Some details were added; others were taken out. Together we have tried to be careful and protect their families. In the end I hope I have done them and their courage justice, and they have told me that they hope people will want to know about them. This is a dispatch from inside extreme suppression, from those who just happen to have been born in the most dangerous place on earth to be a woman.

A Reader's Guide

QUESTIONS AND TOPICS FOR DISCUSSION

1. Before reading *The Underground Girls of Kabul*, what (if anything) did you know about Afghanistan? Was there anything in the book you found surprising about the country and its history?

2. Do you think the practice of *bacha posh* is subversive, with the potential to change the strict gender culture of Afghanistan? Or do you see it as women capitulating to and reinforcing a system of segregation? Do people have the power to challenge Afghanistan's patriarchal society in other ways?

3. Does the practice of *bacha posh* make sense to you, or is it still entirely foreign? How would you explain why this happens?

4. Disguise is a common strategy for coping with subjugation. Can you think of any real-life historical or present-day parallels to *bacha posh*? What examples are there of people of pretend-

ing to be someone or something else in response to segregation or oppression?

5. Many of the women in this book experience the limits of female freedom, even if they have had some success. Is there a limit to what most women can achieve, even in our own society today? Why is that?

6. Jenny Nordberg raises questions about whether or not gender is dichotomous, calling *bacha posh* "a third kind of child"—neither boy nor girl. Do you think we are born a certain way, or do we become our gender?

7. Did you ever wonder how things would have been different had you been born a child of the other gender? Did you ever wish that you could be a different gender, even if only to deal with a particular circumstance?

8. In what way were you treated like a boy or a girl, respectively, when you were a child? Were you told that there were things you absolutely couldn't do because of your gender? Do you see a future where gender roles will be less strictly defined? What would that future offer us?

9. Do you agree with the author's conclusion that women's rights are essential to human rights and to building peaceful civilizations? Why or why not?

10. What would you tell the author or any of these women? They would love to hear from you. We invite you to continue the conversation on bachaposh.com or to connect with Jenny Nordberg on Twitter: @nordbergj